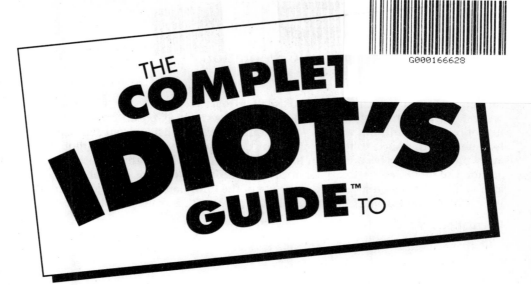

THE COMPLETE IDIOT'S GUIDE™ TO

More Windows 98

by Paul McFedries

A Division of Macmillan Computer Publishing
201 W.103rd Street, Indianapolis, IN 46290

G000166628

To Karen, who makes me laugh.

Copyright © 1998 by Que Corporation

International Standard Book Number: 0-7897-1739-5

Library of Congress Catalog Card Number: 98-85582

01 00 99 98   4   3   2   1

Interpretation of the printing code: the rightmost double-digit number is the year of the book's printing; the rightmost single-digit, the number of the book's printing. For example, a printing code of 98-1 shows that the first printing of the book occurred in 1998.

Composed in Stone Serif and MCPdigital by Macmillan Computer Publishing

Printed in the United States of America

Publisher
Dean Miller

Executive Editor
Christopher Will

Acquisitions Editor
Christopher Will

Development Editor
Kate Shoup Welsh

Technical Reviewer
Coletta Witherspoon

Managing Editor
Brice P. Gosnell

Production Editor
Katie Purdum

Copy Editors
Sara Bosin and Christina Smith

Indexer
Erika Millen

Cover Designer
Michael Freeland

Book Designer
Glenn Larsen

Production
Mona Brown
Michael Dietsch
Ayanna Lacey
Gene Redding

Contents at a Glance

Contents

Part 2 "Just So" Windows: More Customization Tomfoolery   97

7 Customizing Web Integration and the Active Desktop   99

21 Graphics Gadgetry: Working with Video Cards and Monitors 323

Part 6 More Networking Know-How 337

22 Working with Network Connections 339

Appendixes

Tell Us What You Think!

As a reader, you are the most important critic and commentator of our books. We value your opinion and want to know what we're doing right, what we could do better, what areas you'd like to see us publish in, and any other words of wisdom you're willing to pass our way. You can help us make strong books that meet your needs and give you the computer guidance you require.

Do you have access to the World Wide Web? Then check out our site at
http://www.mcp.com.

Note: If you have a technical question about this book, call the technical support line at 317-581-3833 or send email to support@mcp.com.

As the executive editor of the group that created this book, I welcome your comments. You can fax, email, or write me directly to let me know what you did or didn't like about this book—as well as what we can do to make our books stronger. Here's the information:

Fax: 317-581-4663

Email: cwill@mcp.com

Mail: Christopher Will
           Comments Department
           Que Corporation
           201 W. 103rd Street
           Indianapolis, IN 46290

Introduction

The more technique you have, the less you have to worry about it.
—Pablo Picasso

When it comes to movies, "sequel" is a synonym for "so bad, it hurts." Yes, some worthy sequels have been made, but for every *Godfather II*, there are a hundred *Weekend at Bernie's II*. Luckily, however, Redmond, WA (the home of Microsoft) is a long way from Hollywood, CA, so sequels about Windows make sense. After all, Windows 98 is a cranky, complex beast that can't be fully understood in one sitting.

This book, then, is the sequel to *The Complete Idiot's Guide to Windows 98*. The idea behind *The Complete Idiot's Guide to More Windows 98* is simple: to give you *more* coverage of *more* features. Why more? After all, didn't you learn everything you needed to know about Windows in *The Complete Idiot's Guide to Windows 98*? Well, to paraphrase Picasso, the more Windows techniques you have, the less you have to worry about Windows itself. The techniques I'll show you in this book will make your Windows work both more powerful and more efficient. What you'll find then is that Windows fades into the background, and you'll be able to devote all your precious time and energy into getting your work (or play) done.

What kinds of techniques am I talking about? Here's a sample:

➤ Tweaking Windows for maximum performance.

➤ Working faster and smarter with a few simple Start menu and taskbar customizations.

➤ Boosting your productivity with easy file and folder techniques.

➤ Getting the most out of your online sessions by learning about Internet Explorer's most powerful features.

➤ Taking the pain out of dealing with DOS.

➤ Creating better documents by sharing data between two Windows programs.

➤ Preventing Windows crashes (and recovering from them if they happen).

➤ Simple and safe ways to work with the Registry.

➤ Taking the mystery out of networking and the Dial-Up Networking accessory.

The Complete Idiot's Guide to More Windows 98 teaches you all this and, well, *more*. Does that make this a "For Eggheads Only" book? Not at all. The approach I use is the same as in *The Complete Idiot's Guide to Windows 98*: You get just the facts and info you need to know, presented in a lighthearted, poke-fun-at-Windows-at-every-opportunity way.

What You Should Know

This book assumes not only that you've read *The Complete Idiot's Guide to Windows 98*, but that you made it through those Windows wars and are ready to continue the battle. So that I can get to the good stuff quicker, I will assume that you have all the basic knowledge required to survive in the Windows wilderness. Specifically, I assume you know how to

➤ Work your mouse and keyboard

➤ Use the Start menu and taskbar

➤ Manipulate windows

➤ Deal with pull-down menus and dialog boxes

➤ Create, save, open, and print documents

➤ Use standard Windows tools such as WordPad and Paint

➤ Set up and establish an Internet connection

The Lay of the Land: What's In the Book

The Complete Idiot's Guide to More Windows 98 is designed more as a reference book than as a "how-to" that you're supposed to read cover-to-cover. Most of the chapters are self-contained, so you can leap around and read whatever catches your fancy. If a topic requires knowledge of some tidbit discussed earlier, I'll point out the relevant chapter so you can get the info you need.

Here's a summary of how the book is laid out:

Part 1—More Miscellaneous (but Useful) Windows 98 Tricks and Techniques

The first part of the book presents a hodgepodge of sometimes fun, sometimes interesting, but always useful, Windows techniques. You'll learn how to take control of the Windows 98 startup, how to get the most out of files and folders, how to share data between applications, how to make DOS and Windows live together in harmony, how to install and use Microsoft Plus! 98, and more.

Part 2—"Just So" Windows: More Customization Tomfoolery

Although I took you through a ton of customization techniques in the first book, Windows 98 is really a two-ton truck that's loaded with features that positively beg to be tweaked. The chapters in Part 2 take you through that second ton. You learn how to customize Web integration, the Active Desktop, the Start menu and taskbar, color schemes, sound schemes, the keyboard and joystick, and Windows 98's international settings. I also provide not one, but two chapters on the all-important (and all-powerful) Registry.

Part 3—More Online Fun: Communications and the Internet

The five chapters in Part 3 help you not only to get online, but also to be more productive while you're there. I show you the ins and outs of your modem, how to use Internet Explorer's most powerful features, and how to customize the email capabilities of Outlook Express. I also show you how use Microsoft Chat and Personal Web Server.

Part 4—Swifter, Higher, Stronger: More Windows 98 System Tools

The chapters in Part 4 continue the coverage of the long list of Windows 98 system tools from where it left off in *The Complete Idiot's Guide to Windows 98*. Chapter 17, "From Slowpoke to Speed Demon: Making Windows Fly," shows you a number of techniques for eking out every ounce of Windows 98 performance. Chapter 18, "A Windows Lifeline: The Emergency Boot Disk," shows you how to create a boot disk that will get you out of trouble should Windows go weird on you. And Chapter 19, "For the Nerd In You: Higher-End System Tools," runs through the rest of the system tools, from the System Information utility to the Task Scheduler.

Part 5—Hardware Hootenanny: More Device Advice

Part 5 consists of only two chapters, but they're power-packed chapters, for sure. Chapter 20, "Using Device Manager to Take Control of Your Hardware," unveils some of the mysteries behind your computer's hardware and shows you how to work with that hardware from within the friendly confines of Windows 98. Chapter 21, "Graphics Gadgetry: Working with Video Cards and Monitors," shows you how to get the most out of your system's graphics hardware.

Part 6—More Networking Know-How

The last three chapters of the book discuss various aspects of Windows 98 networking. I show you how to set up your machine for networking, access networking resources, share your resources with the network, send email over the network, and use Dial-Up Networking to access the network from remote locales.

Appendixes

The book closes with three appendixes. Appendix A presents a glossary of Windows and computer terms; Appendix B runs through a few useful Windows 98 Web sites; and Appendix C lists the complete Windows 98 ANSI character set.

Some of the Book's Fabulous Features

The Complete Idiot's Guide to More Windows 98 is designed to make your computing life easier. To that end, the book uses the following conventions:

➤ Text that you type, items that you select, and text that you see on your screen appear in **bold**.

➤ As you'll see, Windows 98 uses quite a few keyboard shortcuts. These shortcuts almost invariably require you to hold down one key and press another. For example, one shortcut you may use a lot requires you to hold down the **Ctrl** key, press the **Esc** key, and then release **Ctrl**. To avoid writing out a mouthful like that over and over, we needed an easier way to express these *key combinations* (a sort of "shortcut shorthand," if you will). So key combinations appear with a plus sign (+) in the middle, as in **Ctrl+Esc**.

➤ The names of dialog box controls appear in a special font like this: Select the **Create from File** option button and then click the **Display As Icon** check box.

Also, look for the following features that point out important information:

Check This Out

You'll find these "Check This Out" sidebars scattered throughout the book. I use them to highlight important notes, tips, warnings, and other tidbits that will help further your Windows education.

Techno Talk

This book generally shuns long-winded technical explanations because they tend to be, well, *boring*. However, in cases where a bit of in-depth know-how is too interesting to pass up, I'll plop the text inside one of these "Techno Talk" boxes. This stuff won't help you get your work done any quicker, but it will arm you with a few choice geekisms that will impress the heck out of people at parties.

Note This "Cross-Reference" box points you to other parts of the book that contain related information. To learn more about this element, please see "Some of the Book's Fabulous Features," page xx.

The Standing Ovation Department

Yikes, *another* book! This volume brings my book brood up to an even two dozen (not counting collaborations with other authors), and that double dirty dozen has sold well over a million copies worldwide. However, I wouldn't have sold anywhere near that number if it wasn't for the unmatched competence and unparalleled professionalism of the good folks at Que. Not only that, but everyone at Que is just so darned *nice* to work with. (I'm sure it has something to do with that fine Indiana air.)

So, as usual, there are lots of people to thank, including Publisher Dean Miller, Executive Editor Chris Will, Development Editor Kate Welsh, Production Editor Katie Purdum, Copy Editors Christina Smith and Sara Bosin, and Technical Editor Coletta Witherspoon. Kudos to all of you for another outstanding effort.

Part 1
More Miscellaneous (but Useful) Windows 98 Tricks and Techniques

To get your advanced Windows 98 education off to a rousing start, the chapters here in Part 1 offer a grab bag of handy tips and techniques. You'll learn quite a few high-falutin' methods for things like the Windows 98 startup, files and folders, sharing data, DOS, Microsoft Plus! 98, and more. Don't worry, though. This isn't one of those all-show-and-no-go collections. The emphasis here is on practicality and usefulness, so each chapter is crammed with techniques that you can put to good use .

Chapter 1

Beginning at the Beginning: Windows 98 Startup Techniques

In This Chapter

➤ Understanding the startup process

➤ Using the Windows 98 Startup menu

➤ The proper way to shut down Windows 98

➤ Creating custom startup and shutdown screens

➤ Everything you need to know, from go to whoa

In Lewis Carroll's book *Alice's Adventures in Wonderland*, the White Rabbit is about to read a letter and asks the King where he should begin. The King's answer? "Begin at the beginning, and go on 'till you come to the end; then stop." This chapter follows this sage advice and begins at Windows 98's beginning: the startup process. I go on (and on) until I come to the end—the Windows 98 shutdown process—and then I stop.

Startup and at 'Em: Taking Charge of Startup

The startup process may seem like a surprising topic because the Windows 98 startup seems so uneventful. You power up your machine, various internal beeps and rumblings are sounded, and then Windows 98 shows up for work a minute or two later. End of story, right? Not exactly. There's actually quite a bit going on behind the scenes.

Understanding just a little of what's happening can help you take control of the startup process and is a must for troubleshooting certain types of Windows woes.

The Boot Route: What Happens at Startup

The computer cognoscenti use the term *boot* as a synonym for the startup process.

Boot!?

Yeah, although it has nothing to do with punting the recalcitrant beast across the room (as tempting as this may be from time to time). Instead, as you'll see in a second, your computer sort of lifts itself up by its own bootstraps during startup, so "boot" is short for "bootstraps."

Ever wondered just what was happening under the hood during a typical boot? I didn't think so, but I'll tell you anyway. When you muscle your machine's power switch to the "On" position, the system's microprocessor loads a special chunk of software that busies itself preparing all your hardware for active duty. This is called the Power-On Self Test (POST, for short). If the POST completes without mishap, you hear a single beep. The machine then checks to see if a "bootable" floppy disk is in drive A (see Chapter 18, "A Windows Lifeline: The Emergency Boot Disk"). If not, Windows 98 steps on the stage and takes over the rest of the startup. One of its first chores is to process the CONFIG.SYS and AUTOEXEC.BAT files (which I'll discuss later in this chapter; see "What's All This About CONFIG.SYS and AUTOEXEC.BAT?"). Windows then proceeds to load its own files.

Taking Advantage of the Windows 98 Startup Menu

As I said before, the boot is moot most of the time because it usually doesn't involve the likes of you and me. Aside from the post-POST beep and perhaps a few scary-looking screen messages, the startup is almost always an exercise in sensory deprivation. However, what if you don't want the startup to proceed in its usual fashion? For example:

➤ What if you're having trouble with Windows (such as a messed-up display)?

➤ What if you have both Windows 98 and Windows 3.1 on your system and you want to load Windows 3.1?

➤ What if you have a DOS program (such as a game) that won't run under Windows?

In all these situations, you'll want to bypass the normal Windows loading process, but how?

The secret is a hidden menu called the Windows 98 Startup menu. To see this menu, fire up your system and hold down the Ctrl key. (Make sure you hold down Ctrl before you hear the beep that signals the end of the POST.)

Losing Control with Ctrl

Some systems sense that you're holding down the Ctrl key and interpret this to mean that you want to pause the POST. Grrr. If your system seems to stall when you hold down Ctrl during startup, release Ctrl for a second or two and then hold it down again.

After the POST is toast, you'll see the Startup menu, which looks something like this:

```
Microsoft Windows 98 Startup Menu
=======================================


    1. Normal
    2. Logged (\BOOTLOG.TXT)
    3. Safe mode
    4. Step-by-step confirmation
    5. Command prompt only
    6. Safe mode command prompt only
    7. Previous version of MS-DOS


Enter a choice: 1          Time remaining: 30
```

The number of options you see depends on your Windows 98 configuration, but the ones shown above are the most common. Here's a summary:

➤ **Normal**   This command tells Windows 98 to start in the usual manner.

➤ **Logged (\BOOTLOG.TXT)**   This command runs a normal startup, except that Windows 98 jots down various notes during the startup procedure. These notes are written to a text file named BOOTLOG.TXT, which is stored in your hard drive's main folder (usually C:\). BOOTLOG.TXT is useful as a troubleshooting tool. For example, when you examine the file, you may see a couple of lines that look like this:

```
[0016586B] Loading Vxd = vmouse
[0016586B] LoadFailed  = vmouse
```

The LoadFailed line tells you which driver Windows 98 choked on during the startup.

➤ **Safe mode**   This command is invaluable for those times when Windows won't work. It loads a stripped-down version of Windows 98—called Safe mode—that usually gets on its feet without a hitch. Once you have this "Windows lite" running, you can then proceed to investigate the problem.

5

➤ **Step-by-step confirmation**   This command lets you march through all of Windows 98's startup tasks one at a time, which is a great way to isolate problems. For each task, you see a prompt like this:

```
Perform some impenetrably obscure task [Enter=Y,Esc=N]?
```

To run the task, press **Enter** or **Y**; to skip the task, press **Esc** or **N**. The idea is that you step through the tasks and watch your screen for error messages.

➤ **Command prompt only**   This command takes you directly to the DOS prompt, so it's useful for running DOS programs that don't like running under Windows 98 for some reason. When you're at the prompt, you can start Windows 98 by typing **win** and pressing **Enter**.

➤ **Safe mode command prompt only**   This command also drops you off at the DOS prompt, but it does it in Safe mode, which means it and doesn't process the CONFIG.SYS and AUTOEXEC.BAT files.

➤ **Previous version of MS-DOS**   If your system had an existing version of DOS when you installed Windows 98, Setup saves those old system files. When you select this command, Windows 98 boots the old version of DOS. This is also the command to use if you still have Windows 3.1 on your machine. After this command gets you to the DOS prompt, type **win** and press **Enter** to start Windows 3.1.

Startup Menu Shortcuts

If you know which Startup menu command you want to run, you can bypass the menu by using the shortcut keys listed below. In each case, make sure you press the key or key combo immediately after you hear the end-of-POST beep.

Press...	To run...
F4	Previous version of MS-DOS
F5	Safe mode
Shift+F5	Safe mode command prompt only
Shift+F8	Step-by-step confirmation

What's All This About `CONFIG.SYS` and `AUTOEXEC.BAT`?

I mentioned earlier that once Windows 98 hijacks the boot sequence, one of the first items on its internal to-do list is to process the `CONFIG.SYS` and `AUTOEXEC.BAT` files, in that order. What the heck are these files with names that only a true geek could love? In a nutshell, they're both *initialization files*. They contain instructions that Windows 98 uses to initialize various aspects of your system:

➤ **`CONFIG.SYS`:** The instructions in this file are used mostly to configure some of the devices attached to your computer.

➤ **`AUTOEXEC.BAT`:** This is a special kind of *batch file*, which is a file that runs a series of DOS commands. In this case, the commands usually load programs into memory and set a few parameters that are used by devices and other programs.

The sad truth about `CONFIG.SYS` and `AUTOEXEC.BAT` is that they're digital dinosaurs, relics from a prehistoric time when DOS and Windows 3, whatever ruled the earth. The fact is, unless you have an ancient machine, Windows 98 probably doesn't require the services of these antiquated files and may even run faster without them. To find out, use Windows Explorer or My Computer to find these files (you'll probably find them in the main folder of drive C) and then rename them (to, say, `CONFIG.OLD` and `AUTOEXEC.OLD`).

Check This Out...

Unhiding `CONFIG.SYS`

If you don't see `CONFIG.SYS`, it may just be hiding from you. To make it show its face, select the **View | Folder Options** command in Windows Explorer or My Computer. In the Folder Options dialog box, select the **View** tab, activate the **Show all files** option, and then click **OK**.

Reboot your computer to see if it starts properly and to make sure that all your devices work as advertised. If so, great; you now know that you can live the rest of your life free of the burdens of `CONFIG.SYS` and `AUTOEXEC.BAT`. If not, bummer; you'll need to restore their names and come to terms with your lot in life.

What do you do if Windows won't start at all without having these files around? Try this:

1. Reboot your computer and display the Windows 98 Startup menu.

2. In the Startup menu, run the **Safe mode command prompt only** command.

3. Once you get to the DOS prompt, type the following two commands and press **Enter** (type the commands one at a time and adjust them as necessary depending on the new names you assigned the files earlier):

   ```
   ren config.old config.sys
   ren autoexec.old autoexec.bat
   ```

4. Restart your computer and let Windows 98 load normally.

Creating a Custom Startup Screen

After Windows 98 has put the whip to CONFIG.SYS and AUTOEXEC.BAT, it begins processing its own internal files. This usually takes a while, so rather than have you gawk at a
black screen for the entire operation, the Microsoft programmers decided to toss up a nice
startup screen for you to look at. (If, for some reason, you'd really prefer to look at a black
screen, just press **Esc** once the startup screen appears and the logo returns from whence it
came. Note, however, that the screen you see probably won't be entirely black. That is, it
will probably contain a few cryptic messages, which are just remnants from the first part
of the boot sequence, so they can be safely, even cheerfully, ignored.)

This Windows logo screen is pleasant enough, but it's possible to replace it with another
image that's more to your liking. Paint is the application of choice for this, so start it now
by selecting **Start | Programs | Accessories | Paint**.

If you already have an image that you want to use, follow these steps:

1. Select **File | Open** (or press **Ctrl+O**) to get the Open dialog box on its feet.

2. Find the file you want to use, highlight it, and then click **Open**.

3. Select the **Image | Attributes** command (or press **Ctrl+E**). In the Attributes dialog
   box, eyeball the **Width** and **Height** text boxes to get the current dimensions of the
   image (make sure the **Pixels** option is activated). Click **OK** once you've made a
   mental (or written) note of these numbers.

4. For this to work, the image must have a width of 320 pixels and a height of 400
   pixels. If your image already boasts those dimensions, say "Yes!" and skip to step 5.
   Otherwise, you need to resize the image. First, resize the horizontal dimension to
   320 pixels by selecting **Image | Stretch/Skew** (or by pressing **Ctrl+W**), entering an
   appropriate percentage in the **Horizontal** text box (the one in the **Stretch** group),
   and clicking **OK**. For example, if your bitmap is 640 pixels wide, you'd enter **50**, as
   shown in the following figure.

*Use the Stretch and
Skew dialog box to
size your image to
320×400.*

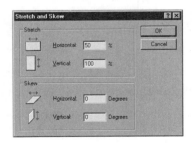

5. Resize the vertical dimension to 400 pixels by selecting **Image | Stretch/Skew** again, entering an appropriate percentage in the **Vertical** text box (again, the one in the **Stretch** group), and clicking **OK**. For example, if your bitmap is 500 pixels wide, you'd enter **80**. Your image should now be 320×400.

Fine-Tuning the Width and Height

It's possible that you might not end up with an image that's exactly 320×400. If that happens, and if you're just a few pixels off either way, you can tweak the dimensions by selecting **Image | Attributes** and then using the Image Attributes dialog box to enter the exact dimensions.

6. Use Paint's tools to modify the image, as necessary.

7. Select **File | Save As** and save the image as `Logo.sys` in your hard drive's main folder (usually `C:\`).

If you want to create a shiny, new image to use as the startup logo, follow these steps:

1. Select **Image | Attributes** (or press **Ctrl+E**) to display the Attributes dialog box.

2. Enter **320** in the **Width** text box and **400** in the **Height** text box.

3. Click **OK** to return to the image.

4. Use Paint's tools to create your image.

5. Select **File | Save** (or press **Ctrl+S**) and save the image as `Logo.sys` in the main folder of your hard drive.

The next time you start Windows 98, your image appears as the startup logo.

Don't Forget the Startup Folder

Another way to customize the Windows 98 startup is to add programs or documents to the Startup folder, which means these items launch automatically each time you boot. I show you how this works in Chapter 8, "Refurbishing the Start Menu and Taskbar."

Ending at the End: Shutting Down Windows 98

After wrestling with Windows and Windows applications all day, you probably can't wait to shut down your machine for the night and get back to the real world. Who can blame you? Before you do, however, you should know a few things about the shutdown process and a few tricks you can use for custom shutdowns.

Giving Windows the Bum's Rush: The Shut Down Command

When Windows 98 is shut down properly (I'll explain what that means in a sec), it performs quite a few mundane—but absolutely vital—chores:

➤ To save time, Windows 98 often holds data in memory until there's a break in the action (that is, in geekspeak, until the microprocessor becomes idle). When a break comes along, or when you shut down Windows properly, it then writes the data to your hard drive for safekeeping. So if you don't perform the proper shutdown procedure, there's a good chance you'll trash some valuable data.

➤ If you changed any settings or options in an application or in Windows itself, these changes often aren't set in stone until the shutdown process. An improper shutdown might mean that these changes are never recorded.

➤ Windows 98 warns you if any of your network cohorts are using your computer's shared resources. Turning off your machine without going through the proper channels disconnects those users and interrupts whatever they're doing (such as a file transfer or a print job). For some reason, people tend to get very upset when this kind of thing happens.

An improper shutdown is clearly a pro-ulcer thing to do, so you should *never* power down your computer willy-nilly. To avoid ill effects on your health, always trudge through the official Windows 98 shutdown procedure before switching off your machine for the night:

1. Select the **Start | Shut Down** command. (Yeah, I know: you have to click "Start" to "stop." It's wacky, but that's Windows for you!) Undaunted, Windows 98 displays the Shut Down Windows dialog box, shown in the following figure.

The Shut Down Windows dialog box: a balanced part of your shutdown diet.

2. Activate one of the following options:

➤ **Stand by**   You see this option only if your system supports something called Advanced Power Management. What happens is your computer goes into "standby mode," which is a kind of electronic slumber where certain components (such as your hard drive and monitor) are powered down. The computer stays on, so you can power up these components by pressing a key or jiggling the mouse.

➤ **Shut down**   Activate this option when you want to turn off your computer.

➤ **Restart**   Choose this option to give Windows 98 a new lease on life. In this case, Windows 98 shuts down, but then it tells your computer to boot once again.

➤ **Restart in MS-DOS mode**   Select this option to exit Windows 98 and get to the DOS prompt. This is useful for those times when you need to fire up a DOS program that won't run under Windows 98. (See Chapter 4, "Taming the DOS Beast," to learn more about MS-DOS mode.)

3. Click **OK**.

4. If you chose the **Shut down** option, you'll eventually see a screen that tells you that **Windows is shutting down**. After Windows 98 has completed its shutdown duties, you then see a screen that says **It's now safe to turn off your computer**. This is your go-ahead to power down the machine.

Logging Off

If you've set up your computer for multiple users (I explained this in *The Complete Idiot's Guide to Windows 98*), or if your machine is part of a network, your Start menu sports a **Log Off** *User* command just above the **Shut Down** command. (Here, *User* is the moniker of the current user.) If you select this command, Windows 98 bails out of all the running programs and then displays a dialog box for you to type another user name and password.

Creating Custom Shutdown Screens

I showed you earlier in this chapter how to create a custom Windows 98 startup screen. If it's your goal to remake as much of the Windows 98 interface in your own image as possible, then you'll be pleased to know that you can create custom shutdown screens as well. That's right: Both the **Windows is shutting down** screen and the **It's now safe to turn off your computer** screen are images that you can replace with your own funky designs.

Even better, if you don't feel like creating new images from scratch, you can modify the existing screens as you see fit. Here's how to load these images into Paint:

1. Select **Start | Programs | Accessories | Paint** to get the Paint window onscreen.

2. Select **File | Open** (or press **Ctrl+O**) to display the Open dialog box.

3. In the **Files of type** list, select **All files**.

4. Use the **Look in** list to select your main Windows folder (it's probably on drive C).

5. Scroll to the left and look for the following files:

   ➤ **Logow.sys**   This is the **Windows is shutting down** image.

   ➤ **Logos.sys**   This is the **It's now safe to turn off your computer** image.

6. Highlight one of these files and then click **Open**. :

The figure below shows two Paint windows displaying the two shutdown screens.

The Windows 98 shutdown screens are images that you can tweak using Paint.

From here, go ahead and use Paint's tools to alter the images to suit your needs. For example, you might want to use the Text tool to change the **It's now safe to turn off your computer** message to something else (such as "Gone to Lunch" or "You can touch me, but then I'll have to kill you"). The only thing you have to remember is that the final image must be the same size (that is 320 pixels wide by 400 pixels tall).

From Here

This chapter got you started by explaining both the startup and shutdown processes and showing you a few ways to control how they work. In the next chapter, "Taking Charge of Your Files and Folders," I'll show you quite a few useful techniques for working with the contents of your hard disk.

Chapter 2

Taking Charge of Your Files and Folders

In This Chapter

➤ Make sense (and good use) of file types, extensions, and attributes

➤ Powerful techniques for shortcuts

➤ The amazing **Send To** command

➤ Everything you've ever wanted to know about drag-and-drop

➤ Oodles of secrets, shortcuts, and show-stopping shenanigans

Computers can be a pain, but they're worth the hassle once you've cajoled them into producing a professional-looking résumé, creating a slick presentation, or finding useful information on the Web. Contrast this more glamorous side of computing with the relative drudgery of the file and folder maintenance that's a routine part of the workaday Windows world. Whether it's renaming or deleting files, creating folders, or moving documents hither and yon, most file and folder chores are lifelong members of the "Necessary But Dull" club.

File maintenance may seem like nothing more than unproductive busywork, but there's a host of handy file and folder techniques that can actually make you *more* productive. This chapter shows you how these techniques can help you take charge of your files and folders and so free up extra time for more useful pursuits.

File Style: Downright Useful File Know-How and Secrets

Let's begin by looking at files. The next few sections expand your file knowledge and run through quite a few techniques that will help you master the intricacies and subtleties of the file universe.

Figuring Out File Types

Windows 98 has an often weird and confusing relationship with files. In the Windows world view, things are supposed to be "document-centric." That is, instead of thinking about the applications you work with, you're supposed to think only of the documents you create with those applications. So how does Windows implement this approach? There are two main ways:

➤ Each type of file—oops, I mean *document*—is associated with a particular application. Text documents, for example, are associated with the Notepad text editor. This means that to open a text document, you find it in Windows Explorer and then double-click its icon. Notepad hauls itself onto the screen and loads the document automatically.

➤ In Windows Explorer's default folder view, each document shows only its name and an icon that's unique to the type of document. Text documents, for example, display an icon that looks like a little spiral-bound notepad (which helps remind you that Notepad is the associated application).

This all sounds admirable enough, I suppose, but it can get confusing. For example, what if a folder has two or more files with the same name? Check out the following figure. In this admittedly extreme example, there are no fewer than 15 files all with the name Project! Can you tell from the figure which of those files is the MIDI music file? Probably not, unless you have an advanced degree in iconology.

Document dilemma: which one is which?

So how's a body to tell one file from the next? There are a number of methods you can use, but here are the best two:

➤ **Switch to Web view.** Activate the **View | as Web Page** command. As you can see in the next figure, when you highlight a file in Web view, Windows 98 displays a description of the file on the left side of the Contents area. This description includes the file type. Note, too, that the description also tells you the *full name* of the file; that is, the file's main name plus its three-digit *extension*. More on this in the next section.

The file type.   The full name of the highlighted file.   The highlighted file.

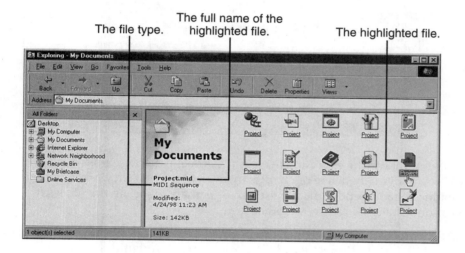

When you highlight a file in Web view, the description tells you what type of file you're dealing with.

➤ **Switch to Details view.** Activate the **View | Details** command. In this view, which is shown in the following figure, the file info is displayed in columns, including a **Type** column that tells you the file type.

More File Flapdoodle: Understanding File Extensions

When a folder has multiple files with the same name, how does Windows itself keep track of which is which? The answer is that the file name you see isn't the full name of the file. As you saw earlier in the Web view figure, each file name actually consists of a primary name (the name you see), followed by a period (.), followed by a three-character code (some of these codes are four characters long). The latter is called the *file extension*. This means that all those Project files in my example only *appear* to have the same name. In reality, they all have different extensions, so there's no conflict (at least from Windows' point of view).

Okay, so that's one mystery solved. Another mystery is how Windows keeps track of the file type of a given document. Once again, the secret lies with the file extensions. Specifically, Windows associates each three-character extension with a particular file type. In the

Web view figure shown earlier, you saw that the full name of the highlighted file was **Project.mid**. The **.mid** extension is associated with the "MIDI Sequence" file type, so that file is a MIDI music file.

Details view includes a Type column that lets you in on the file type of each document.

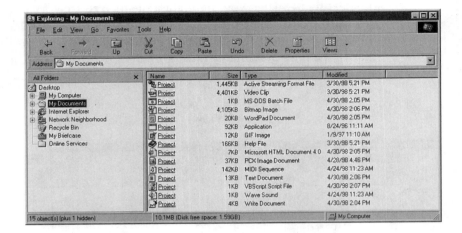

So why doesn't Windows show the extensions? Well, it's probably because they don't want unwary users to accidentally delete or change an extension when they're renaming a file. Doing so would probably render the file useless, or perhaps associate the file with some other application. Chaos, of course, would ensue.

Can't you change the extension anyway when you rename a file? For example, what if I renamed the **Project** MIDI file to **Project.wav**? (The **.wav** extension signifies a regular sound file.) That's a no go, Joe, because Windows is hip to that trick. All this does is change the file's full name to **Project.wav.mid**!

But what if you really do want to change the extension? For example, suppose you want to create a Web page from scratch. Web pages are just text files, so you could start by right-clicking the folder and then clicking **New | Text Document** to create a new text file. However, for Web pages to work they must use either the **.htm** or **.html** extension. Unfortunately, the text document you created will have the **.txt** extension. Hmmm. There's a head-scratcher. Are you doomed? Nope. The trick is that if you convince Windows to display the file extensions, you can rename extensions at will. Here's how to get Windows to display file extensions:

1. In Windows Explorer, select the **View | Folder Options** command to display the Folder Options dialog box.
2. Select the **View** tab.
3. Deactivate the **Hide file extensions for known file types** check box.
4. Click **OK**.

The following figure shows Explorer with file extensions displayed for all to see. You can now adjust any extension as necessary. Be careful, though: If you don't change the extension to something sensible, your document may no longer be accessible. In recognition of this potential liability, Windows 98 always asks of you're sure you want to change an extension.

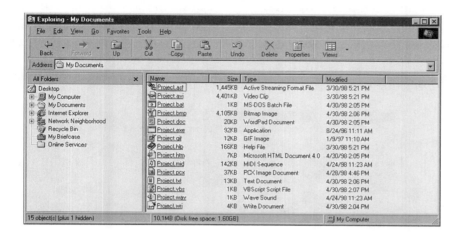

If you need to change an extension, you must first tell Explorer to display the file extensions.

A Fast Look at File Attributes

Have you ever opened a file, made some changes, and then tried to save the file, only to be thwarted by the constant appearance of the Save As dialog box? Have you ever opened a folder in Windows Explorer and seen something like **10 object(s) (plus 15 hidden)** in the status bar, and wondered why Windows was hiding files on you?

Both these perplexing behaviors are the result of special file properties called *attributes*. There are four in all:

➤ **Read-only**   When this attribute is set, you can't make changes to the file (that is, you can only read the file). If you can't save a file, it's probably because it's been set as read-only.

➤ **Hidden**   When this attribute is set, the file is hidden from view. If you'd prefer to see these files, select Explorer's **View | Folder Options** command, select the **View** tab, and then activate the **Show all files** option.

➤ **System**   This attribute applies only to files that Windows uses to perform its internal system chores. By default, Windows doesn't show system files in Windows Explorer. Again, you can force Windows to show these files. Select the **View | Folder Options** command, display the **View** tab, and then activate either **Do not show hidden files** or **Show all files**.

➤ **Archive** When this attribute is set, it tells you that the file has changed since the last time you backed it up (that is, it needs to be archived).

If you like, you can toggle three of these attributes—read-only, hidden, and archive—on and off for a given file. To do so, follow these steps:

1. Right-click the file and then click **Properties**. As you can see in the following figure, the Properties dialog box contains check boxes for these three attributes.

2. Activate a check box to set the attribute; deactivate a check box to clear the attribute.

3. Click **OK** when you're done.

A file's Properties dialog box contains check boxes to toggle three of the attributes on and off.

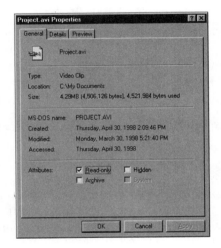

Getting the Most Out of Shortcuts

Software seems to have a built-in "impatience factor." That is, no matter how quickly something happens, after a while you'll wish that it happened even faster. Take firing up FreeCell, for example. Getting there—**Start** | **Programs** | **Accessories** | **Games** | **FreeCell**—takes only five clicks, but if you do it regularly, it can seem like *forever*. Similarly, opening a document can easily take a dozen clicks, depending on the application involved and where the file is housed.

Programmers are people too, and they're affected by the impatience factor as much as the rest of us. That must be why the Microsoft programmers created a feature that seems to be designed with the impatient in mind: *shortcuts*. A shortcut is a special file that serves only to point to something else. If a shortcut points to a document, for example, you need only double-click the shortcut (single-click if Web integration is turned on), and Windows 98 does all the hard work for you. That is, it will load the appropriate application and tell it to display the document automatically. In other words, a dozen clicks gets knocked down to a mere two (or even one). Impatient no more!

Shortcuts are a powerful feature and are one of the best ways to become ridiculously productive with only a bit of effort on your part. This section shows you how to create and work with shortcuts.

Windows always seems to offer us a few hundred methods for doing something, and creating shortcuts is no exception. It can be a bit confusing, so let's run through the best methods to use.

First, let's look at the method to use for creating a shortcut to just about anything that you can see in Windows Explorer. This includes a document, a file that starts a program, a folder, a disk drive, a printer, a computer on your network, even a Control Panel item. Follow these steps:

1. Use Windows Explorer or My Computer to find the item.

2. Right-drag the item and then drop it where you want the shortcut to appear (such as the desktop).

3. In the mini-menu that appears, click **Create Shortcut(s) Here**.

When the shortcut shows up, notice that Windows 98 tacks on a little arrow to the lower-left corner of the icon. This is a thoughtful reminder that the shortcut *points to* something else. Windows 98 also adds the phrase **Shortcut to** to the name of the original item. There's no problem renaming shortcuts, so feel free to delete this extra phrase. (I'll show you a better way to eliminate the annoying **Shortcut to** phrase in Chapter 9, "A Few Other Ways to Dress Windows for Success." See the section titled "Geek Chic: Customizing with TweakUI.")

Easy Program Shortcuts

If you want to create a shortcut for a Start menu program (such as FreeCell), click **Start** and open the menus until the program is displayed. Then right-drag the item and drop it on the desktop (or wherever). When the mini-menu pops up, click **Create Shortcut(s) Here**.

What do you do if you can't right-drag the file to create the shortcut? No problemo:

1. In Windows Explorer or My Computer, highlight the item you want to create the shortcut for.

2. Select the **Edit | Copy** command.

3. Move to the folder you want to use to hold the shortcut.

4. Select the **Edit | Paste Shortcut** command. (You can also right-click the desktop and then click **Paste Shortcut** in the menu that appears.)

Once the shortcut is in place, you'll probably just leave it as is and enjoy its handiness. However, shortcuts have a few options you can set, so let's look at what's available. To see the options, right-click the shortcut and then click **Properties**. In the dialog box that comes marching in, head for the **Shortcut** tab, which will look something like the one shown in the following figure.

Use the Shortcut tab to play with various shortcut options.

Here's a quick run-through on the various options:

Target This text box tells you the name and location of the item the shortcut points to (which is known in WinLingo as the *target*).

Start in If your shortcut starts a program, this text box sets the application's working folder. This means, for example, that when you select **File | Open** in the program, the specified folder will be displayed automatically in the Open dialog box. So you could use this text box to specify a folder that contains documents you might need to access while using the program.

Shortcut key Use this box to assign a key combination that will launch the shortcut. The idea is that you click inside this box, and then press any character. This sets up a key combo of the form **Ctrl+Alt+***character* (where *character* is the keyboard character you pressed). If you prefer a key combination that begins with **Ctrl+Shift**, hold down both **Ctrl** and **Shift** and then press a character; for a **Ctrl+Alt+Shift** finger-bender, hold down all three keys and then press a character.

Run If the shortcut starts a program, this drop-down list determines how the program window is displayed. Select Normal window, Minimized, or Maximized.

Find Target This command button opens a folder window and highlights the original file or folder. This gives you with a quick way to get to the original item. This is handy if, for example, you want to make a copy of the target.

Change Icon Clicking this button displays the Change Icon dialog box, shown in next figure. Highlight the new icon you want to use, and then click **OK**. Windows also has a few other icon collections you can check out. Try entering either of the following items into the **File name** text box (then press **Tab** to see the new set of icons):

```
C:\WINDOWS\MORICONS.DLL
C:\WINDOWS\PROGMAN.EXE
```

Use the Change Icon dialog box to pick out a snazzier icon for a shortcut.

The Complete Drag-and-Drop

Drag-and-drop is one of those features that, once you've used it, you wonder how in the world you ever got along without it. It really is amazing just how much it can simplify all kinds of everyday tasks. To celebrate this indispensable feature, this section presents a complete review of all the different hoops you can make drag-and-drop jump through.

Before we get to that, however, let's recap the basic drag-and-drop dance steps. And-a-one, and-a-two:

1. You begin by highlighting whatever it is you want to work with (such as one or more files or folders).

2. Position the mouse pointer over one of the highlighted objects, and then hold down the left mouse button.

3. Move the mouse (this is the dragging part), and position the pointer over the destination.

4. Release the mouse button (this is the dropping part).

To save a bit of verbiage in the rest of this section, I'll use the term *object* as a shorthand for all the things you can move or copy with drag and drop: files, folders, shortcuts, multiple items, and so on.

Drag-and-drop is a true time saver, but its arcane rules are enough to trip up even the most nimble of brains. Here's a recap:

➤ **Copying**   If you drag the object to a folder on a *different* disk drive, Explorer copies the object. Note, too, that you can force a copy operation by holding down **Ctrl** while you drop the object.

➤ **Moving**   If you drag the object to a folder on the *same* disk drive, Explorer moves the object. To force a move, hold down **Shift** while dropping the object.

➤ **Dragging a program**   If the object is a file that runs a program (that is, it has an .exe or .com extension), Explorer creates a shortcut in the destination folder.

➤ **The special drag**   If you don't feel like wasting valuable brain storage space memorizing these drag-and-drop rules, just use the *special drag*, instead. What's special about it is that you use the right mouse button to drag an object. When you drop it on the destination folder, Explorer displays the menu shown below. From here, simply click the action you want.

Isn't that special: If you right-drag-and-drop an object, Explorer offers you a menu of choices.

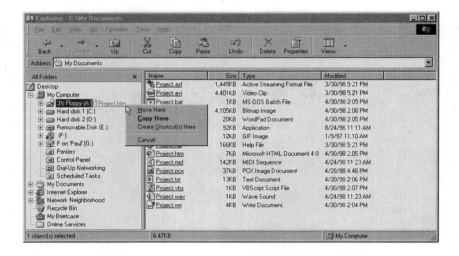

Here are a few more tasty drag-and-drop tidbits to savor:

➤ You can cancel a drag at any time by pressing **Esc**.

➤ It's possible to drag and scroll at the same time. For example, what do you do if you drag an object into the All Folders list and then realize you can't see the destination folder? Instead of canceling, drag the object to either the top or the bottom of the

All Folders list (depending on where the destination folder is). Explorer either scrolls the folders down (if you're at the top of the pane) or scrolls the folders up (if you're at the bottom of the pane).

➤ Windows 98's Explorer is also happy to open folder branches in mid-drag. To open a branch, drag the file over to the branch to highlight it. After a second or two, Explorer opens the branch.

➤ You might think that you could start a program and then drag a document onto the program's taskbar button to open the document. Ha! The taskbar just scoffs at your efforts. There is a way to get around this, however. Drag the document and let the mouse pointer hover over the taskbar button for a couple of seconds. Windows 98 then opens the program window so that you can drop the document into the program.

The Handy Send To Command

In *The Complete Idiot's Guide to Windows 98*, I showed you how to use the **Send To** command to simplify some file operations. To recap, you first do one of the following:

➤ Highlight a file and select **File | Send To**.

➤ Right-click a file and then click **Send To** in the menu.

Either way, a submenu with several potential destinations slides onto the screen, as shown in the next figure. The choices depend on the configuration of your computer and which Windows 98 components you have installed, but you'll at least see commands for your floppy disk and the My Documents folder.

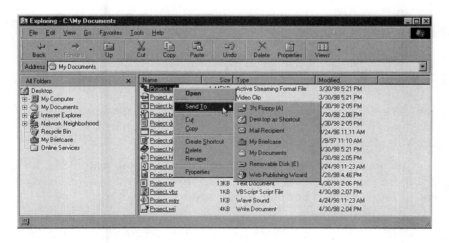

The Send To command offers an easy method of copying or moving files to floppy disks and other locations.

That's not bad, but here's the great part: Each of those items on the Send To menu is a shortcut. Therefore, clicking an item on this menu is exactly the same thing as dragging and dropping the object on the destination. This means you just click the destination you want and Windows 98 moves or copies the file. (As you would expect, Send To uses the same rules for moving and copying as those I subjected you to for drag-and-drop a bit earlier.)

Now here's the insanely great part: Those shortcuts in the Send To menu reside in a special folder named **SendTo** that sits inside your main Windows folder. To see for yourself, open the **Windows** folder and select the **SendTo** subfolder. As you can see below, all the residents of the Send To menu are present and accounted for.

Each member of the Send To menu has a corresponding shortcut in the SendTo folder.

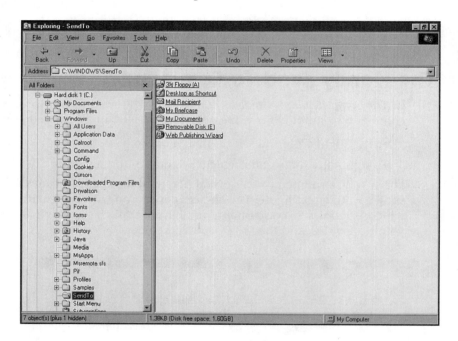

Why is this so wonderful? Well, you can create your own shortcuts in the SendTo folder and they'll end up as commands on the Send To menu as well. This means you can add shortcuts for commonly used folders, for example.

However, no one says that you have to restrict the Send To commands to just folders and disk drives. Because you can create shortcuts for just about anything in Windows 98, you can populate the SendTo folder with any number of interesting destinations:

➤ **Printers**   If you add a printer shortcut to the Send To menu, you can print a document just by sending it to the printer. Explorer's All Folders list has a **Printers** folder that contains icons for your installed printers.

➤ **The Recycle Bin**   Adding the Recycle Bin to the Send To menu is handy when you want to delete something but you can't see the Recycle Bin icon on your desktop. It also offers one advantage over deleting files in Explorer: You don't have to confirm that you want to send the object to the Recycle Bin.

➤ **Programs**   If you create a shortcut to a program on the Send To menu, you can then send a document to the program. For example, if you add a shortcut to Notepad, you can send a text file (even one that doesn't have a **.txt** extension) to the shortcut, and Notepad opens with the document loaded.

Expediting Explorer: More Shortcuts and Options

To complete your look at taking charge of files and folders, this section runs through a few topnotch tricks and techniques for making Windows Explorer easier to use.

A Compendium of Keyboard Shortcuts

In most of the Explorer techniques you've seen so far, you've used your mouse to click, drag, and drop just about everything in sight. If your clicking finger is getting tired, or if you're just an old-fashioned keyboardist at heart, you'll be happy to know that Explorer offers tons of keyboard time savers. The following table lists them all.

Press this...	To do this...
+	Open the next level of folders below the current folder. Use the + on the numeric keypad.
–	Close the current folder. Use the – on the numeric keypad.
*	Open all levels of folders below the current folder. Use the * on the numeric keypad.
Alt+Enter	Display the Properties dialog box for the selected object.
Alt+F4	Close Explorer.
Alt+left arrow	Go back to a previously displayed folder.
Alt+right arrow	Go forward to a previously displayed folder.
Backspace	Go to the parent folder of the current folder.
Ctrl+A	Select all the objects in the current folder.
Ctrl+arrow key	Scroll up, down, left, or right (depending on the arrow key used) without losing the highlight on the currently selected objects.
Ctrl+C	Copy the selected objects.
Ctrl+V	Paste the most recently cut or copied objects.
Ctrl+X	Cut the selected objects.
Ctrl+Z	Reverse the most recent action.

continues

continued

Press this...	To do this...
Delete	Send the currently selected objects to the Recycle Bin.
F2	Rename the selected object.
F3	Display the Find dialog box with the current folder as the default.
F4	Open the Address toolbar's drop-down list.
F5	Refresh the Explorer window. This is handy if you've made changes to a folder via the command line or a DOS program and you want to update the Explorer window to display the changes.
F6	Cycle the highlight among the All Folders list, the Contents list, and the Address toolbar. **Tab** does the same thing.
Shift+Delete	Delete the currently selected objects without sending them to the Recycle Bin.
Shift+F10	Display the context menu for the selected objects.
Tab	Cycle the highlight among the All Folders list, the Contents list, and the Address toolbar. **F6** does the same thing

Microsoft Natural Keyboard Shortcuts

If you have a Microsoft Natural Keyboard (or a compatible keyboard), the Windows logo key ⊞ gives you two Explorer-related shortcuts: Press ⊞+E to start Explorer; press ⊞+F to display the Find dialog box.

Opportunistic Opening: How to Open a File in Another Program

I mentioned earlier that most files are associated with a particular program. For example, double-clicking a text file opens that file in Notepad. Similarly, double-clicking an HTML file (a file that contains the instructions for a World Wide Web page) displays the Web page in Internet Explorer. However, what do you do if you want to open the file in a different application? For example, what if you want to open an HTML file in Notepad for editing?

A similar dilemma occurs when you come across a file that isn't associated with any program. For example, many installation disks come with files named **Readme.1st** or **Read.me**. These are text files that contain installation notes, but Windows 98 has no associations for weirdo extensions like **.1st** and **.me**. Therefore, double-clicking these files produces a curt error message.

To get around both of these situations, you can ask Windows 98 to open any file in another application. As long as that application can handle the file, it will open without a hitch and you're off to the races. Here's what you do:

1. In Explorer, highlight the document you want to open.
2. Hold down **Shift** and either select **File | Open With** or right-click the document and click **Open With** from the menu. The Open With dialog box, shown in the following figure, appears.

Use the Open With dialog box to choose the application you want to use to open the file.

3. In the **Choose the program you want to use** list, highlight the application you want to use to open the file.
4. If you want to use this application for this file type all the time, activate the **Always use this program to open this file** check box.
5. Click **OK**. Windows 98 uses the selected program to open the file.

Giving Explorer a Facelift: The View Options

You saw earlier that the Folder Options dialog box enabled you to toggle file extensions on and off and to show hidden and system files. You no doubt noticed that this dialog box was chock full of other options, so it's time now to see what fun you can have with them.

Once again, in Windows Explorer or My Computer, select **View | Folder Options** to get the Folder Options dialog box up and running, and then select the **View** tab, which is shown in the following figure.

First off, you can use the **Folder views** group to set up a common look to all your folders.

Note
I tell you about a couple more powerful file-type techniques in Chapter 6, "A Few of My Favorite Windows Things." See "File Type Tweak I: Modifying Actions," p. 84, and "File Type Tweak II: Creating New Actions," p. 86.

29

*Use the Folder
Options dialog box to
set up Explorer to suit
your style.*

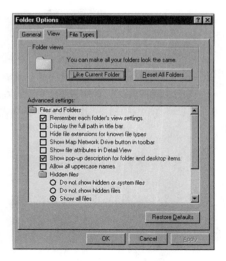

The idea is that you first use the commands on the **View** menu to set up a folder the way
you like. (For example, you might activate the **Details** command and select **Arrange
Icons | by Type** to sort everything by file type. Note, however, that this feature doesn't
apply to the toolbars.) You would then head for the **Folder views** group:

➤ **Like Current Folder** Click this button to apply the current view to all your
folders.

➤ **Reset All Folders** Click this button to change all your folders back to the default
folder view.

Here's a look at the options that reside in the **Advanced settings** list:

➤ **Remember each folder's view settings** When this check box is turned on, Windows 98 keeps an eye on the folders you work with and "remembers" the View
menu options (Large Icons, Details, sorting, and so on) that you set. The next time
you open the folder, Windows 98 grabs these saved options and uses them to
display the folder the way you had it before.

➤ **Display the full path in title bar** If you activate this check box, Explorer displays
the full path of the current folder in the title bar. *Path* is the official geekoid word
for the exact location of the folder. This includes the disk drive, any folders in
which the current folder is contained, and the name of the folder. For example, the
full path of the **Fonts** folder is **C:\Windows\Fonts**.

➤ **Hide file extensions for known file types** As you saw before, this check box
toggles file extensions on and off.

➤ **Show Map Network Drive button in toolbar** If you activate this check box,
Explorer adds two new buttons to the toolbar. Click the Map Network Drive button

to map the current network resource as a drive on your system. Click the Disconnect Network Drive button to unmap a network resource. See Chapter 22, "Working with Network Connections."

➤ **Show file attributes in Detail View**   Activating the check box adds an extra Attributes column to Explorer's Details view. This column displays letters that represent the attributes for a folder or file: **R** for read-only, **H** for hidden, **A** for archive, and **S** for system.

➤ **Show pop-up description for folder and desktop items**   Some Windows 98 icons—particularly those on the desktop and in the Control Panel—have an associated InfoTip that pops up when you point at them. This check box toggles those InfoTips on and off.

➤ **Allow all uppercase names**   When this check box is deactivated, Explorer displays all uppercase filenames with only the first letter as uppercase. To display all uppercase filenames, activate this check box.

➤ **Hidden files**   I showed you earlier how these three options determine which files Explorer displays. (See "A Fast Look at File Attributes.")

➤ **Hide icons when desktop is viewed as Web page**   This check box toggles the desktop icons on and off. That is, when this option is activated, Windows 98 removes the desktop icons when you view the desktop as a Web page.

➤ **Smooth edges of screen fonts**   If you activate this check box, Windows 98 smoothes the jagged edges of large fonts, which makes them more readable.

➤ **Show window contents while dragging**   This check box toggles the *full-window drag* feature on and off. When it's deactivated, Windows 98 shows only the outline of any window you drag with the mouse (by dragging the title bar); if you activate full-window drag, however, Windows 98 displays the window's contents while you're dragging. You need a fast video card to make the full-window drag feature worthwhile.

Note, too, that you can return to Windows 98's regular settings at any time by clicking the **Restore Defaults** button.

From Here

This chapter showed you quite a few techniques for dealing successfully and efficiently with files and folders. Chapter 3, "Sharing Data: The Mysterious Snake Oil of OLE," offers more file fun as you learn how to share data between programs. Note, too, that many of Windows 98's system tools are useful for keeping your files and folders on the straight and narrow. Check out Chapter 19, "For the Nerd In You: Higher-End System Tools," for details.

Sharing Data: The Mysterious Snake Oil of OLE

In This Chapter

➤ Data sharing without OLE

➤ What OLE is and how it can change your life

➤ Linking data between two applications

➤ Embedding data inside a document

➤ A no-bull approach that emphasizes the practical side of OLE

Okay, let's get a couple of things straight right off the bat. First of all, OLE is pronounced *OH-lay* (this allows you to get the bad pun in this chapter's title). Secondly, despite this pronunciation, OLE has nothing whatsoever to do with *olé*, the bullfight chant. It stands for *object linking and embedding*, which sounds scary, but it's just a method for sharing data between some Windows applications.

This chapter will attempt to knock some sense into this OLE business by keeping theory to a minimum, and by placing OLE in its most practical, hands-on light. The examples you'll see will show you how to harness the power of OLE to make your life easier, and to accomplish tasks you'd never have thought possible a few minutes ago.

Dividing the Spoils: Data Sharing Basics

Windows was foisted upon an unsuspecting computing public for many reasons—the fancy graphics, the easy interface, the multitasking fun—but one of Windows' biggest reasons for being is to share data between programs. Gone are the days when our word-processing documents were expected to contain only text, and our spreadsheets were expected to contain only numbers. Today's modern files often include alien elements, such as images from a graphics program, or sound files from a library of sound clips.

Windows makes it easy to combine data from separate programs by acting as the middle-man to make sure things go smoothly. Windows has a number of tricks up its electronic sleeve to accomplish this, but the two most common are the Clipboard and OLE. You'll examine the Clipboard in this section, and then the rest of the chapter will focus in on the hocus pocus of OLE.

Any time you cut or copy something in an application, Windows stores the data in a special place called the *Clipboard*. The data sits there, waiting patiently(maybe reading a magazine or two) until you issue a Paste command. Windows then copies the info from the Clipboard to the current cursor position in the application. The trick here is that Windows, for the most part, doesn't care which application sends out the paste message. In other words, you can cut or copy data from one application, and then paste it into something completely different.

For clarity's sake, let's go through the specific steps required to exchange data via the Clipboard:

1. Activate the application containing the data you want to share.
2. Select the data you want to work with.

Selecting Stuff

Selecting data is more or less the same in most Windows applications. If you have a mouse, you can usually drag the pointer over the data. From the keyboard, position the cursor where the data starts, hold down the **Shift** key, and then use the application's navigation keys (usually the arrow keys, Page Up, Page Down, and so on) to select the data. Some applications may require an extra step or two. In Paint, for example, you first need to click the Select or Free-Form Select tool.

3. Select the **Edit | Copy** command. Windows transfers the data to the Clipboard.
4. Switch to the application you want to receive the data.
5. Move to where you want the data to appear, then select the **Edit | Paste** command. Windows grabs the data from the Clipboard and pastes it into the application. A

copy of the data remains on the Clipboard, however, so you can run as many Paste commands as you need.

The Clipboard sounds like some mysterious place, but it's actually just a special chunk of your computer's memory that Windows sets aside for all this cut-and-paste malarkey. In fact, it's possible to actually view the current contents of the Clipboard. To do this, select **Start | Programs | Accessories | System Tools | Clipboard Viewer**. The Clipboard Viewer window that appears will display your most recently cut or copied data. (The Clipboard can only hold the contents of a single Cut or Copy command.)

For example, take a look at the three windows in the picture below. The window on the left is an Outlook Express email message that shows an address that I've copied. The Clipboard Viewer window in the middle shows the copied data, intact and ready to paste. (To open the Clipboard Viewer, select **Start | Programs | Accessories | System Tools | Clipboard Viewer**.) The window on the right shows the same data pasted into a WordPad document.

The original data.

The data sitting in the Clipboard after being copied.

The data pasted into WordPad.

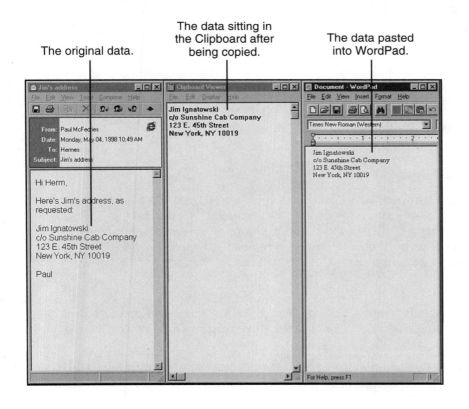

An address copied from Outlook Express to the Clipboard, and then pasted from the Clipboard to WordPad.

OLE: Can You See?

The Clipboard method's greatest virtue is its simplicity, but it suffers from two major drawbacks. First, if the data gets changed in the original application, the document containing the copy will become out-of-date. This has two consequences:

➤ If you know the data needs to be updated, you have to repeat the whole copy-and-paste procedure to get the latest version of the data.

➤ If you don't know the data needs to be updated (for example, if someone else changes the original data without telling you), then you're out of luck because you'll be stuck with an old version of the data.

Secondly, what if you want to make changes to the copied data? You may be able to edit the data directly (if it's just text, for example), but more often than not you'll need to crank up the original application, change the data there, and then do the Clipboard thing all over again. However, problems can arise if you're not sure which application to use, or which file contains the original data.

It would be nice if we didn't have to worry about the updating of our shared data. If we put together a wish list, it would probably contain two items:

➤ If the data changes in the other application, I want the copied data updated automatically.

➤ If I want to make changes to the copied data, make it easy to find both the original application and the original data file.

OLE Lingo

To get through the rest of this chapter, you'll need some terminology for the application that creates the original data, and for the application that gets the copy. The official terms are *server* and *client*, respectively, but most people can never remember which is which. Instead, I'll use the terms *source* and *destination*.

Well, my friends, I'm here today to tell you that wishes *can* come true, because OLE addresses both of these issues. Let's examine the three parts of OLE—object, linking, and embedding:

➤ **Object**   This is the data that is inserted into the destination application. The basic Clipboard method sends raw data, but OLE is more sophisticated because it also sends information that lets you easily update and work with the data.

➤ **Linking**   This is an OLE method you can use to insert an object into a destination document. When you link an object, OLE sets up and maintains a link between the source application and the object, which means that if the original data is changed, OLE updates the copy automatically. For example, suppose you insert a linked spreadsheet object into a word-processor document. If you revise some of the numbers in the spreadsheet sometime down the road, the copy inside the document is automatically updated to reflect the new numbers.

➤ **Embedding**   This is an OLE technique you can use to insert an object into a destination file. When you embed an object, OLE copies not only the source data, but also all kinds of info about the source application. It's easy to make changes to the embedded object because OLE knows where it came from and can start the source application for you automatically. For example, you can make changes to a Paint picture embedded in a WordPad document simply by double-clicking it. OLE starts up Paint (the source application) and automatically loads the picture so you can make your changes. Note, however, that OLE maintains no connection between an embedded object and the original object. In particular, any changes you make to the embedded object have no effect on the original file.

Should I Link or Embed?

This question, while not quite up there with the major philosophical conundrums of our times, illustrates what is perhaps the most confusing aspect of OLE: Under what circumstances should you link your objects or embed them? The answer lies in how OLE treats the source data. When you link an object, OLE doesn't even bother sending the data to the destination. Instead, it sends a "reference" that tells the destination application which file contains the source data. This is enough to maintain the link between the two applications. When you embed an object, however, the actual data is crammed holus-bolus into the destination document.

So, you should link your objects if:

➤ You want to keep your destination documents small. The destination just gets the link info, and not the data itself, so there's much less overhead associated with linking.

➤ You're sure the source file won't be moved or deleted. To maintain the link, OLE requires that the source file remain in the same place (that is, the same disk drive and folder). If it's moved or deleted, the link is broken.

➤ You need to keep the source file as a separate document in case you want to make changes to it later, or in case you need it for more OLE fun. You're free to link an object to as many destination files as you like. If you think you'll be using the source data in multiple places, you should link it so you can maintain a separate file.

➤ You won't be sending the destination file via email or floppy disk. Again, OLE expects the linked source data to appear in a specific place. If you send the destination file to someone else, they might not have the proper source file to maintain the link.

On the other hand, you should embed your objects if:

➤ You don't care how big your destination files get. Embedding works best in situations where you have lots of hard disk space and lots of memory.

➤ You don't need to keep the source file as a separate document. If you only need to use the source data once, embedding it means you can get rid of the source file and reduce the clutter on your hard disk.

➤ You'll be sending the destination file and you want to make sure the object arrives intact. If you send a file containing an embedded object, the other person sees the data, complete and unaltered.

Doing the Linking and Embedding Thing

If all this seems a bit confusing, don't worry; that's a normal reaction to this High Geek techno stuff. If it's any consolation, however, deciding whether you want to link or embed is actually the hardest part of OLE. Once you know what you want to do, the rest is straightforward. Yet, just to keep us all on our toes, OLE gives us a few different methods to use to link or embed an object. The following two are the most common:

➤ You can copy the object from the source application and paste it in the destination application as a linked or embedded object.

➤ You can insert a new embedded object from within the destination application.

Linking or Embedding an Object by Pasting

If the object you want to link or embed already exists, you can place it on the Clipboard and then paste it in the destination document. If you think this sounds like what we did earlier...well, you're close. The difference, as the following steps show, is that you paste *not* with the Paste command, but with the Paste Special command:

1. Activate the source application, and open or create the document that contains the object.

2. Select the object you want to link or embed, and run the **Edit | Copy** command to place the data on the Clipboard.

3. Switch to the destination application and move where you want the object to appear.

4. Select the **Edit | Paste Special** command. A Paste Special dialog box appears. The layout of the Paste Special dialog box varies from application to application. The next figure shows the one that WordPad uses.

No Paste Special, No OLE

If the destination application doesn't have a Paste Special command, it's bad news: it means the program doesn't support object linking and embedding.

Alternatively, some applications (such as the old Cardfile program in Windows 3.1) have a Paste Link command on their Edit menus. If you want to link the object, you can use this command to bypass the Paste Special dialog box.

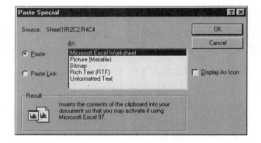

WordPad's Paste Special dialog box.

5. In the list of data types (the **As** list in the previous figure), select the first item (such as **Microsoft Excel Worksheet**).

6. To embed the object, activate the **Paste** option button; to link the object, activate the **Paste Link** option button.

7. Click **OK**. The destination application inserts the object.

Inserting a New Embedded Object

If the object you want to embed doesn't exist, and you don't need to create a separate file, OLE lets you insert (that is, embed) the new object directly into the destination application. For example, suppose you want to embed a Paint drawing into a WordPad document, but the drawing doesn't exist and you don't need a separate Paint file for the drawing. In this case, OLE lets you embed a new Paint object in the WordPad document and create the drawing right from WordPad. Here's how it works:

39

1. In the destination application, move where you want the new object to appear.

2. In most applications, you then select the **Insert | Object** command. (Some older programs use the **Edit | Insert Object** command.) The Insert Object dialog box appears, as shown in the next figure (this is the Insert Object dialog box from WordPad).

WordPad's Insert Object dialog box.

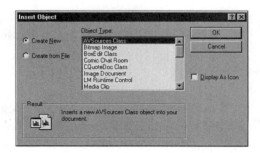

3. Make sure the **Create New** option is activated.

4. In the **Object Type** list, select the type of object you want to create. If you want to create a Paint drawing, for example, select the **Bitmap Image** object type.

5. Click **OK**. Windows 98 starts the source application for the object type you selected.

6. Create the object you want to embed.

Check This Out...

Updating Your Work

In most source applications, you can embed the object without leaving the application simply by selecting the **File** menu's **Update** command. Since you won't be creating a separate file for the object, this is sort of like saving your work.

7. Exit the source application. In most cases, you'll do this by pulling down the **File** menu and selecting the **Exit & Return to document** command, where **document** is the name of the active document in the destination application. Otherwise, you exit just by clicking outside of the work area.

8. The source application may ask if you want to update the embedded object. If so, click **Yes**, and Windows 98 embeds the object.

Editing a Linked or Embedded Object

If you need to make changes to a linked or embedded object, you can start the source application and load the object automatically by using either of the following methods:

➤ Double-click the object in your document.

➤ Select the object, and pull down the **Edit** menu. Now either select the **Edit Type Object** command, where **Type** is the type of object you selected (for example, Bitmap Image or Document), or select the **Type Object** command, and then select **Edit**.

Working with the Latest OLE Applications

The latest version of object linking and embedding (sometimes called OLE 2) includes a fistful of new features that make creating and maintaining embedded objects even easier. Here's a summary of just a few of these features:

Drag and drop objects between applications   You can move information from one open OLE 2 application to another simply by dragging selected data from one and dropping it in the other. If you want to copy the data, you need to hold down **Ctrl** while dragging.

In-place inserting   If you insert a new OLE 2 object, Windows 98 activates *in-place* inserting. This means that instead of displaying the source application in a separate window, certain features of the destination application's window are temporarily hidden in favor of the source application's features:

➤ The title bar changes to tell you what kind of object you're now working with.

➤ The menu bar (with the exception of the File and Window menus) is replaced by the source application's menu bar.

➤ The toolbars are replaced by the source application's toolbars.

To exit in-place inserting and embed the object, click outside the object.

In-place editing   When you edit an OLE 2 object, the object remains where it is, and the destination application's window changes as it does with in-place inserting. Make your changes, and then click outside the object to complete the edit.

Let's look at an example to see OLE 2 in action. First off, the following picture shows the normal Microsoft Excel window. For an extra point of reference, I've displayed the Help menu.

Your basic Microsoft Excel window.

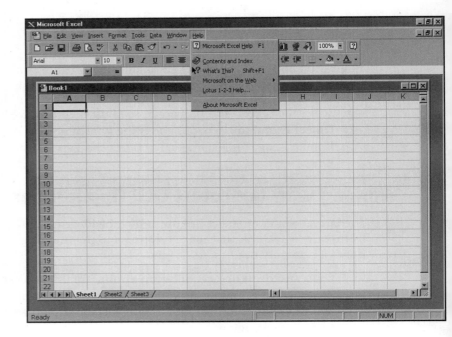

Now I'll insert a Microsoft Word document into Excel. Word (versions 6.0 and later) which is an OLE 2 application, so it supports in-place inserting. As the following picture shows, OLE 2 changes the menu bar and toolbars from Excel's to Word's. (For example, compare Excel's Help menu shown earlier with the Help menu shown in the following figure.)

Word's menu bar.   Word's toolbars.

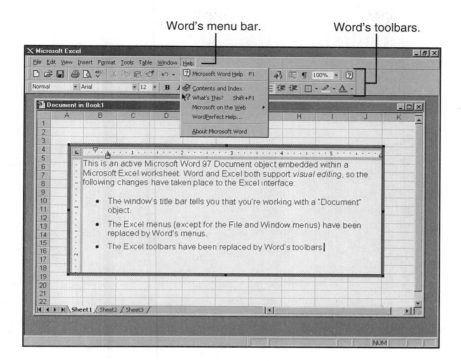

With in-place inserting, the destination window (Excel) assumes many features of the source window (Word 97).

From Here

This chapter took you on a tour of the strange and wonderful world of OLE. We covered a lot of ground, but you'll find you use these techniques regularly, so everything will sink in before too long. Speaking of strange, it's time now to leave the friendly confines of Windows and investigate the alien world of DOS. Chapter 4, "Taming the DOS Beast," takes you through.

Taming the DOS Beast

In This Chapter

➤ Cranking up a DOS session

➤ Doling out DOS commands

➤ Understanding MS-DOS mode

➤ Customizing the DOS window

➤ Valuable tips and techniques that let you show DOS who's boss

If you've ever read the letters section of a computer magazine, or spent any time online, you've probably come across a "holy war" or two. In computing circles, a holy war is a never-ending debate on the merits of one thing versus another, where people use the same arguments over and over, and nobody's opinion ever budges even the slightest one way or the other. (A holy war is also known as a FAWOMPT: a Frequently Argued Waste Of My Precious Time.)

Until a few years ago, the mother of all holy wars was the DOS versus Windows debate. I shudder to think how much energy some people spent extolling the virtues of one system and the shortcomings of the other. It's all moot nowadays, of course. Windows long ago trounced DOS both technologically and in the marketplace. However, DOS is still around, only now it has been relegated to just another Windows accessory. If you still have some old DOS programs kicking around, or if you still use DOS for file maintenance (renaming multiple files at once, for example), this chapter shows you how to get the most out of your DOS sessions.

Dirty DOS Dancing: Starting a DOS Session

From Windows' point of view, DOS is just a program more or less like any other. You start it up, work in it, and then shut it down when you're done. You can even display your DOS session in a window and move that window around onscreen, or even minimize it to an icon.

To start a DOS session, you have two choices: you can load a DOS application, or you can run **COMMAND.COM**, the DOS *command interpreter*.

Running a DOS Application

To run a DOS program, use either of the following techniques:

➤ Create a Start menu command for the program, and then select that command.

➤ Select **Start | Run** to display the Run dialog box. Click **Browse** and use the Browse dialog box to select the file that launches the program. When you're back in the Run dialog box, click **OK**.

Either way, Windows 98 loads the program in its own DOS session and you're off.

Starting a DOS Prompt Session

A **COMMAND.COM** session is a little different, however. What does a command interpreter do? It displays the DOS prompt to let you enter DOS commands, then it translates those commands into a language DOS can understand.

To start a **COMMAND.COM** DOS session, you have two ways to go:

➤ Select **Start | Programs | MS-DOS Prompt**.

➤ Select **Start | Run**, enter **command.com** in the Run dialog box, and then click **OK**.

Starting DOS in a Particular Folder

If you highlight a folder in Windows Explorer and then use the **Start | Run** method to launch a **COMMAND.COM** DOS session, Windows will begin the DOS session in the highlighted folder.

Working at the DOS Prompt

Once the DOS prompt appears, you're free to enter DOS commands, start DOS programs, or do whatever other DOS stuff suits your fancy. Here are a few things to remember:

➤ Windows treats each DOS session like any other program. Therefore, if you need to switch to another application, you can use the **Alt+Tab** "cool switch" (hold down **Alt** and press **Tab** until you get to the application you want).

➤ You can toggle your DOS session between a window and full-screen by pressing **Alt+Enter**.

➤ When you're done dealing with DOS, type **exit** and press **Enter** to return to Windows.

Running DOS Commands

What if you want to run just a single DOS command in your DOS session? It seems like a lot of work to first open the DOS session and then run the command. Can't you just run the command directly? Well, it depends. Some DOS commands are actually separate, stand-alone programs in their own right. (These are called *external* commands.) Examples include **EDIT**—the DOS text editor—and **FORMAT**—the DOS command that formats floppy disks. To run these commands, select **Start | Run**, enter the name of the command in the **Run** dialog box, then click **OK**.

DOS also has a collection of commands that are part of **COMMAND.COM**. (These are called *internal commands*.) An example is **DIR**, which produces a listing of files in the current directory. To run these commands, select **Start | Run**, and enter the following in the **Run** dialog box:

```
command.com /k command
```

Here, *command* is the name of the DOS command you want to run. For example, to get a directory listing for **C:\Windows**, enter the following command in the Run dialog box:

```
command.com /k dir c:\windows
```

The **/k** thing (it's called a *switch*) tells DOS not to exit the **COMMAND.COM** session automatically. This enables you to see the results of the command.

In some cases, you may prefer to run a temporary **COMMAND.COM** session. This means that when the command is finished executing, the entire DOS session ends and you're plopped back in Windows. In this case, use **/c** instead of **/k**, like so:

```
COMMAND.COM /c command
```

Note

If you plan on spending a fair bit of time at the DOS prompt, the **DOSKEY** command can make your life a lot easier. I show you how to use **DOSKEY** in Chapter 6. See "Loading **DOSKEY** for Smoother DOS Prompt Sessions," p. 81.

Dealing with Long Filenames

Before Windows 95 came along, Windows users had to struggle under the yoke of the DOS "8.3" filename rule: A primary name consisting of no more than eight characters, followed by a period (.), followed by an extension of no more than three characters. These procrustean restrictions resulted in hard disks the world over being littered with semi-comprehensible names such as **FY94BDGT.XLS** and **LTR2MOM5.DOC**.

Windows 95 changed all that by allowing long-suffering users to work with luxuriously long filenames (up to about 250 characters), and Windows 98 carries on this support.

The Real Filename Deal

Why did I say that filenames can be "about" 250 characters? Well, here's the correct rule: The total number of characters in the pathname—that's the filename plus the file's drive and folder—can't be more that 253.

For example, if you create a file in the root folder of drive C, your path is three characters long (C:\), so the maximum length of the filename is 250 characters. If you create a verbosely named file and then try to copy it into, say, the C:\WINDOWS folder, you get an error message because the new pathname is actually 260 characters (250 for the filename plus 10 for the path).

However, long filenames can be a bit tricky at the DOS prompt, so let's examine the issues. First off, the Windows 98 version of DOS *does* support long filenames. To prove it for yourself, run the following **DIR** (directory listing) command in your main Windows folder:

```
dir *.bmp
```

The following figure shows the results. The first two columns show the old "DOS" name for each file (primary name on the left and extension on the right), while the last column shows the "Windows 98" name for each file.

Notice that many of the files actually seem to use two different names. Take the file **Pinstripe.bmp** as an example. Its DOS name is **PINSTR~1.BMP**. What gives? Well, long filenames are supported only by programs designed to run with Windows 95 or Windows 98 (also Windows NT). Older programs would choke on these long names, so Windows tracks two names for every file: the nice long name, and a shorter name that conforms to the "8.3" rule. Programs that don't know how to deal with long filenames will still work because they only see the shorter name.

*Run the **DIR** command at the DOS prompt to see both DOS (short) and Windows 98 (long) filenames.*

Why do some of the short names look so weird?

That's thanks to the formula that Windows uses to derive the shorter name. If the primary name is longer than eight characters, all spaces are removed, only the first six characters are taken, and then ~**1** is tacked on to the end. That ~**1** weirdness is used to avoid having multiple files with the same short name. For example, consider the following two long filenames:

```
Pinstripe.bmp
Pinstripes.bmp
```

They have the same first six letters, so to get short names that don't conflict, ~**1** would be added to the first one and ~**2** would be added to the second one, like so:

```
PINSTR~1.BMP
PINSTR~2.BMP
```

When you're running file-related DOS commands, you can use either the short names or the long names. If you want to use the latter, however, you need to watch out. If the long name contains a space or any other character that's illegal in an 8.3 name, you need to surround the long name with quotation marks. For example, the following command will generate an error:

```
copy carved stone.bmp stoned carve.bmp
```

Instead, you need to enter this command as follows:

```
copy "carved stone.bmp" "stoned carve.bmp"
```

Sharing Data between DOS and Windows

In the previous chapter, I showed you how to copy and paste data between Windows programs. Sharing data with a DOS program is another kettle of digital fish entirely. This section shows you how to copy text and graphics from a DOS program, and it also shows you how to paste graphics from a DOS program.

The best way to copy text from a DOS application is to place the program in a window and highlight the text you want. Here are the steps you need to plow through:

1. Open the DOS application, and place it in a window (if it's not already) by pressing **Alt+Enter**. (The program is in a window if you can see the Minimize, Maximize, and Close buttons in the upper-right corner.)

2. Click the **Mark** button in the toolbar, or pull down the window's Control menu (by pressing **Alt+Spacebar**) and select **Edit | Mark**. A blinking cursor appears on the left, just below the toolbar. (If you don't see the toolbar across the top of the DOS window, pull down the window's **Control** menu and activate the **Toolbar** command.) The Mark command tells Windows 98 that you want to select some text in the DOS program.

3. Select the information you want to copy. (You can use the normal text selection techniques that you'd use in a Windows application.) Your screen should look something like the one shown in the following figure.

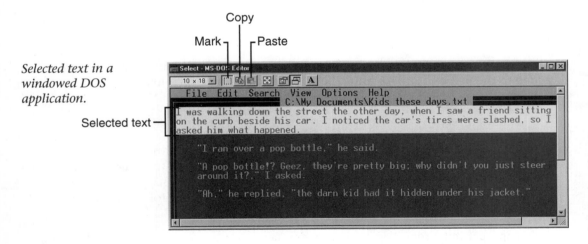

Selected text in a windowed DOS application.

4. Click on the toolbar's **Copy** button, or open the Control menu and select **Edit | Copy** (you can also just press **Enter**). This copies the selection to the Clipboard.

50

If the DOS program has a picture that you want to copy, you first need to display the application in a window. Set up your window so that you can see the image, and then press **Alt+Print Screen**.

Alt Print Screen Gives You More than You Bargained For

The **Alt+Print Screen** method makes a copy of the *entire* window—the title bar, scroll bars, the whole shootin' match. If you don't want these things included in your image, you should first paste the picture into Paint and remove the extraneous matter from there.

When you copy data from a DOS program, it sits quietly in the Clipboard until you issue a Paste command from a Windows application.

Pasting text *into* a DOS application takes a bit more effort, as the following steps demonstrate:

1. Open the Windows application and copy the text from the document you want to work with.

2. Open the DOS application and place it in a window (if it's not already) by pressing **Alt+Enter**.

3. Position the cursor where you want to insert the text.

4. Click the toolbar's **Paste** button, or open the Control menu and select **Edit | Paste**. The Clipboard copies your text before your very eyes!

Using MS-DOS Mode for DOS Games and Other Finicky Programs

Windows programs are inherently cooperative and are happy to share a computer's resources amongst themselves. DOS programs, on the other hand, are the greedy-guts of the computing world. The computer is for their sole benefit, and any other programs that want in on the action can just wait in line. Fortunately, Windows 98 is able to fool most DOS programs into thinking they have a monopoly on the computer's resources, which enables you to run DOS and Windows programs at the same time.

However, there are a few DOS programs that are just plain finicky. No matter how hard Windows tries to please them, these programs simply won't run under Windows. The Microsoft programmers realized this, so they came up with something called *MS-DOS mode*, which is designed to give a program exclusive access to the computer.

In some cases, Windows will recognize when a program requires MS-DOS mode and will set things up accordingly when you run the program. You can also specify MS-DOS mode by hand. You have two choices:

➤ Restart your computer in MS-DOS mode. You do this by first selecting **Start | Shut Down** to display the Shut Down Windows dialog box. Activate the **Restart in MS-DOS mode** option, and then click **OK**. When you get to the DOS prompt, start the DOS program.

➤ Adjust the program's settings to that it runs in MS-DOS mode automatically.

Here's how you do the latter:

1. Use Windows Explorer to locate the file that runs the program.

2. Right-click that file and then click **Properties** in the menu. Windows 98 displays the Properties dialog box for the program.

3. Select the **Program** tab and then click the **Advanced** button. Windows 98 displays the Advanced Program Settings dialog box.

4. Activate the **MS-DOS mode** check box, as shown in the following figure.

Use this dialog box to let Windows 98 know that you want to run a program in MS-DOS mode.

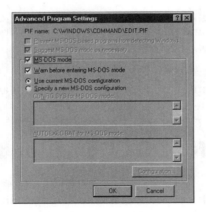

5. Click **OK** to return to the Properties dialog box.

6. Click **OK**.

When you run the program, Windows 98 displays the warning shown in the following dialog box. Click **Yes** to run the program. Remember that MS-DOS mode means the program has exclusive access to the computer, so you won't be able to run other programs or access any Windows features.

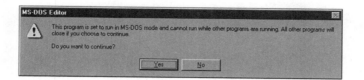

Windows 98 displays this warning when you attempt to run an MS-DOS mode program.

DOS Deluxe: Customizing DOS Windows

I'll close this DOS diatribe by showing you a few options for customizing the DOS window. To view these options, you have two choices:

➤ In Windows Explorer, right-click the file that runs the DOS program, and then click **Properties** in the menu.

➤ If the program's DOS window is already open, click the toolbar's Properties button (shown in the following figure).

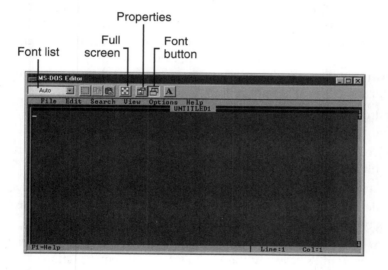

The toolbar buttons for customizing a Windows 98 DOS window.

Either way, you see the program's Properties dialog box, which will look a lot like the one shown below.

Let's start with the various settings found in the **Program** tab:

➤ **Cmd line** This text box specifies the path (drive, folders, and filename) of the file that runs the program.

➤ **Working** Use this text box to set the program's default working folder. (This is the folder that first appears when you select **File | Open** or **File | Save As**.)

➤ **Batch file** You can use this box to enter the name of a batch file or DOS command to run before starting the program.

The Properties dialog box for a DOS program.

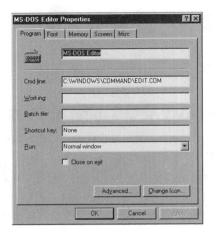

➤ **Shortcut key**   Use this box to assign a key combination that will launch the program. Click inside this box, then press any character. This sets up a key combo of the form **Ctrl+Alt+*character*** (where ***character*** is the keyboard character you pressed). To get a key combination that begins with **Ctrl+Shift**, hold down both **Ctrl** and **Shift** and then press a character; for a **Ctrl+Alt+Shift** combo, hold down all three keys and then press a character.

➤ **Run**   This drop-down list determines how the program window is displayed. Select Normal window, Minimized, or Maximized.

➤ **Close on exit**   If you activate this check box, the DOS window closes automatically when you quit the program.

➤ **Advanced**   This button displays a dialog box that controls various MS-DOS mode settings. As described earlier, the only one you need to bother with is the **MS-DOS mode** check box.

➤ **Change Icon**   Clicking this button displays the Change Icon dialog box, which I discussed in Chapter 2's "Getting the Most Out of Shortcuts" section.

If you don't like the size of the characters you see in your DOS windows, it's no problem changing them. Use either of the following methods:

➤ Use the DOS window's **Font** drop-down list to choose a font size. (If you select **Auto** in this list, you can also adjust the font size by resizing the window.)

➤ Display the program's Properties dialog box, and then select the **Font** tab, which is shown in the following figure. (You can get to the Font tab quickly by clicking the Font button in the toolbar.) Use the **Font size** list to choose the font size you want.

Continuing along the Properties dialog box (and skipping the scary Memory tab), you come to the **Screen** tab, shown in the next figure.

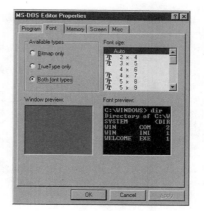

The Font tab offers a selection of font sizes for your DOS viewing pleasure.

The Screen tab settings determine the look of the DOS program's screen.

Here's a look at the most useful of these options:

➤ **Full-screen** Activate this option to have the program always start full-screen.

➤ **Window** Activate this option to have the program always start in a window.

➤ **Initial size** This list sets the number of screen lines that appear (25, 43, or 50). This setting doesn't take effect until you restart the program.

➤ **Display toolbar** Activating this check box means that Windows 98 displays the DOS window toolbar automatically.

➤ **Restore settings on startup** Activating this check box tells Windows 98 to "remember" the last window position and size and to use these settings again the next time you run the program.

Last, and probably least, is the **Misc** tab, shown in the following figure.

The Misc tab: miscellaneous settings for mucking around with a DOS window.

Here's what you get (again, I've skipped some of the more arcane settings):

➤ **Allow screen saver**   While this check box is on, Windows 98 allows your Windows screen saver to do its duty while you're using the DOS program.

➤ **QuickEdit**   When you activate this check box, you can highlight DOS text with your mouse without having to worry about the Mark command that I described earlier. (On the downside, you won't be able to use your mouse within the DOS program itself.)

➤ **Exclusive mode**   If you find that your mouse won't work within the DOS program, try activating this check box. This means that only the DOS program has access to the mouse.

➤ **Warn if still active**   When this check box is activated, Windows 98 displays a warning if you attempt to close a DOS window without first quitting the DOS program. This is a good thing because it's possible to lose unsaved data if you don't perform the proper shutdown procedure in the DOS program.

➤ **Fast pasting**   If you find that Windows 98 isn't pasting DOS text properly (as described earlier in this chapter), it may be because the text is coming in too fast. Try deactivating this check box.

➤ **Windows shortcut keys**   The check boxes in this group represent various Windows 98 shortcut keys. However, it's possible that the DOS program might be set up to use one or more of these shortcuts for its own nefarious purposes. To allow the program to use a key or key combo, deactivate the appropriate check box. Here's a review of what each key combination does in Windows 98:

Alt+Tab   Cycles through the icons of the open applications

Ctrl+Esc   Opens the Start menu

Alt+PrtSc	Takes a screen shot of the active window and copies it to the Clipboard
Alt+Space	Pulls down the control menu for the active window
Alt+Esc	Cycles through the open applications, showing the entire window for each program
PrtSc	Takes a screen shot of the entire desktop and copies it to the Clipboard
Alt+Enter	Toggles a DOS program between a window and full-screen:

From Here

This chapter gave you the real DOS deal: starting DOS sessions, working at the DOS prompt, using MS-DOS mode, and customizing DOS windows. That's quite enough of that, thank you very much. In Chapter 5, "More Windows Goodies: Microsoft Plus! 98," you return to the safety of Windows and examine the basket of treats that come in the Microsoft Plus! 98 package.

More Windows Goodies: Microsoft Plus! 98

In This Chapter

➤ How to install Plus! 98

➤ Protecting your system against viruses

➤ Understanding the rejigged system tools

➤ The Plus! 98 graphics and multimedia tidbits

➤ What the Plus! fuss is all about

Windows 98 is a decent program right out of the box, but Microsoft left out a few goodies in the push to get the program out the door on time. Microsoft gathered these leftover knickknacks, tossed them on a CD-ROM, called it Microsoft Plus! 98, and slapped a price tag on it. Is it worth the extra bucks? Well, most of the Plus! 98 paraphernalia probably should have been included with Windows 98, so you need to get your head around that, for starters. If you do, then, yes, it's definitely worth the price of admission because you get some very useful tools and some fun stuff to play with. This chapter runs through most of the Plus! 98 components.

Installing Microsoft Plus! 98

Let's get the Plus! 98 show on the road by seeing how you install it:

1. Insert the Plus! 98 CD. After a few seconds, you should see the Plus! 98 CD-ROM window.

2. Click **Install Plus!**. (If the Plus! 98 CD-ROM window didn't show up, select **Start | Settings | Control Panel**, open the **Add/Remove Programs** icon, and then click **Install** and follow the wizard's instructions.)

3. When the Plus! 98 Setup loads, click **Next**. The License Agreement rears its ugly head.

4. Activate **I accept the Agreement** (you do, don't you?) and then click **Next**. Setup asks for some user information.

5. Your **Name** and **Organization** should be filled in already (feel free to edit these fields as necessary), so you should only need to enter your **CD Key**. Click **Next** when you're done.

6. Setup now asks if you want to scan your system for viruses. You'll be running a virus scan a bit later, so you don't need to do it now. (The exception to this would be if you suspect your system is infected with a virus.) Deactivate the **Scan system for viruses** check box, and then click **Next**.

7. The next Setup dialog box gives you two options (click **Next** when you've made your choice):

   ➤ **Complete**   Activate this option to install the entire Plus! 98 package. This is the easiest way to go, provided you have the 200MB of disk space required.

   ➤ **Custom**   If you don't have the room (or the inclination) to install all the Plus! 98 components, activate this option. After you click **Next**, you're presented with a list of the components. Deactivate the check boxes beside the components you don't want, and then click **Next**.

8. Setup is now ready to start copying the Plus! 98 files to your machine. Click **Next** to get things rolling.

9. Once the copying is complete, Setup will offer to configure a desktop theme or run the Maintenance Wizard. I'll show you how to do this stuff later on, so deactivate the check boxes and click **Finish**.

10. If you installed VirusScan, Setup will ask if you want to restart your computer. Click **Yes**.

What You Get For Your Money: The Plus! 98 Components

When you return to your regularly scheduled Windows program, select **Start** | **Programs**, and you'll notice that a new **Microsoft Plus! 98** menu has appeared. As you can see in the following figure, this menu gives you access to all of the Plus! 98 components. Note, too, that there is also a new VShield icon in the taskbar (more on this in the next section). The rest of this chapter gives you a quick look at most of these Plus! 98 bits and pieces.

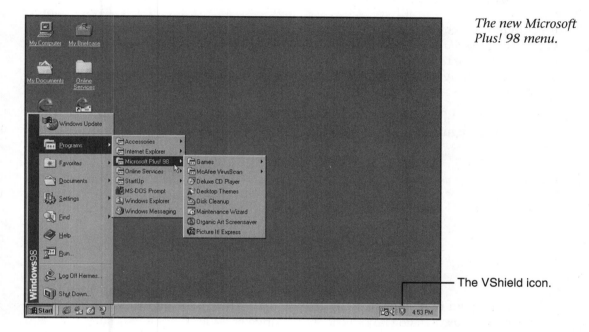

The new Microsoft Plus! 98 menu.

The VShield icon.

VirusScan: Inoculating Windows Against Viruses

Viruses are nasty little programs that live for the sheer thrill of trashing your valuable data. They're crafted in dank basements by repressed, pimple-faced, Jolt cola-fueled deviants—programming wizards who've succumbed to the dark side of The Force. These amoral hackers like to muddy the waters by describing their wicked offspring as "self-propagating, autonomous computer programs" and giving them innocent-sounding names such as Michelangelo and Christmas. But don't be fooled: these small slices of evil can do irreparable harm to your files. (Just so you know, many viruses have names that more directly reflect their intentions. These include Armageddon, Beast, Black Monday, Dark Avenger, and Darth Vader. I'll show you how to see a list of the known viruses a little later.)

Although virus infections are, fortunately, still relatively rare, they *do* happen. Why Microsoft refuses to include virus protection as a standard Windows feature is beyond me. At least they were smart enough to include one of the best anti-virus programs—McAfee VirusScan—in the Plus! 98 package. This program is actually two programs in one:

➤ **VirusScan**   This program checks the files on your hard disk (or floppy disk) for virus infections.

➤ **VShield**   This program runs in the background and constantly monitors your system for signs of virus activity.

Let's begin with VirusScan. To be safe, you should use VirusScan to perform a checkup on your system regularly. I'd recommend running the program at least once a week (even daily if you regularly download files from the Internet) or anytime your computer seems to behave strangely (I know, I know: computers *always* behave strangely). Here's how it works:

1. Select **Start | Programs | Microsoft Plus! 98 | McAfee VirusScan | VirusScan**. The following figure shows the window that appears.

The McAfee VirusScan window.

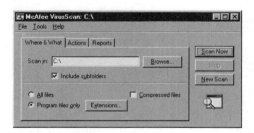

2. Use the **Scan in** box to select the drive or folder that you want to scan. (Click **Browse** to use a dialog box to choose the drive or folder.)

3. Click **Scan Now**. VirusScan proceeds to check every file in the location you selected. The scan takes a few minutes, so this would be a good time to go grab a cup of coffee or see what's happening around the water cooler.

4. If VirusScan comes across an infected file, it will let you know and ask what you want to do next (clean the file, delete it, and so on). In most cases, you'll want to clean the file.

5. When the scan is complete, the VirusScan window displays a list of the infected files, if any.

VirusScan is great at hunting down viral intruders that have invaded your files. What happens, though, if a virus outbreak occurs between scans? That's where VShield rides to the rescue. It's VShield's job to monitor your system constantly and look for suspicious (that is, virus-like) activity. VShield monitors the programs you run and the documents you open; it monitors the files you copy, rename, create, and so on.

Viruses: A Pox On All Our Houses

If you think there are only a few viruses out there, think again. There are, in fact, *thousands*. To see for yourself, select the **Tools | Virus list** command. This displays the Virus List dialog box, which gives you information on all the known viruses. At the time of writing, this list contained well over 3,000 viruses, and the list was growing at over 200 new viruses per month!

VShield loads automatically at startup (recall the new taskbar icon I pointed out earlier), and it does its job without getting in your face (unless, of course, it detects a virus). This means that most of the time you can just ignore it. Your only job will be to sleep better at night knowing your system is well-protected.

Besides using VirusScan regularly, here are a few other tips to help keep your system disease-free:

➤ These days, most viruses are transmitted via file downloads from the Internet, an online service, or a network connection. Set up a special folder for downloads and scan this folder every time you download a file. (To learn how to scan ZIP files before decompressing them, see "ZIP Files as Compressed Folders" later in this chapter.)

➤ The second leading cause of viral infections is the lowly floppy disk, so you should always be careful about which used disks you trust in your computer. If you've inherited some old disks, you can make sure there are no viruses lurking in the weeds by formatting all the disks before you use them.

➤ Trust no one when it comes to loading programs on your machine. Whether they come from family, friends, the Internet, or a BBS, use VirusScan to scan the files *before* using them on your hard disk.

➤ Keep your virus list up to date. As you read this, there are probably dozens, maybe even hundreds, of morally challenged scumnerds designing even nastier viruses. Regular updates will help you keep up. Fortunately, VirusScan has an Update feature that uses the Internet or a modem connection to grab new anti-virus detection code and foil the latest virus plagues. To perform this update, select **File | Update VirusScan**.

Maintenance Wizard does VirusScan

When you install Plus! 98, Setup tweaks the Maintenance Wizard (**Start** | **Programs** | **Accessories** | **System Tools** | **Maintenance Wizard**) to enable you to schedule regular virus scans. I showed you how to use the Maintenance Wizard in *The Complete Idiot's Guide to Windows 98*.

A Cleaner Disk Cleanup

Plus! 98 also beefs up the Disk Cleanup utility. When you run this program (select **Start** | **Programs** | **Accessories** | **System Tools** | **Disk Cleanup**), you see a new "Non-Critical files" option, as shown in the following figure. This option helps you rid your system of unused (and therefore deletable) files.

Thanks to Plus! 98, Disk Cleanup can also wipe out non-critical files to help you recoup even more disk space.

Here's how this new option works:

1. Activate the **Non-Critical files** option and then click **OK**.

2. When Disk Cleanup asks if you're sure you want to delete files, click **Yes**. Disk Cleanup examines your system and then displays the CyberMedia Non-Critical File Cleaner window.

3. Select a category in the **Cleanup Types** list, and you'll see a list of files on the right, as shown in the following figure.

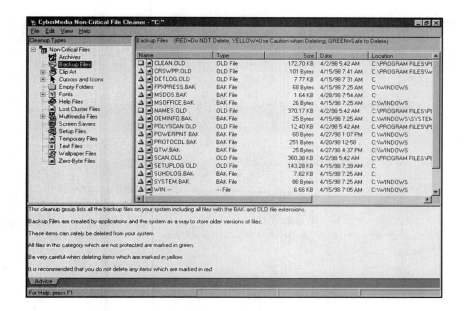

Each category in the Cleanup Types list displays a list of files that are considered non-critical to the health of your system.

4. You now have the following choices:

   ➤ If you want to check out a file, highlight it and select **File | Open**. (If that doesn't work, try **File | Quick View**, instead. To learn about QuickView, head for Chapter 6, "A Few of My Favorite Windows Things," and read the section "Using QuickView to Sneak a Peek at a File.")

   ➤ Files marked with a green icon can be deleted without danger (although, to be safe, you should probably view the file's contents first). Highlight the file (or files) and select **File | Delete**.

   ➤ Files marked with a yellow icon are candidates for deletion, but you should take a more cautious approach. That is, first rename the file and see if your system misses it. To rename a highlighted file, select **File | Rename** (or press F2), type the new name, and then press **Enter**. For easier deleting down the road, leave the current filename as is and insert a common prefix, such as **JUNK-**. For example, if a file is named **SCAN.OLD**, rename it **JUNK-SCAN.OLD**.

   ➤ Files marked with a red icon should not be touched.

5. Repeat steps 3 and 4 as necessary.
6. When you're done, select **File | Exit**.

ZIP Files as Compressed Folders

If you spend any time on the Internet, online services, or bulletin board systems, you've probably tripped over more than your share of ZIP files. A ZIP file is a *compressed archive*, which means two things:

➤ The "archive" part means that the ZIP file may hold multiple files.

➤ The "compressed" part means that all the files in the ZIP have been shrunk to their smallest possible sizes. This is very similar to the way DriveSpace gives you more hard disk room by compressing files so that they take up less space.

In other words, a ZIP file acts much like a folder that has been compressed, and with Plus! 98 installed, that's exactly how Windows 98 views these files. For example, the **Downloads** folder shown in the following figure contains a number of ZIP files (notice the **.zip** extension). In the Type column, see how Windows 98 now describes these files using the **Compressed Folder** type.

Thanks to Plus! 98, Windows now knows what to make of ZIP files.

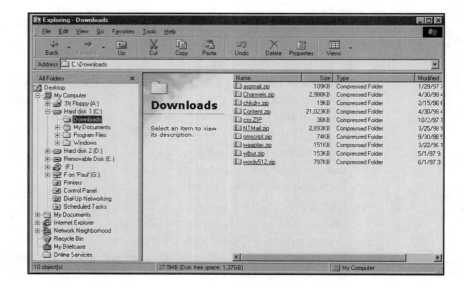

In the past, you needed a special program to access the contents of a ZIP file. But Plus! 98 supplies Windows with various ways to deal with these files:

➤ To check the ZIP file's contents for viruses (always a good idea), highlight the file and select **File | Scan for Viruses**. This starts VirusScan with the ZIP file selected automatically. Click **Scan Now** to run the scan.

➤ Windows now regards ZIP files as folders, so opening a ZIP file just displays the contents of the file within a folder window.

➤ To extract the contents of a ZIP file, highlight it and select **File | Extract** to display the Extract Wizard, as shown in the following figure. Use the **Files will be extracted to this directory** text box (or the **Browse** button) to select a location for the extracted files, and then click **Next**. (If the wizard asks if you want to create the directory, click **Yes**.)

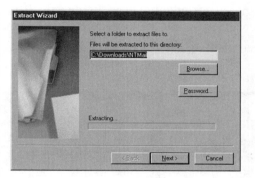

Plus! 98 includes the Extract Wizard for extracting the contents of a ZIP file.

What if you want to take one or more files and compress them into a new ZIP file? No problem. Here's how it works:

1. Use Windows Explorer or My Computer to highlight the file or files you want to compress into the ZIP.

2. Select **File | Send To | Compressed Folder**. Windows gathers the files, compresses them, and then stuffs them into a new ZIP file in the same folder.

3. Press **F5** to refresh the display and see the new file (it will be named after one of the files you compressed, except with a **.zip** extension).

New Desktop Themes

Most of the Plus! 98 improvements you've seen so far are strictly left brain treats. If your right brain is feeling left out of the loop, don't worry because Plus! 98 has plenty of eye candy. This section gives you the lowdown on the new desktop themes. The next section discusses the Picture It! Express photo editor.

In *The Complete Idiot's Guide to Windows 98*, I showed you how to select desktop schemes that govern the look of various objects, including menu bars, window borders and title bars, icons, and more. Plus! 98 takes this idea a step further with desktop *themes*. A theme is also a collection of object properties, but it covers more ground than a simple scheme. Each theme specifies various settings for not only windows and message boxes, but also a screen saver, a wallpaper, mouse pointers, sounds, desktop icons, and more.

To choose a desktop theme, follow these steps:

1. Select **Start | Programs | Microsoft Plus! 98 | Desktop Themes**. Windows 98 loads the Desktop Themes dialog box.

2. Use the **Theme** drop-down list to choose the theme you want to use. The window that takes up the bulk of the dialog box shows you a preview of the theme (see the following figure). You see not only how the theme will affect the various window objects, but also the wallpaper and desktop icons the theme uses.

3. To preview the screen saver associated with the theme, click the **Screen Saver** button.

Use the Desktop Themes dialog box to choose one of the wild desktop themes that come with Plus! 98.

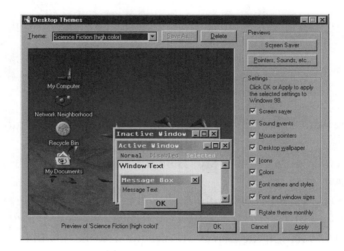

4. To preview the mouse pointers and sounds associated with the theme, click the **Pointers, Sounds, etc** button.

Plus! 98 Screen Savers

Even if you don't bother with a desktop theme, you can still set up your system with any of the wacky screen savers that were installed by Plus! 98. In particular, check out the new "Organic Art" screen saver for some real mind-blowing fun. (As a reminder, you choose a screen saver by right-clicking the desktop, clicking **Properties**, and then selecting the **Screen Saver** tab.)

5. The **Settings** group contains check boxes for each object contained in the theme. To remove an object from the theme, deactivate its check box.

6. If you want the theme to change each month, activate the **Rotate theme monthly** check box.

7. When you're done, click **OK**.

Many of the desktop themes tell you how many colors they require (usually either 256 colors or high color—65,356 colors). If you choose one of these themes, make sure your display is set up with at least that many colors. To do this, right-click the desktop, click **Properties**, and then select the **Settings** tab. Use the **Colors** list to choose the number of colors you need.

Photo Touch-Ups with Picture It! Express

If you have a scanner or digital camera, you can use Windows 98's Imaging program to grab an image and store it as a file on your computer. (I explained how this is done in *The Complete Idiot's Guide to Windows 98*.) Of course, once you've got the image file safely stowed on your machine, the next question is what the heck do you do with it? That is, what do you do if you want to apply special effects to the image, correct the tint, crop out part of the image, and so on?

These kinds of tasks normally require the use of a dedicated (and often expensive) photo-editing program. However, Plus! 98 comes with a photo editor as part of the package. It's called Picture It! Express, and although it's pretty limited in what it can do, it should serve you well for most basic touch-ups.

To start the program, select **Start | Programs | Microsoft Plus! 98 | Picture It! Express**. The following figure shows the Picture It! Express window with an image ready for editing.

Here's a quick summary of various tasks you can perform with the program:

➤ **Scan a photo.** To scan in a photo, click **Get Picture** and then click **Scan Picture**. Follow the steps shown in the Scan Picture pane, and then click **Scan**.

➤ **Get an image from a digital camera.** To download an image from a digital camera, click **Get Picture** and then click **Digital Camera**. Follow the steps shown in the Digital Camera pane, and then click **Download pictures**.

➤ **Open an existing file.** To open an image file from your hard disk, click **Get Picture** and then click **My Picture**. Use the **Click a folder** list to pick out the location of the file, click the image you want, and then click **Open**.

➤ **Zoom in and out.** Click the vertical strip of buttons in the lower right corner to zoom in and out of the picture.

➤ **Crop a picture.** If you need only part of a picture, you can crop out the stuff you don't need. Click **Size & Position** and then click **Crop**. Follow the steps in the Crop pane, and then click **Done**.

The Picture It!
Express window.

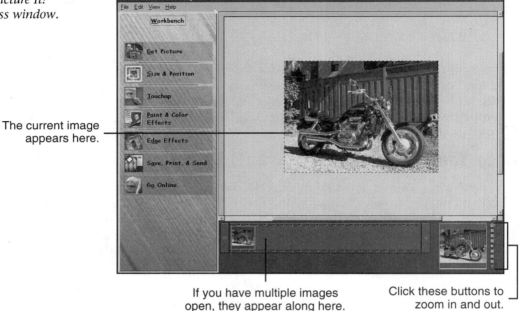

The current image
appears here.

If you have multiple images
open, they appear along here.

Click these buttons to
zoom in and out.

➤ **Rotate or flip a picture.** To rotate a picture or flip it along an axis, click **Size &**
Position and then click either **Rotate** or **Flip**. Select the type of rotation or flip that
you want, and then click **Done**.

➤ **Eliminate red eye.** If your photo subjects are suffering from a bad case of red eye,
you can get the red out by clicking **Touchup** and then **Fix Red Eye**. Follow the steps
in the Fix Red Eye pane, then click **Done.**

➤ **Adjust the brightness and contrast.** Adjusting the brightness and contrast represents the most common of photo repair jobs. To do this, click **Paint & Color Effects**
and then click **Brightness & Contrast**. In the Brightness & Contrast pane, click
Smart Task Fix to have Picture It! Express repair the image automatically. Otherwise, use the controls in this pane to make your adjustments by hand. Click **Done**
when you're, well, done.

➤ **Correct the tint.** If your reds aren't quite red and your blues aren't quite blue, you
need to correct the tint. To do this, click **Paint & Color Effects** and then click
Correct Tint. To have Picture It! Express correct the tint automatically, click an area
of the image that's supposed to be white. If there's no white in sight, use the color
ring to adjust the tint by hand. When you're finished, click **Done**.

➤ **Soften the edges of the image.** Softening the edges means replacing the edges of
the image with a soft, white border that fades into the image. To apply this nice

effect, click **Edge Effects** and then click **Soft Edges**. In the Soft Edges pane, drag the slider to the right for a softer edge, or drag it to the left for a harder edge. Click **Done** when you have the effect you want.

➤ **Finishing up.** When you complete your photo editing chores, click **Save, Print, & Send** for a list of options. Choose **Save As** to save the image under a different name; choose **Save** to save the image; choose **Close This Picture** to remove the image from the Picture It! Express window; choose **Print This Picture** to send the image to your printer; choose **Save As Wallpaper** to use the image as your desktop wallpaper.

Most Valuable Player: The Deluxe CD Player

As you may know, Windows 98 ships with a little program called CD Player that lets you play audio CDs in your computer's CD-ROM drive. CD Player is decent enough, but you'll forget it ever existed once you've used the Deluxe CD Player that comes with Plus! 98. Deluxe CD Player has a layout that's both simple and slick, and it offers tons of options for playing your CDs. The big news with Deluxe CD Player, however, is that it can use the Internet to download the title, artist, and track names for many CDs, as well as to search for information on the artist and to access music sites on the Web.

To give Deluxe CD Player a spin, just insert an audio CD into your CD-ROM drive. Windows 98 will probably launch Deluxe CD Player automatically and your disc will start playing. (If you don't see the Deluxe CD Player window, you can load it by hand by selecting **Start | Programs | Microsoft Plus! 98 | Deluxe CD Player**.)

Whenever you insert a new disc, Deluxe CD Player asks if you want to download information for the disc (title, artist, and track data). I'll show you how this works later on, so click **Cancel** for now. The following figure shows the Deluxe CD Player window that shows up.

Use the Deluxe CD Player window to wail your favorite tunes through your CD-ROM drive.

71

The basic Deluxe CD Player controls operate in the same way as those in the regular CD Player. That is, you click Play to start the music, click Previous track and Next track to shuffle from track to track, and click Stop to get some peace and quiet. You can also use the **Track** drop-down list to choose a specific track to play. If you have more than one CD-ROM drive, use the **Disc** list to select the one that you want to work with.

The Mode list gives you the following options:

➤ **Standard** Plays the tracks in their predefined order and runs through all of the tracks once.

➤ **Random** Plays the tracks in random order.

➤ **Repeat Track** Repeats the current track.

➤ **Repeat All** Returns to the first track after the last track is done).

➤ **Preview** Plays just the first five seconds of each track.

As I mentioned earlier, Deluxe CD Player is "wired" and will happily access the Internet for you to get disc data, search for music topics, and more. Assuming you have an Internet connection established, the available Net commands can be found by opening the **Internet** list:

➤ **Download track names** By default, Deluxe CD Player displays the disc title as "New Title," the artist as "New Artist," and the track names as "Track 1," "Track 2," and so on. For more meaningful monikers, select the **Download track names** command to download the disc data from the Internet. Deluxe CD Player connects to an Internet music site and then grabs the disc title, artist, and track names.

➤ **Internet music sites** This command throws open a submenu that contains links to music-related Web sites.

Once you've downloaded the disc particulars, the following **Internet** menu commands become available:

➤ **Search the net** This command displays a submenu with various search options for the current artist and album.

➤ **More about *Artist*** Select this command to visit a Web site that gives you information about the current artist.

➤ **More about this album** Select this command to visit a Web site that gives you information about the current disc.

➤ **Other *Genre* albums** Select this command to visit a Web site that displays a list of other albums in the same music genre as the current album.

From Here

This chapter looked at all the shiny baubles and bangles that come with the Microsoft Plus! 98 package. After showing you how to install Plus! 98, I talked about VirusScan, the enhanced Disk Cleanup, ZIP files as compressed folders, desktop themes, Picture It! Express, and Deluxe CD Player. The only Plus! 98 stones left unturned were the various games, but I'll leave the fun stuff up to you.

Speaking of baubles and bangles, I have quite a few of them in my own bag of Windows 98 tricks. I'll hold many of these trinkets up to the light in Chapter 6, "A Few of My Favorite Windows Things."

A Few of My Favorite Windows Things

In This Chapter

➤ Windows 98 tips and tricks

➤ More fun with file types

➤ Fancy financial tricks with Calculator

➤ An Internet Explorer Easter egg hunt

➤ An exercise in Windows self-indulgence

This chapter presents an assortment, a miscellany, a grab bag, a hodgepodge, a mish-mash, a treasure trove, a veritable potpourri of Windows stuff. You'll find tips, tricks, arcana, even strange but fascinating animations called "Easter eggs." They're all things I've come across in my long treks across the Windows 98 landscape, and I've collected them all in one place for your browsing pleasure.

Ten Transcendental Tips and Tricks

There's no doubt that Windows is a complicated, arcane, and sometimes just plain weird program. To survive over the long haul, you need to develop your own arsenal of short-cuts and handy techniques that will smooth your Windows work and get you out of jams. As a starter kit, here's a list—in no particular order—of 10 of my favorite tips and tricks.

1. Press Ctrl Alt Delete for Stuck Programs

Windows 98 does a fair job of intercepting rogue programs that have run amok. It will usually tell you that a program has "performed an illegal operation" and offer to shut down the wayward application for you.

Every now and then, however, a program locks up completely, and no amount of shouting or gesticulating on your part will unlock it. In these cases, press the "three-fingered salute": **Ctrl+Alt+Delete** (also known in the trade as the "Vulcan nerve pinch"). Windows 98 should display the Close Program dialog box with a list of your open programs. In particular, you should see the name of the crashed program with **Not responding** tacked on to the end. Highlight the offending application, say "Yeah, well respond to *this*," and click the **End Task** button. Windows 98 terminates the recalcitrant program with extreme prejudice.

2. Microsoft Natural Keyboard Shortcuts

The split-keys design of the curvaceous Microsoft Natural Keyboard is a great defense against the ravages of Carpal Tunnel Syndrome and other typing-related repetitive stress injuries. However, this keyboard also saves wear and tear on your wrists and fingers by offering a useful Windows logo shortcut key—[wl]. (This key is also available on most new keyboards these days.) Pressing this key by itself opens the Start menu, which is a lot easier than pressing the tough-to-reach **Ctrl+Esc** key combination. But you also can use it in various key combinations to gain quick access to many Windows 98 features. The following table summarizes these key combinations.

Press...	To...
⊞	Open the Start menu.
⊞+E	Open Explorer.
⊞+F	Find a file or folder.
Ctrl+⊞+F	Find a computer.
⊞+M	Minimize all open windows.
Shift+⊞+M	Undo minimize all.
⊞+R	Display the Run dialog box.
⊞+F1	Display Windows Help.
⊞+Break	Display the System Properties dialog box.
⊞+Spacebar	Scroll down one page (supported only in certain applications, such as Internet Explorer).
⊞+Tab	Cycle through the taskbar buttons.

For good measure, the Microsoft Natural Keyboard also includes an **Application** key. It has a picture of a little pulled-down menu. Pressing this key activates the shortcut menu for the current object.

3. Faster Deleting

When you send a file to the Recycle Bin, Windows 98 always asks if you're sure you want to delete the file. If you're absotively, posolutely certain that a particular file can be deleted, press **Shift+Delete**. This bypasses the Recycle Bin (and, so, the annoying confirmation prompt) and just deletes the file without so much as a how do you do. The downside? If you nuke the wrong file by accident, it's toast, and there's zip you can do to get it back.

4. A Double Double-Click Treat

Here are two little-known double-click shortcuts that you should find handy:

➤ If you find the Maximize button in Windows is too small a target, or if you keep accidentally clicking the neighboring Close button, there's an easier way to max out a window: just double-click its title bar.

➤ Many icons have a Properties dialog box that gives you access to various settings and options related to the icon. To get to this dialog box, you either highlight the icon and select **File | Properties**, or right-click the icon and then click **Properties** in the shortcut menu. Here's another method that might be quicker in some cases: hold down **Alt** and double-click the icon (single-click if Web integration is turned on).

5. Back Up the Registry

You'll learn all about the Windows Registry in Chapter 10, "The Registry: The Soul of the Windows Machine." As the name of that chapter implies, the Registry is a crucial Windows body part. However, unlike real body parts, you can save a backup copy of the Registry and then restore that backup down the road should anything untoward happen to your machine.

The good news is that Windows 98's Backup program (select **Start | Programs | Accessories | System Tools | Backup**) makes backing up the Registry a breeze. To include the Registry files in a backup job, follow these steps:

1. In the Microsoft Backup window, click **Options** to display the Backup Job Options dialog box.

2. Activate the **Advanced** tab.

3. Activate the **Back up Windows Registry** check box, as shown in the following figure.

4. Click **OK**.

Activate the Back up Windows Registry check box to, well, you know.

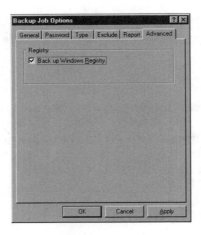

6. A Faster Way to Restart

Back in Chapter 1, "Beginning at the Beginning: Windows 98 Startup Techniques," I told you about the Restart option in the Shut Down Windows dialog box (select **Start | Shut Down** to get there). If you need to restart your computer, but are too impatient to run through the entire reboot process, never fear: a faster way is here.

With the **Restart** option selected, hold down **Shift** and then click **OK**. This tells Windows 98 not to bother with a full reboot. Instead, you see a **Windows is now restarting** message (at which point it's okay to let go of the **Shift** key) and, true to its word, Windows 98 restarts.

7. The Explorers Do Double Duty

As you know, Windows Explorer is the program for performing file and folder maintenance chores, and Internet Explorer is the program for browsing the World Wide Web. What you may not know, however, is that both programs are fully capable of filling in for the other in a pinch.

The secret is the Address bar that appears in both windows (if you don't see it, select **View | Toolbars | Address Bar**):

➤ If you're using Windows Explorer, type a Web address into the Address bar and press **Enter**. Windows Explorer not only displays the Web page, but it also converts its menus and toolbars to those used by Internet Explorer. Note, too, that this works for any folder window, including My Computer, Control Panel, Printers, Scheduled Tasks, and so on.

➤ For Internet Explorer, use the Address toolbar to type a location on your machine (such as **My Computer** or a drive and folder, such as **c:**) and press **Enter**. Internet Explorer displays the location, and it also displays the menus and toolbars normally seen in Windows Explorer. For example, the following figure shows Internet Explorer displaying the My Computer folder.

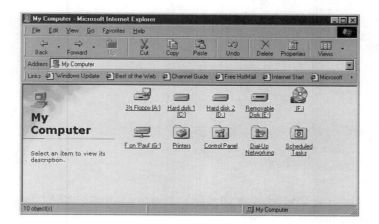

Internet Explorer is happy to display not only Web pages, but also local stuff, such as the My Computer folder.

The Taskbar's Address Bar

The Address bar—in a clear bid for ubiquity—can also be displayed right on the taskbar. To get it there, right-click an empty chunk of the taskbar, and then click **Toolbars | Address**. Once the Address bar is in place, you can use it to enter Web addresses and locations on your computer.

8. Easier Access to Disk Drive Tools

Windows 98 offers tons of tools for keeping your disk drives humming, including Disk Cleanup, ScanDisk, Backup, and Disk Defragmenter. (I showed you how to use these tools in *The Complete Idiot's Guide to Windows 98*.) Unfortunately, most of these tools reside way over in the System Tools menu. That's a multi-mouse-click journey by itself, but if you only want to run the tool on a specific disk drive, you'll be clicking until the cows come home.

Is there an easier route to take? You bet:

1. Using Windows Explorer or My Computer, right-click the disk drive that you want to work with, and then click **Properties** when the little menu shows up. Windows 98 displays the Properties dialog box, which will be similar to the one shown below.

2. If you want, you can use the **Label** text box to change the name of the drive. (This isn't strictly a system tool issue, but I thought while you're here, what the heck.)

*A disk drive's
Properties dialog box
gives you easy access
to several system
tools.*

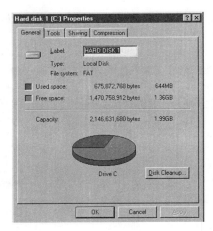

3. If you want to remove unnecessary files from the disk, click **Disk Cleanup** to run the Disk Cleanup utility.

4. Display the **Tools** tab, as shown in the following figure. The three groups correspond to three different drive maintenance chores, and each one tells you when you last performed the chore.

*Use the Tools tab to
monitor when you
last performed
maintenance on the
disk.*

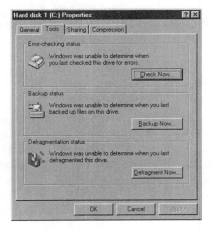

5. To check the drive for errors, click **Check Now** to run ScanDisk on the drive.

6. To back up the drive's files, click **Backup Now** to launch Microsoft Backup.

7. To defragment the drive, click **Defragment Now** to run Disk Defragmenter on the drive.

8. To compress the drive, display the **Compression** tab and then click either **Compress Drive** (to compress the drive's files) or **Create New Drive** (to create a new compressed drive from the free space on the current drive).

9. Click **OK** to exit the dialog box.

9. Loading DOSKEY for Smoother DOS Prompt Sessions

Chapter 4, "Taming the DOS Beast," showed you a few pointers for working at the DOS prompt. If you plan on spending any time at all dealing with DOS, I highly recommend that you install the DOSKEY command at the beginning of each DOS session. Among other things, DOSKEY lets you recall previous commands and edit the current command line, which are real time savers. (I explain how this works in a bit.) To install DOSKEY, simply type **doskey** and press **Enter** at the DOS prompt.

To make this highly useful command available all the time in your MS-DOS prompt sessions, tell Windows 98 to load it automatically whenever you start a DOS session. To do this, follow these steps:

1. How you proceed depends on how you start your DOS sessions:

   ➤ For those DOS prompt sessions that you launch by selecting **Start | Programs | MS-DOS Prompt**, open your main Windows 98 folder, open the **Start Menu** folder, then open the **Programs** folder. Right-click the **MS-DOS Prompt** icon and then click **Properties**.

   ➤ For those DOS prompt sessions that you invoke by typing **command.com** in the Run dialog box, use Windows Explorer to find the **Command.com** file (it's probably in **C:**), right-click the file, and then click **Properties**.

2. With the Properties dialog box displayed, select the **Program** tab.

3. In the **Batch file** text box, type **doskey**.

4. Click **OK**.

The simplest DOSKEY feature is command-recall. To see how this works, try entering the following commands at the DOS prompt:

```
cd\windows
dir
cd\
```

Now try pressing the up arrow key. You should see the **cd** command. Press the up arrow again to see the **dir** command. DOSKEY keeps a list of the commands that you enter, and you use the up and down arrow keys to move through the list. To rerun a command, simply use the arrow keys to find it and then press **Enter**. Is technology great, or what?

The following table offers a rundown of the various keys and key combos that DOSKEY responds to.

Press...	To...
Page Up	Recall the oldest command in the list.
Page Down	Recall the newest command in the list.
F7	Display the entire command list.
Alt+F7	Delete all commands from the recall list.
F8	Have DOSKEY recall a command that begins with the letter or letters you've typed on the command line.
F9	Have DOSKEY prompt you for a command list number (you can see the numbers with the **F7** key). Type the number and press **Enter** to recall the command.

Over the years, I've perfected (if that's the right word) my own four-fingered typing style (well, five-fingered, actually; I use my right thumb for the spacebar). But no matter how good I get as a typist, I still fumble certain words. For example, I always type "propmt" instead of "prompt." Before DOSKEY came along, I'd type some long-winded DOS command, realize that I made a typo at the beginning, and then end up pounding my head against the wall because I had to retype the whole thing.

With DOSKEY loaded, however, you can edit the command line. Instead of retyping commands, you can just use various keys to move the cursor to the offending letters and replace them. Ah, the promised land, at last! The following table summarizes DOSKEY's command-line editing keys.

Press...	To...
Left arrow	Move the cursor one character to the left.
Right arrow	Move the cursor one character to the right.
Ctrl+left arrow	Move the cursor one word to the left.
Ctrl+right arrow	Move the cursor one word to the right.
Home	Move the cursor to the beginning of the line.
End	Move the cursor to the end of the line.
Delete	Delete the character over the cursor.
Backspace	Delete the character to the left of the cursor.
Ctrl+Home	Delete from the cursor to the beginning of the line.
Ctrl+End	Delete from the cursor to the end of the line.
Insert	Toggle DOSKEY between "insert" mode (your typing is inserted between existing letters on the command line) and "overstrike" mode (your typing replaces existing letters on the command line).

Check This Out...

Overcoming Overstrike

By default, DOSKEY is in overstrike mode. If you prefer to use insert mode as the default, start DOSKEY with the following command

`doskey /insert.`

10. CD-ROMs: Taking the "Auto" Out of AutoPlay

When you're working with CD-ROM discs, the AutoPlay feature can be quite handy. For discs that support this feature (most new ones do), one of the following will happen when you insert the disc:

➤ If the disc's program hasn't been installed, AutoPlay automatically loads the installation software.

➤ If the disc has been installed, AutoPlay automatically starts the program.

Sounds nice enough, but there will be plenty of times when you'll prefer that AutoPlay wasn't so automatic. For example, you might insert a disc for later use, or you might just need to grab a file from the disc.

If you'd prefer that Windows 98 not run AutoPlay when you plop a CD-ROM in its drive, hold down the **Shift** key while you insert the disc. This tells Windows 98 to skip the AutoPlay.

If you're totally anti-AutoPlay for some reason, it's possible to convince Windows 98 to *never* use it. Here are the steps:

1. Right-click the desktop's **My Computer** icon and then click **Properties** in the menu. (You can also launch Control Panel's **System** icon.) This displays the System Properties dialog box.

2. Display the **Device Manager** tab.

3. Open the **CD-ROM** branch, click your CD-ROM drive, and then click **Properties**.

4. Display the **Settings** tab.

5. Deactivate the **Auto insert notification** check box, as shown in the following figure.

6. Click **OK** to return to the System Properties dialog box.

7. Click **OK**. When Windows 98 asks if you want to restart your computer, click **Yes**.

To turn off AutoPlay permanently, deactivate the Auto insert notification check box.

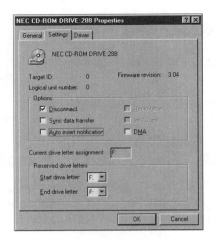

A Few of My Favorite Practical Windows Things

This section offers a few Windows tricks for things like file types, using QuickView to examine documents, and converting your old Windows 3.1 program groups. The emphasis here is on practical techniques that you should find useful in your day-to-day Windows sessions. (Don't worry: you'll get to some fun stuff a bit later.)

File Type Tweak I: Modifying Actions

In Chapter 2, "Taking Charge of Your Files and Folders," you learned about *file types*. In particular, you learned three things:

➤ That a file type describes the format of the file (such as a text document).

➤ That a file type defines an association between an application and the documents created with the application (such as between Notepad and text documents).

➤ That a file type is determined by the file extension—the three-letter code after the period (.) in the file name (such as TXT for a text document).

Another file type characteristic is that it defines one or more *actions* that can be performed with its associated files. Most file types have an Open action (which opens the file within its associated application) and a Print action (which prints the file using its associated application). One of these actions is always set up as the *default*, which means it's the action that's performed when you either highlight the file and press **Enter**, or double-click the file.

What's the big whoop? Well, suppose you deal with a file type that has an action you don't like. For example, one of Notepad's limitations is that it just doesn't have the horsepower to handle large text files. If you try to open a large text file, Windows 98 will ask if you want to use WordPad instead. To avoid this hassle, you might prefer to use WordPad to open text files and just forget about Notepad altogether.

To do that, you must alter the Open action for the Text Document file type. Here's how:

1. In Windows Explorer or My Computer, select **View | Folder Options**.
2. Display the **File Types** tab.
3. In the **Registered file types** list, click the file type that you want to work with. (For our WordPad example, click **Text Document**.)
4. Click the **Edit** button. The Edit File Type dialog box shows up for work. The following figure shows the dialog box that appears for the Text Document file type.

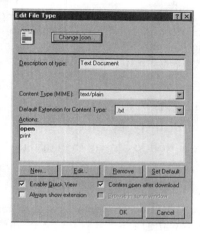

Use the Edit File Type dialog box to alter the actions for a file type.

5. The **Actions** list displays the available actions for this file type. Highlight the action you want to change (such as **open** for our example) and then click **Edit**. An editing action dialog box appears, similar to the one shown in the following figure.

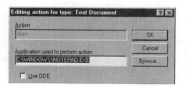

Use this dialog box to edit the action you highlighted.

6. In the **Application used to perform action** text box, enter the location of the application that you want to use. If you're not sure, click **Browse**, highlight the appropriate file in the Open With dialog box, and click **Open**. (**WordPad.exe** is usually stored in **C:\Program Files\Accessories**.)

7. Click **OK** to return to the Edit File Type dialog box.

8. Click **Close** to return to the File Types tab.

9. Click **OK** to exit the Folder Options dialog box and put the new action into effect.

File Type Tweak II: Creating New Actions

Completely replacing the application associated with a particular action is sometimes a bit too drastic. For example, you might still want to use Notepad for small text files because Notepad loads quite a bit faster than its bulkier WordPad cousin.

The solution is to create *new* actions for a file type. In our text file example, you could keep the Open action as is and create a new action—called, for example, Open with WordPad—that uses WordPad to open a text file. How does that help? Well, when you highlight a text file and pull down the File menu, or right-click a text file, the menus that appear will show both commands: Open (for Notepad) and Open with WordPad (for WordPad). Here are the steps to stride through to set up a new action for a file type:

1. In Windows Explorer or My Computer, select **View | Folder Options**.

2. Display the **File Types** tab.

3. In the **Registered file types** list, click the file type you want to work with.

4. Click the **Edit** button to display the Edit File Type dialog box once again.

5. Click **New**. The New Action dialog box parachutes onto the screen.

6. Use the **Action** text box to enter a name for the new action.

7. In the **Application used to perform action** text box, enter the location of the application you want to use. If you're not sure, click **Browse**, highlight the appropriate file in the Open With dialog box, and click **Open**. The following figure shows a filled-in version of the New Action dialog box.

Use the New Action dialog box to set up a new action for a file type.

8. Click **OK** to return to the Edit File Type dialog box. The new action appears in the Actions list.

9. If you want to make the new action the default, highlight it and click the **Set Default** button.

10. Click **Close** to return to the File Types tab.

Check This Out...

Accelerator Keys

What's with the & thingy in the Action text box? It's called an ampersand, and it tells Windows 98 to set up the following letter as the command's accelerator key. For example, as shown in the figure, entering **Open with &WordPad** defines **W** as the accelerator key. You can then press this letter's key to select the command on either the File menu or the Context menu (see the following figure).

11. Click **OK** to exit the Folder Options dialog box.

With the new action in place, you'll see it on the File menu when you highlight a document of that file type. You also see the new action in the menu that appears when you right-click one of the file type documents. For example, the following figure shows the menu that appears when you right-click a text file. Notice the new Open with WordPad action. (And, as promised in the previous Check This Out sidebar, the "W" is underlined to indicate that it's an accelerator key.)

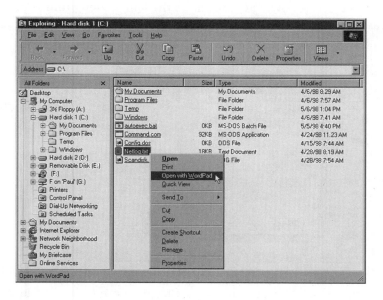

New actions show up on the shortcut menu for the file type.

Using QuickView to Sneak a Peek at a Document

If you want to see what's inside a document, the easiest method is to double-click the document to open it within its associated application. There are two times when this might not be the route you want to take:

➤ If the associated application is a large program, it might be overkill to load the program just to take a quick look at a document.

➤ If you don't have the associated application installed on your system. For example, if you want to look at an Excel workbook but you don't have Excel installed.

To solve both problems, try Windows 98's Quick View program on for size. Quick View's forte is that it "understands" tons of file types and can display a file even if you don't have the appropriate application installed. You can't use Quick View to edit a file, but it's great for sneaking a peek.

To use Quick View, follow these steps:

1. In Windows Explorer or My Computer, highlight the document you want to view.

2. Either select **File | Quick View**, or right-click the document and then click **Quick View** in the menu. The following figure shows the Quick View window that pops up. In this case, Quick View is displaying the contents of an Excel workbook.

Quick View lets you see the contents of a file, even if you don't have the appropriate application installed.

	A	B	C	D	E
1					
2		Jan	Feb	Mar	1st Quarter
3	*Sales*				
4	Division I	23,500	23,000	24,000	70,500
5	Division II	28,750	27,800	29,500	86,050
6	Division III	24,400	24,000	25,250	73,650
7	SALES TOTAL	76,650	74,800	78,750	230,200
8	*Expenses*				
9	Cost of Goods	6,132	5,984	6,300	18,416
10	Advertising	4,600	4,200	5,200	14,000
11	Rent	2,100	2,100	2,100	6,300
12	Supplies	1,300	1,200	1,400	3,900
13	Salaries	16,000	16,000	16,500	48,500
14	Shipping	14,250	13,750	14,500	42,500
15	Utilities	500	600	600	1,700
16	EXPENSES TOTAL	44,882	43,834	46,600	135,316
17	GROSS PROFIT	31,768	30,966	32,150	94,884

3. If you do have the associated application installed, you can open the file in that application by selecting **File | Open File for Editing**.

4. When you're done, quit Quick View by selecting File | Exit.

Converting Windows 3.1 Program Groups

If you're upgrading from Windows 3.1 and you install Windows 98 into a separate directory, Windows Setup just ignores all of your carefully constructed Windows 3.1 program groups. If you don't like that idea, Windows 98 has a utility called Program Group Converter that can convert existing Program Manager groups into Windows 98 Start menu folders. Here's how it works:

1. Select **Start | Run** to display the Run dialog box.
2. Type **grpconv /m** and click **OK**. The Select a Group to Convert dialog box appears.
3. Open your Windows 3.1 folder. The dialog box displays a list of program group files.
4. Highlight one of the program group files and click **Open**. The program asks whether you're sure you want to convert the group.
5. Click **Yes**. The group is converted and the Select a Group to Convert dialog box is redisplayed.
6. Repeat Steps 4 and 5 for any other groups you want to convert.
7. When you're done, click **Cancel**.

Now select **Start | Programs** and you'll see your converted program groups as commands on the Programs menu.

Not-So-Stupid Calculator Tricks

Most folks use Windows 98's Calculator accessory for quick additions, subtractions, multiplications, and divisions. However, Calculator is no mere four-trick pony. In fact, it's possible to cajole Calculator into spitting out a loan payment, the future value of an investment, the remaining balance on a loan, and other feats of financial legerdemain.

To get started, whip out the Calculator by selecting **Start | Programs | Accessories | Calculator**. You need the Scientific version of the Calculator for this, so select the **View | Scientific** command to display the Calculator window shown in the following figure. Note, in particular, the following two buttons:

➤ **x^y** This button raises x to the power of y. For example, to calculate 2^4 (2 to the power of 4), you click **2**, then **x^y**, then **4**. The shortcut key for this button is **Y**.

➤ **+/-** This button changes the sign of the current value displayed in Calculator's results box. For example, if the box shows 100, pressing +/- changes that value to -100. The shortcut key for this button is **F9**.

You must use the Scientific Calculator for the financial wizardry in this section.

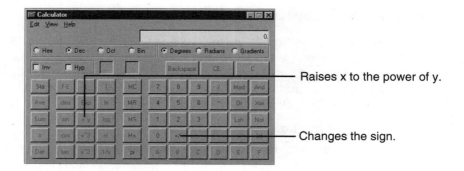

Raises x to the power of y.

Changes the sign.

In the financial projects that follow, I'll be using the following terms:

Term	What It Means
FV	The future value of an investment.
I	The interest rate for an investment or loan.
N	The number of periods in an investment or loan.
PMT	The regular payment into an investment or loan.
PV	The present value of an investment or loan.

Okay, let's get to it:

Calculating Loan Payments

Loans and mortgages are a fact of financial life, and it's a rare household that doesn't have or need a loan of some kind. If you're contemplating a loan, the crucial question is how large is the chunk of change you have to fork out every month. Calculator can figure this out for you using the following formula:

$PV*I/(1-(1+I)^{-N})$

Looks like fun, doesn't it? Well, it's not as bad as it appears. Here's how this looks as the sequence of Calculator buttons and values that you click:

$PV * I / (1 - (1 + I) \ x^y \ N +/-) =$

Let's try an example. Suppose you have a $100,000 mortgage over 30 years with an 9% annual interest rate. To get the monthly payment, you must first translate everything into monthly values: 30 years is 360 months and 9% (0.09) annually is 0.75% (0.0075) monthly. Plugging these values into the above formula, we get the following:

$100000*.0075/(1-(1+.0075)^{-360})$

Here's the exact sequence of buttons to click in Calculator:

100000 * .0075 / (1 - (1 + .0075) x^y 360 +/-) =

The answer works out to approximately $804.62 per month.

Calculating a Loan Balance

If you want to know how much principal is remaining on an outstanding loan, use this formula:

$PV = PMT*(1-(1+I)^{-N})/I$

In this case, N is the number of payments left on the loan. Here's the general Calculator sequence:

PMT * (1 - (1 + *I*) x^y *N* +/-) / *I* =

For example, suppose you're paying $200 per month on a car loan that has 24 months to go at 9% annual interest (0.0075 monthly). Here's how to calculate the remaining principal:

200 * (1 - (1 + .0075) x^y 24 +/-) / .0075 =

The answer is approximately $4,377.83.

Calculating the Future Value of an Investment

Whether you're saving for your kid's education or for your own retirement, you need to know how much your investments will be worth in the future. In other words, if you deposit *PMT* dollars into an investment earning interest rate *I* for *N* years, what's the future value? Here's the formula that figures this out:

$PMT*((1+I)^N-1)/I$

Here's the general Calculator sequence for this formula:

PMT * ((1 + *I*) x^y *N* - 1) / *I* =

Suppose you deposit $1,000 annually into an IRA earning 8% interest (0.08) over 20 years. To calculate the future value, use the following Calculator sequence:

1000 * ((1 + .08) x^y 20 - 1) / .08 =

The result is approximately $45,761.96.

If you're making monthly payments, don't forget to multiply the number of years by 12 to get the total number of months (*N*), and to divide the annual interest rate by 12 to get the monthly rate (*I*).

Calculating Required Investment Deposits

A slightly different problem is when you have a financial goal in mind and you need to know what it will take to get there. For example, if you think you'll need $50,000 for your child's education in 18 years, what do you have to put aside every year (assuming 8% annual interest)? Here's the formula:

$FV*I/((1+I)^N-1)$

Here's the general Calculator sequence for this formula:

FV * I / ((1 + I) x^y N - 1) =

For the above example, click the following Calculator buttons:

50000 * .08 / ((1 + .08) x^y 18 - 1) =

The result: You must sock away approximately $1,335.10 each year to give your kids the gift of a good education.

Factoring Inflation Into Your Investments

If you've started planning for your retirement, you've probably calculated how much money you'll need to live (in the style you're accustomed to, of course). However, many people make the mistake of not factoring inflation into their calculations. For example, $500,000 in an IRA might be enough money in today's dollars, but what about 20 years from now?

To find out, you can use the following formula:

$FV/(1+I)^N$

Here's the general Calculator sequence for this formula:

FV / (1 + I) x^y N =

Let's assume a 3% (0.03) inflation rate and see what $500,000 will be worth in today's dollars. Here's the Calculator sequence to plug in:

500000 / (1 + .03) x^y 20 =

The answer, somewhat surprisingly, is approximately $276,837.88. Aren't you glad you checked!

A Few of My Favorite Fun Windows Things

Okay, now that we have all that serious stuff out of the way, it's time to have a little fun. The rest of this chapter takes you through a few Windows tricks that are decidedly frivolous and silly.

A-Hunting We Will Go: Tracking Down the Internet Explorer Easter Egg

Programmers usually toil thanklessly in obscurity and, I'm sure, most prefer it that way. However, we all like to get at least a little recognition in our lives, and programmers are no exception. To that end, many Windows applications include *Easter eggs*—animated boxes that display cute characters and list the names of the programming wizards who created the program. (These animations are also called *gang screens*.)

Internet Explorer has its own Easter egg and, as a diversion from our labors, here are the steps to follow to display it:

1. Open Internet Explorer (you don't need to establish an Internet connection for this).

2. Select the **Help | About Internet Explorer** command. The About Internet Explorer dialog box slides onscreen and displays a short animation.

3. Hold down the **Ctrl** key and use your mouse to drag the "e" icon in the upper-right corner. Position the icon so that it's just to the left of the words "Microsoft Internet Explorer," as shown in the following figure (don't drop the icon just yet).

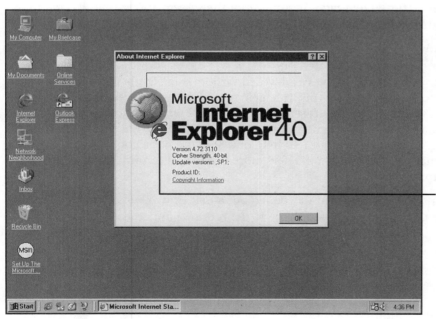

If you drag the "e" icon strategically, you'll eventually activate the Internet Explorer Easter egg.

First drag the "e" icon to here.

4. Drag the icon slowly to the right until the "Microsoft Internet Explorer 4.0" text slides out of the dialog box (you should now see an Unlock button).

5. Drop the icon in the middle of the world.

6. Click **Unlock**. A new window appears and displays the animated Easter egg. Hang in there long enough and you'll get to some comedy material. (My favorite? The list of features that didn't make it into the product, including the "Scratch n Sniff Toolbar.")

Volcanic Screen Saver

The "3D Text" screen saver renders a world in 3D and then tosses it around the screen. For some variety, try this:

1. Right-click the desktop and then click **Properties** to open the Display Properties dialog box.

2. Select the **Screen Saver** tab.

3. In the **Screen Saver** list, select **3D Text**.

4. Click **Settings**, enter **Volcano** in the **Text** box, and then click **OK**.

5. Click **Preview**. The 3D text fades in and out of the screen, and with each fade-in, it displays the name of a different mountain or volcano.

Cheating at Solitaire

Many people I know count themselves as devoted Windows fans only because they've become addicted to Solitaire! While this little gem of a game is certainly one of the world's great time wasters, it can be frustrating if you don't win as often as you like. (The card "waterfall" that appears at the end of each successful game is, I'm sure, something we all enjoy seeing as much as we can.) To help out, Solitaire has a couple of built-in "cheat" features that you can use to put a few more in the win column (how well you'll sleep at night is up to you):

➤ I'm sure many a Solitaire savant has pulled out a hair or two when, during a Draw Three game, the card you've been dying to get is drawn underneath one or two cards in the pile. To get at that pesky devil, select **Game | Undo** to reverse the draw. Now hold down the **Ctrl**, **Alt**, and **Shift** keys and click the deck. Solitaire draws only one card this time! Keep clicking until you turn over the card you want, and then resume the game normally.

➤ The quickest road to Solitaire defeat is to miss adding a drawn card to the row stacks. To prevent this from happening, select **Game | Options**. In the Options dialog box, activate the **Outline dragging** check box, and then click **OK**. Now drag each card you draw over the bottom card in each row stack. If one of the bottom cards turns black, you know you've found a match.

From Here

This chapter ran through a few of my fave rave Windows tips and tidbits. I hope you'll find these baubles useful in your Windows work.

That ends Part 1. In Part 2, "'Just So' Windows: More Customization Tomfoolery," I'll show you quite a few ways to customize Windows 98 to suit your own inimitable style.

Part 2
"Just So" Windows: More Customization Tomfoolery

Many people live in neighborhoods where all the houses look more or less the same. To make their humble abodes stick out from the crowd, most folks customize their domiciles with everything from a simple paint job to ornate shrubs and lawn sculptures.

Your Windows house is the same way. Right out of the box you get the same old Windows 98 as everyone else. However, Windows is crammed with the electronic equivalents of paint, plants, and pink flamingos. These customization features are the subject of the chapters here in Part 2. I'll show you how to remodel Web integration, the desktop, the Start menu and taskbar, the keyboard, and more. I'll also give you an introduction to the most powerful Windows 98 customization tool of all: the Registry.

Chapter 7

Customizing Web Integration and the Active Desktop

In This Chapter

➤ A review of Web integration basics

➤ How to customize the folder Web view

➤ Working with Web view templates

➤ Setting up a custom Active Desktop

➤ Handy methods to help you integrate Web integration and activate the Active Desktop

Although Windows 98 has a lengthy list of new and improved features, the one that gets the most attention (good and bad) is Web integration. This is as it should be because Web integration represents both a new way to look at data (what's on your machine is treated more or less the same as what's on the Internet) and a new way to interact with Windows (for example, single-click versus double-click).

Another reason Web integration is a big deal is that it gives you unprecedented power to remake the Windows interface in your own image. To that end, this chapter focuses on the customizable aspects of Web integration.

Which Windows: Web or Classic?

Before diving into the deep end of Web integration's customization features, let's dip a toe into the waters and review what Web integration is all about. When the Web integration switch is flipped, the way you operate Windows 98 gets flipped, as well:

Everything's a link: In a Web page, links are displayed underlined in a different color font to make them stand out from the rest of the page text. In most cases, colored, underlined text in a Web page acts as a "Click me!" sign. The same thing happens when Web integration is powered up: icon titles sprout an underline, and when you use your mouse to point at an icon, the title text turns blue.

Launch icons with a single click: One of the problems that most novices had with Windows 95 was that they were never sure when to click and when to double-click. Web integration eliminates this confusion by making just about everything launchable with a single click.

Clickless highlighting: To highlight an icon in the Web integration world, just point your mouse at it. Windows 98 waits for a second or two, just to be sure, and then highlights the icon. There are also clickless methods for highlighting two or more icons:

➤ If the icons are displayed in a row, point your mouse at the first icon until it's highlighted. Then hold down **Shift** and point the mouse at the last icon. After a brief pause for the cause, Windows 98 highlights all the icons.

➤ To highlight icons willy-nilly, hold down **Ctrl** and point your mouse at each icon in turn. Remember to pause for a second or two to get the icon safely highlighted before moving on.

Folders turn into Web pages: With Web integration on, Windows 98 displays your folders as though they were Web pages. As you'll see later in this chapter, it's possible to customize your folders to add links to Web pages or even other folders.

Okay, so just how do you get Web integration into your life? Here's a whack of ways to get started:

➤ Select **Start | Settings | Folder Options**.

➤ In Windows Explorer or My Computer, select the **View | Folder Options** command.

➤ If you're in the Display Properties dialog box (right-click the desktop and then click Properties), display the **Web** tab and then click **Folder Options**. In the dialog box that pops up, click **Yes**.

Whichever road you take, you end up at the Folder Options dialog box, shown in the following figure. The **General** tab has two options that ping pong Windows 98 between Web integration and the old Windows 95 way of doing things:

➤ **Web style:** Activate this option to activate Web integration.

➤ **Classic style:** This option turns off Web integration and takes you back to the old way of doings (such as double-clicking to launch icons).

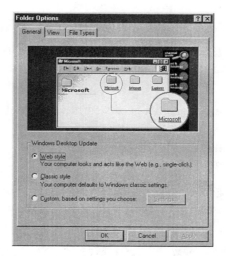

The Folder Options dialog box is where you turn Web integration on and off.

What's with the third option, **Custom, based on settings you choose**? If you activate this option and then slam the **Settings** button that comes alive, Windows 98 lobs the Custom Settings dialog box your way (see the next figure). You use this dialog box to set up, among other things, the specific Web integration features you want to use.

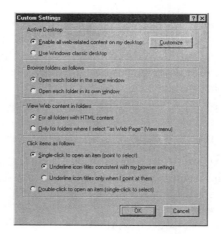

The options in this dialog box enable you to define a hybrid setup somewhere between the "Web" and "classic" styles.

For starters, the two options in the **View Web content in folders** group control when Windows 98 displays folders as Web pages:

For all folders with HTML content: Windows 98 displays every folder as a Web page.

Only for folders where I select "as Web Page" (View menu): You have to display each folder as a Web page by selecting the **View | as Web page** command.

The options in the **Click items as follows** groups determine your clicking options:

Single-click to open an item (point to select): This option turns on the one-click launching and clickless highlighting features. You also gain access to two related options:

➤ **Underline icon titles consistent with my browser settings**: Windows 98 underlines all the icon titles.

➤ **Underline icon titles only when I point at them**: Windows 98 applies the title underlining only when you point your mouse at an icon.

Double-click to open an item (single-click to select): Windows 98 uses the "classic" mouse techniques for launching and selecting icons.

Creating a Custom Web View for a Folder

When Windows 98 displays a folder in Web view, the folder turns into a Web page. One of the advantages of this is that when you place the mouse pointer over an icon, Windows 98 displays a description of the icon on the left. For some files—such as graphics files and Web page files—Windows 98 also displays a "preview" of the file. For example, the following figure shows a highlighted image file and its preview.

This is interesting enough, I suppose. But the Web view becomes downright useful when you realize that the view is fully customizable. In *The Complete Idiot's Guide to Windows 98*, I showed you some simple tweaks, such as changing the folder background. However, you can also perform full-blown renovations using HTML and other Web technologies, and that's the topic of the next few sections.

What's HTML?

HTML stands for Hypertext Markup Language, and it's what's used to create Web pages. HTML consists of a few codes that tell a Web browser how to display the page (format text and paragraphs, define links, and so on). If you'd like to get up-to-speed on this important technology, may I not-so-humbly suggest that you check out my book *The Complete Idiot's Guide to Creating an HTML 4 Web Page*. Here's the address of the book's home page:

```
http://www.mcfedries.com/books/cightml/
```

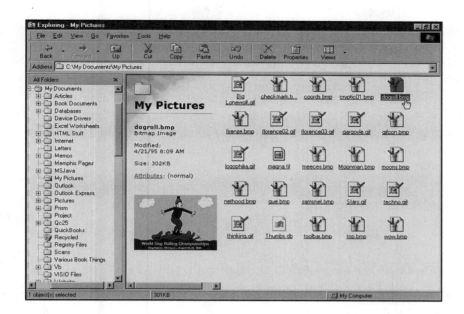

In Web view, Windows 98 shows previews of images and Web pages.

Getting a Grip on the Web View Folder Template

Before continuing, you need to understand just what you're dealing with when you display a folder in Web view. At first it might seem that Windows 98 is only displaying the folder *as though* it were a Web page, but that's not the case. No, you really are looking at an honest-to-goodness HTML document. The folder contents are displayed courtesy of a special feature, but the rest of the "page" is standard (albeit advanced) HTML. This means that you can customize any folder to your heart's content just by modifying the underlying HTML document. You have two ways to proceed:

➤ Use Notepad to modify the HTML document for a single folder.

➤ Use Windows 98's HTML folder template to modify the layout of all the folders on your system.

Note that I don't recommend modifying a folder template using FrontPage Express because it doesn't understand some of the more advanced features of the template. This means FrontPage Express doesn't show the template properly, which makes it difficult to modify the template safely.

Messing Around with the Web View Folder Template

If you're comfortable with HTML, the easiest way to modify a folder's HTML document is to edit the HTML tags directly using Notepad. There are three ways to go about this:

➤ Select **View | Customize this Folder** to display the Customize This Folder dialog box. Activate **Create or edit an HTML document** and click **Next**. When Windows 98 tells you that you're about to start the template editor, click **Next** again to open the template within Notepad.

➤ In Windows Explorer or My Computer, open your main Windows 98 folder, and then open the **Web** subfolder. Copy the file named **Folder.htt** and paste it inside the folder you want to customize. (Note that this is a hidden file, so you have to tell Windows 98 to display all files. Select **View | Folder Options**, display the **View** tab, and then active **Show all files.**)

➤ In the folder you want to customize, select **File | New | Text Document** to start a new text file, and name it **Folder.htt**.

For the latter two techniques, you need to open **Folder.htt** in Notepad by following these steps:

1. Right-click the file and click **Open With** in the shortcut menu.
2. In the program list that appears, highlight **NOTEPAD**.
3. If you always want to edit HTT files in Notepad, leave the **Always use this program to open this file** check box activated.
4. Click **OK**. The file opens in Notepad.
5. For easiest editing, maximize the Notepad window, and make sure the word wrap feature is turned off (deactivate the **Edit | Word Wrap** command).

Once you have the file opened, you'll see screen after screen of HTML and text. This will either look like gold (if you're familiar with HTML) or gobbledygook (if you're not). I won't run through the entire file here. Instead, I'll show you how to perform the simplest (and certainly the most useful) customization: adding links.

Scroll down the file until you see the following line:

```
<!-- HERE'S A GOOD PLACE TO ADD A FEW LINKS OF YOUR OWN -->
```

Below this line is where you add the links. Here's the default text:

```
<!-- (examples commented out)
        <p>
        <br>
        <a href="http://www.mylink1.com/">Custom Link 1</a>
        <p class=Links>
        <a href="http://www.mylink2.com/">Custom Link 2</a>
-->
```

The first line and the last line are HTML "comment" tags that prevent the text in between from being displayed. So your first order of business is to delete those lines.

For the links themselves, you edit the lines that begin with <a href. This is the HTML tag that defines a link. Here's the general format to use:

```
<a href="address">text</a>
```

Here, *address* is the address of the Web page, and *text* is the link text that you click on. Note, too, that the *address* part can also be a folder on your system. Here is some text and links that you can insert:

```
<b>Web Links:</b>
<br>
<a href="http://www.mcfedries.com/s">Paul McFedries</a>
<br>
<a href="http://www.microsoft.com/">Microsoft</a>
<br>
<a href="http://www.yahoo.com/">Yahoo!</a>
<p>
<b>Local Links:</b>
<br>
<a href="C:\My Documents">My Documents</a>
<br>
<a href="F:\">CD-ROM Drive</a>
<br>
<a href="C:\Windows">Windows</a>
```

The following figure shows a folder in Web view with the links in place.

More Web Page Folder Templates

The methods that I outlined in the previous section for customizing the HTML behind the folder Web view have one major drawback: You have to customize all your folders individually. Yes, you could modify **Folder.htt** and then copy it into your other folders, but that's still a lot of work.

Fortunately, Windows 98 also supports Web page folder *templates*. It works like this:

➤ If Windows 98 finds a file named **Folder.htt** inside a folder, it uses that file to display the folder in Web view.

➤ If Windows 98 doesn't find a file named **Folder.htt** inside a folder, it displays the folder in Web view using the **Folder.htt** template, which can be found in the **Web** subfolder of your main **Windows 98** folder.

A folder Web view customized with a few links.

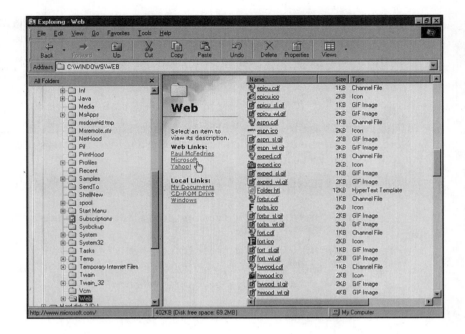

This template is a sort of global HTML document that Windows 98 uses as the default if there is no other **Folder.htt** file in sight. This file is identical to the **Folder.htt** you looked at in the last section, so you can customize it in the same way.

The Web folder actually has several HTT files, eight of which you may find useful:

Controlp.htt: This is the HTML document that Windows 98 uses to display the Control Panel folder as a Web page.

Dialup.htt: This is the HTML document that Windows 98 uses to display the Dial-Up Networking folder as a Web page.

Mycomp.htt: This is the HTML document that Windows 98 uses to display the My Computer folder as a Web page.

Nethood.htt: This is the HTML document that Windows 98 uses to display the Network Neighborhood folder as a Web page.

Printers.htt: This is the HTML document that Windows 98 uses to display the Printers folder as a Web page.

Recycle.htt: This is the HTML document that Windows 98 uses to display the Recycle Bin folder as a Web page.

Safemode.htt: This is the HTML document that Windows 98 uses to display the Active Desktop as a Web page during safe mode.

Schedule.htt: This is the HTML document that Windows 98 uses to display the Scheduled Tasks folder as a Web page.

Customizing the Active Desktop

Windows 98's Active Desktop is a step forward from the static desktop featured in Windows 95. The Active Desktop is "active" because, like the folder Web view you worked with earlier, you're dealing with a Web page. In this case, Windows 98 treats the Web page as a special kind of wallpaper. So, as before, you can customize the Active Desktop by performing HTML surgery on the underlying Web page.

To review, you can use the following methods to activate the Active Desktop:

➤ Select **Start | Settings | Active Desktop**, then activate the **View as Web Page** command.

➤ Right-click the desktop, click **Active Desktop** in the menu, then activate the **View as Web Page** command.

➤ In the Display Properties dialog box (right-click the desktop and then click **Properties**), display the **Web** tab and then activate the **View my Active Desktop as a web page** check box.

Once you have the Active Desktop enabled, you can customize the HTML desktop wallpaper layer. There are two ways to go about it:

➤ Customize the default desktop Web page.

➤ Specify a Web page that already exists locally or on your company's network.

Tweaking the Default Desktop Web Page

Windows 98's default HTML document for the desktop is **Windows98.htm**. Here's how to open this file in Notepad:

1. Using Windows Explorer or My Computer, open your main Windows 98 folder, open the **Web** subfolder, and then open the **Wallpaper** subfolder.
2. Hold down **Shift**, right-click the file, and then click **Open With** in the shortcut menu.
3. In the program list that appears, highlight **NOTEPAD**.
4. Click **OK**. The following figure shows the file opened in Notepad.

This is a regular HTML document that sets a background color and displays the Windows 98 logo, which is also set up as a link to the Windows 98 Web site.

107

Windows98.htm is Windows 98's default Active Desktop Web page.

So modifying the default Active Desktop Web page is a simple matter of editing this file with your own tags. To update the desktop after you've saved your changes, right-click the desktop, then click **Refresh** in the shortcut menu.

Specifying a Custom Desktop Web Page

The other way to customize the Active Desktop is to create a custom Web page. Here are a few things to think about as you create the page:

➤ You can specify only a local page or a page on your network (intranet). You can't use pages that reside on the Internet.

➤ Along similar lines, use either local paths or network paths for things like images and videos. If you use URLs, Windows 98 won't display the resources.

➤ Keep the layout and dimensions of the desktop in mind as you construct the page. Set up your content so that it isn't obscured by the desktop icons. Also, there's no way to scroll down or to the right, so make sure your content fits inside the desktop area.

When your page is ready to roll, follow these steps to set it up as your desktop Web page:

1. Right-click the desktop and then click **Properties** to open the Display Properties dialog box.

2. Display the **Background** tab.

Hiding Those Pesky Desktop Icons

If you like, you can tell Windows 98 not to display the desktop icons when you view the desktop as a Web page. To do this, first select **Start** | **Settings** | **Folder Options**. In the Folder Options dialog box, display the **View** tab and then activate the **Hide icons when desktop is viewed as a Web page** check box. Click **OK**.

3. Click **Browse**.
4. Use the Browse dialog box to highlight the Web page you want to use, and then click **Open**.
5. Click **OK**.

How to Avoid Hunting for Web Pages

If you created the Web page yourself, you can avoid having to browse for it by copying or moving the HTML file to the **Web\Wallpaper** folder. This way, the file will appear in the **Wallpaper** list in the **Background** tab.

Dealing with Desktop Items

The figure below shows a desktop with a couple of items added from the Active Desktop Gallery. (I showed you how to add stuff to the Active Desktop in *The Complete Idiot's Guide to Windows 98*.) Notice that when you pass the mouse over an item, the item sprouts a border. You can use the following techniques to work with the item:

➤ Drag a border to resize the item.

➤ Drag the top border to move the item.

➤ Click the arrow in the upper-left corner to display the Control menu.

➤ Click the Close button in the upper-right corner to remove the item from the desktop.

You can also work with your items from the Web tab in the Display Properties dialog box. As you can see in the following figure, Windows 98 keeps a list of each installed item. Here's a rundown of the techniques you can use to work with the items from this tab:

➤ To modify an item's properties (such as the subscription schedule), highlight the item and then click **Properties**.

An Active Desktop with a couple of items on display.

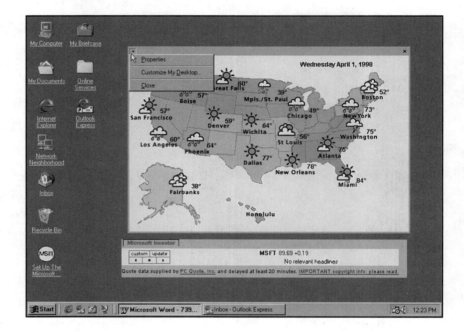

➤ To disable an item, deactivate its check box.

➤ To remove an item from the list, highlight it and click **Delete**. When Windows 98 asks whether you're sure, click **Yes**.

➤ To disable all the desktop items (as well as the underlying desktop Web page), deactivate the **View my Active Desktop as a web page** check box. When you click OK, Windows 98 may warn you that the current wallpaper can be shown only if the Active Desktop is enabled. Click **No** to disable the wallpaper.

110

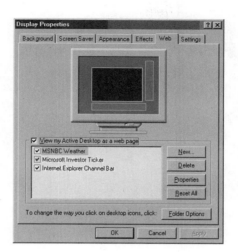

The Web tab lists all the installed desktop items.

From Here

This chapter showed you a few ways to customize Web integration and the Active Desktop. After a quick Web integration review, I showed you how to create a custom Web view for a folder. You also learned how to work with Windows 98's Web view folder templates. For the Active Desktop, I showed you how to edit the default Web page, how to specify a custom Web page, and how to deal with Active Desktop items.

Next up: more interface interference as Chapter 8 shows you some ways to customize the Start menu and taskbar.

Refurbishing the Start Menu and Taskbar

In This Chapter

➤ The lowdown on the **Start Menu** folder

➤ Downright useful Start menu customizations

➤ Trying taskbar toolbars on for size

➤ Lots of slick tricks for taking control of the bottom part of your screen

It doesn't take much mucking about in Windows 98 before you realize that the Start menu and taskbar are crucial chunks of Windows 98 real estate. In Windows 95, it was bad enough using the Start menu to launch programs (and shut down your computer), the taskbar to switch from one program to another, and the system tray to deal in various ways with the myriad other programs that lurk inside your machine. Windows 98 adds to all this by shoehorning the Quick Launch toolbar between the Start button and the taskbar.

To become a truly productive Windows 98 user, you *must* usurp control of that entire strip that runs along the bottom of your screen. *The Complete Idiot's Guide to Windows 98* showed you a few ways to do this, and this chapter takes those customizations even further. You'll learn some powerful methods for renovating the Start menu, how to create your own taskbar toolbars, how to customize the Quick Launch toolbar, and much more.

Understanding the Start Menu Folder

In *The Complete Idiot's Guide to Windows 98*, you learned how to create new Start menu items by using the built-in wizard that's available from the Taskbar Properties dialog box (select **Start | Settings | Taskbar & Start Menu**). That's a convenient and straightforward approach, but there's a more powerful method that utilizes two important facts:

➤ Just about everything you see on the Start menu's menu is a shortcut.

➤ All those shortcuts are stored inside a special folder called **Start Menu**, which resides within your main Windows 98 folder (usually **C:\Windows**).

In other words, you can customize most of the Start menu simply by adding, renaming, and deleting shortcuts within the **Start Menu** folder. (All those shortcut shenanigans I showed you back in Chapter 2's "Getting the Most Out of Shortcuts" section will come in handy here.) And, as you learned in Chapter 2, shortcuts can point not only to programs, but also to things like documents, folders, and Web sites, so there's no end to the fun (if that's the right word) .

Windows offers a whack of ways to get to the **Start Menu** folder, but the following two are the best:

➤ In Windows Explorer, open your main Windows 98 folder and then highlight the **Start Menu** folder.

➤ Right-click the **Start** button and then click **Explore** from the little menu that pops up.

The following figure shows Windows Explorer with the **Start Menu** folder highlighted.

*The most powerful way to play with the Start menu is to work with the **Start Menu** folder directly.*

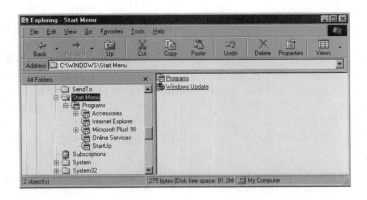

The first bit of weirdness you have to deal with is the fact that the **Start Menu** folder doesn't contain an icon for everything on the Start menu. In fact, the default **Start Menu** folder contains a measly collection of just two shortcuts: **Programs** and **Windows Update**. What about all that other stuff on the Start menu: **Settings**, **Find**, **Run**, and so on? Everything below Programs on the Start menu is, I'm afraid, off limits to the likes of you and me. They're built right into the fabric of Windows 98, and there's no way to mess with them (which is probably just as well). That's no big deal, because you still have tons of customization possibilities.

As I said, what you *can* see in the **Start Menu** folder are two items: a **Programs** folder and a **Windows Update** item, which are shortcuts to the Windows Update Web site. The **Programs** folder (which corresponds to the Programs item on the Start menu), has several subfolders, such as **Accessories** and **Internet Explorer**, which, also have corresponding Start menu items.

So, one way to customize the Start menu is with the existing items within the **Start Menu** folder and its subfolders. You can move, copy, rename, and delete the existing shortcuts, and you can also create new subfolders. Thankfully, there are no esoteric hoops to jump through for this; just use any of the techniques for copying, moving, renaming, and deleting objects that you'd normally use in Windows Explorer. Some notes to bear in mind:

➤ Feel free to move any of the **Start Menu** subfolders to a different location. For example, if you find that you constantly use the programs in the **System Tools** folder, you can put it within closer reach by moving it to the **Programs** folder or even the **Start Menu** folder itself.

➤ You can create new folders, and they'll appear as new menus off the Start menu (depending on where you create the new folder).

➤ If you move or copy a shortcut or folder to the **Start Menu** folder, it appears above the Programs command at the top of the Start menu. In the following figure, for example, I've moved three objects into the **Start Menu** folder: the **Games** folder and the shortcuts for Calculator and Deluxe CD Player.

Besides dealing with the items in the **Start Menu** folder directly, you can also customize the Start menu by creating new shortcuts for other programs and documents. The crucial word here is *shortcuts*. Be very careful that you don't move or copy an *object*—that is, a program, document, or folder—to the **Start Menu**, because that could mess up your system.

To ensure that you always create a shortcut, use the following techniques to create new items with the **Start Menu** folders:

➤ Copy the item, highlight the **Start Menu** folder you want to use as the destination, and select **Edit | Paste Shortcut**.

➤ If you prefer the drag-and-drop technique, make sure you right-drag the object (hold down the right mouse button and drag the object) and then drop it on the destination folder. In the menu that appears, click **Create Shortcut(s) Here**.

115

*Options copied or moved to the **Start Menu** folder appears at the top of the Start menu.*

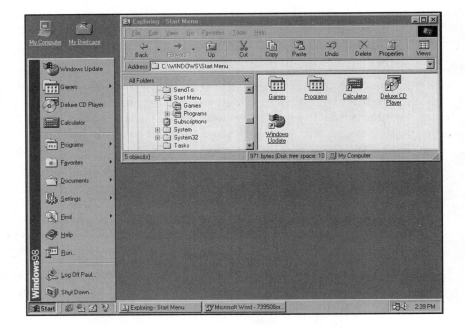

Putting Some Tricks Up Your Start Menu's Sleeve

Okay, now let's move this Start menu customizing stuff into high gear with a few interesting tricks and techniques.

A Faster Way to Toss Something Onto the Start Menu

I put shortcuts on the main Start menu for all the programs and documents that I use every day. This puts these important items just a couple of mouse clicks away.

Here's a quick way to create shortcuts that appear at the top of the Start menu:

1. Use Windows Explorer or My Computer to find the file or folder for which you want to create a shortcut.
2. Drag the item to the **Start** button.
3. Drop it on the **Start** button. Windows 98 adds a shortcut for the file at the top of the Start menu.

Pressing Keys to Select Start Menu Stuff

Once you have the Start menu displayed, click the item you want to run (or the submenu you want to open). You can also select Start menu items by pressing the first letter of the item's name. For example, with the Start menu displayed, you can open the **Programs** menu by pressing **P**.

With all this adding and renaming of Start menu shortcuts, it's quite possible that you'll end up with multiple items sharing the same first letter. One workaround is to keep pressing the first letter until Windows 98 selects the item you want. A better solution is to rename your Start menu shortcuts so that they begin with a number (0 to 9). For example, renaming **Calculator** to **1. Calculator** means you can select this item by pecking **1** on your keyboard. The figure below shows a sample Start menu that uses this technique.

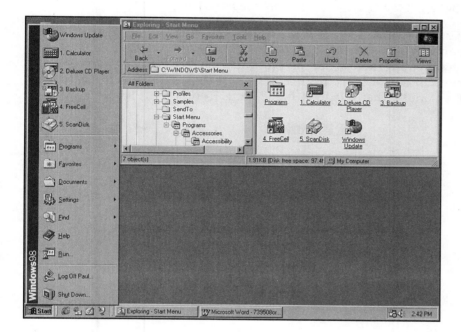

Tacking a unique number onto the front of a Start menu shortcut means that you can select any item by pressing its number.

Adding Control Panel Icons to the Start Menu

If the Start menu commands are really just shortcuts, what's to stop someone from creating shortcuts to Control Panel items in the **Start Menu** folder? Not a thing. In fact, this can be quite handy if you find there are some Control Panel icons you play with regularly.

To try this, highlight the **Control Panel** folder in Windows Explorer and then drag the icon you want onto the Start button. (If you're feeling confident, you can do the same thing with items in the **Printers** folder and the **Dial-Up Networking** folder.)

*What about dragging the **Control Panel** folder itself to the **Start Menu** folder? Won't that give me a menu of the Control panel icons?*

That's a good idea, but it won't work. All Windows 98 does is create a shortcut that opens the **Control Panel** folder in its own window.

One solution would be to create a new folder off the **Start Menu** folder—called, **Control Panel**—and then drag all the Control Panel icons into this new folder.

This technique works, but it means that every time an application adds an icon to the Control Panel (and there's no shortage of programs that do this), you have to remember to update your new **Start Menu** folder. To avoid this chore, create a new folder inside the **Start Menu** folder, and give it the following finger-numbing name:

```
Control Panel.{21EC2020-3AEA-1069-A2DD-08002B30309D}
```

That dog's breakfast of letters and numbers within the curly braces ({ and }) is Windows 98's unique ID number for the Control Panel. Thank the deity of your choice that you don't have to know anything more about this . All you really need to know is that it works. As you can see in the following figure, the menu it creates contains all the Control Panel icons. (A nice bonus is that Windows 98 hides the ID number.)

A menu of Control Panel icons at your fingertips.

If you don't mind messing with more of those lengthy ID numbers, you can achieve the same effect with the **Printers**, **Dial-Up Networking**, and **Scheduled Tasks** folders.

For the **Printers** folder, create a new folder with the following name:

```
Printers.{2227A280-3AEA-1069-A2DE-08002B30309D}
```

For the **Dial-Up Networking** folder, create a new folder and give it this name:

```
Dial-Up Networking.{992CFFA0-F557-101A-88EC-00DD010CCC48}
```

For the **Scheduled Tasks** folder, create a new folder with the following name:

Scheduled Tasks.{D6277990-4C6A-11CF-8D87-00AA0060F5BF}

The "Look, Ma, No Hands" Approach: The Startup Folder

Putting items on the main Start menu means you get to launch these items with only a couple of mouse clicks or keystrokes. That's nice, but what if I told you that it's possible to launch programs and documents without using *any* mouse clicks or keystrokes?

It's for real, and the secret is a special folder called **StartUp**, which you'll find in the **Start Menu\Programs** folder. Shortcuts in the **StartUp** folder load automatically each time you start Windows 98. So if you have any programs or documents that you use first thing, or that you use all day, create shortcuts for them within the **StartUp** folder.

Ignoring the StartUp Folder at Startup

If, for some reason, you don't want Windows 98 to load the **StartUp** folder shortcuts, hold down the **Shift** key while Windows 98 loads.

Some Taskbar Tweaks

With the Start menu now under your control, it's time to tame the taskbar. The rest of this chapter runs you through various techniques for moving the taskbar, creating taskbar toolbars, customizing the Quick Launch toolbar, and more.

Moving the Taskbar

In *The Complete Idiot's Guide to Windows 98*, I showed you that it's possible to change the size of the taskbar. (Drag the top edge of the taskbar up or down.) Another taskbar property that's not set in stone is its position on the desktop. Although it normally resides at the bottom of the screen, you're free to toss the taskbar onto the top edge of the screen, or onto the left or right side of the screen.

For example, when I'm writing, I like to maximize the vertical area of my word processor's window so that I can see as much text as possible. One easy way to gain more vertical space is to move the taskbar to one of the side edges.

To move the taskbar, position the mouse pointer over an empty part of the taskbar. Now drag the pointer to the edge of the screen where you want to position the taskbar. As you approach the edge, the taskbar leaps into place. The following figure shows the taskbar on the left edge of the screen. Notice how the desktop icons shift to the right to remain visible.

Feel free to drag the taskbar to any edge of the screen.

Working with Taskbar Toolbars

In Windows 95, the taskbar's role was limited: it showed buttons for each running program and enabled you to click those buttons in order to switch to a particular program. The Windows 98 taskbar also does these things, but its job description has been expanded to include program launching. It does this by sharing its space with various "toolbars" that contain icons for running programs and opening documents and Web sites. The Windows 98 taskbar comes with four built-in toolbars:

Address: This toolbar contains a text box into which you can type Internet addresses. When you press Enter, Windows 98 loads the address into Internet Explorer. (In other words, this toolbar works just like the Address Bar used by Internet Explorer.)

Links: This toolbar contains several buttons that link you to predefined Internet sites. This is the same as the Links toolbar in Internet Explorer.

Quick Launch: This is a collection of one-click icons that launch Internet Explorer, Outlook Express, TV Viewer (if it's installed), and the Internet Explorer channels. There's also a Show Desktop icon that clears the desktop by minimizing all running programs in one fell swoop.

Desktop: This toolbar contains all the desktop icons.

120

Customizing Quick Launch

The Quick Launch toolbar offers handy one-click access to icons. Fortunately, you can take full advantage of this by customizing Quick Launch with your own icons. Again, you deal with shortcuts within a folder. In this case, open your main Windows 98 folder and head for the following subfolder:

```
\Application Data\Microsoft\Internet Explorer\Quick Launch
```

To toggle these toolbars on and off, first right-click an empty spot on the taskbar. In the shortcut menu that shows up, click **Toolbars** and then click the toolbar you want to work with.

Taskbar Toolbar Options

After you've displayed a toolbar, there are a number of options you can work with to customize the look of the toolbar. Right-click an empty section of the toolbar and then click one of the following commands:

View: This command displays a submenu with two options: **Large** and **Small**. These commands determine the size of the toolbar's icons.

Show Text: This command toggles the icon titles on and off.

Refresh: This command refreshes the toolbar's contents.

Show Title: This command toggles the toolbar title (displayed to the left of the icons) on and off.

Creating New Taskbar Toolbars

Besides the predefined taskbar toolbars, you can also create new toolbars that display the contents of any folder on your system. Here are the steps to follow:

1. Right-click an empty spot on the toolbar to display the shortcut menu.
2. Click **Toolbars | New Toolbar**. Windows 98 displays the New Toolbar dialog box, shown below.
3. Use the folder list provided to highlight the folder you want to display as a toolbar.
4. Click **OK**. Windows 98 creates the new toolbar.

The following figure shows the **Control Panel** folder as a toolbar. Notice that I've turned off the icon titles (that is, I deactivated the **Show Text** command).

121

Use the New Toolbar dialog box to choose the folder you want to display as a taskbar toolbar.

The **Control Panel** *folder as a taskbar toolbar.*

From Here

This chapter shows you a few tricks for customizing the Start menu and taskbar. For the Start menu, I explained the **Start Menu** folder and then showed you how to work with shortcuts within that folder. You also learned a few advanced techniques, such as adding a menu of Control Panel icons and working with the **StartUp** folder. You also learned how to move the taskbar, open taskbar toolbars, and create your own taskbar toolbars.

Chapter 9, "A Few Other Ways to Dress Windows for Success," presents some miscellaneous customizations, including creating custom wallpapers, colors schemes, and sound schemes, making keyboard and joystick adjustments, working with international settings, and more.

A Few Other Ways to Dress Windows for Success

In This Chapter

➤ Creating custom wallpaper

➤ Creating custom color and sound schemes

➤ Customizing your keyboard

➤ Calibrating your joystick

➤ Working with Windows' regional settings

➤ How to ditch Windows' old duds and replace them with fashionable togs

Many restaurants offer a "bottomless" cup of coffee that gives you free refills until either you're full or you're too hopped up on caffeine to successfully request another cup. Windows 98 offers the electronic equivalent: a seemingly bottomless cup of customization options and settings. You'll take a few more gulps from that cup in this chapter as I show you how to create custom wallpapers, color schemes, and sound schemes, how to customize your keyboard, how to calibrate your joystick, how to work with international settings, and more.

Rolling Your Own Windows 98

Windows 98 offers plenty of pre-fab customization components. There are lots of wallpapers for the desktop, oodles of color schemes for doing Windows' colors, and a decent collection of sound schemes for changing how Windows beeps and bops. These ready-made components are fine for quickie customizations, but the true rugged individualist wants nothing less than to remake Windows in his own image. To that end, this section shows you how to create your own custom wallpapers, color schemes, and sound schemes.

Roll Your Own I: Creating a Custom Wallpaper

I showed you how to cover the desktop with a snazzy wallpaper in *The Complete Idiot's Guide to Windows 98*. (Open Control Panel's Display icon and then use the Background tab in the Display Properties dialog box.) The interesting thing(for some of us, anyway) about wallpapers is they're all just simple graphics files that use Paint's BMP (bitmap) format. For example, the "Carved Stone" wallpaper is really just the file named **Carved Stone.bmp**. Not only that, but all of these files reside within your main Windows 98 folder (usually C:**Windows**). So what? So this: To create your own custom wallpaper, you need to do only two things:

1. Use Paint to create an image.
2. Save that image as a bitmap file in your main Windows 98 folder.

The next time you open the Background tab in the Display Properties dialog box, your custom wallpaper will show up in the **Wallpaper** list.

That's all pretty easy, but Paint can actually make it easier because the program offers the following File menu commands:

➤ **Set As Wallpaper (Tiled)**   This command sets the current image as the desktop wallpaper and displays the image tiled. ("Tiled" means that Windows 98 repeats the image until it fills the entire desktop.)

➤ **Set As Wallpaper (Centered)**   This command sets the current image as the desktop wallpaper and displays the image in the center of the desktop.

Roll Your Own II: Creating a Custom Color Scheme

In *The Complete Idiot's Guide to Windows 98*, I discussed assigning a color scheme to change the look of Windows 98's windows, icons, menus, buttons, text, and more. (In the Appearance tab of the Display Properties dialog box, use the Scheme list.)

Unfortunately, some of the predefined schemes look as though they were created in the Phyllis Diller House of Design. If you think you can do better, it's easy enough to cobble together your own scheme. Here's how it works:

1. Open Control Panel's **Display** icon and select the **Appearance** tab, shown in the following figure.

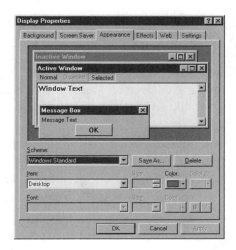

Use the Appearance tab to create your own Windows 98 color scheme.

2. Use the **Item** drop-down list to choose an element of the Windows 98 interface to work with. (I'll run through the list of the available items after these steps.)

Easier Item Selecting

Another way to select some of objects in the Item list is to click the appropriate part of the fake desktop. For example, clicking the title bar of the active window selects the Active Title Bar item.

3. Use the other controls—such as **Size**, **Color**, and **Font**—to customize the item.

4. Repeat Steps 2 and 3 until you're done.

5. Click the **Save As** button. Windows 98 displays the Save Scheme dialog box.

6. Enter a name for the scheme in the text box provided and click **OK**. Your newly created color scheme appears in the **Scheme** list.

7. Click **OK**.

Here's a rundown of the various objects available in the **Item** list:

➤ **3D Objects** Dialog box command buttons and tabs, caption buttons (see the "Caption Buttons" entry), scrollbars, status bars, taskbar, and window borders. You can set the background color and font color for these objects.

➤ **Active Title Bar** The title bar of the window that you're working in (the "active" window). Windows 98 can display title bar backgrounds as a gradient. To control

125

this gradient, use both the **Color** and **Color 2** palettes. You can also set the size (height) of the title bar, as well as the font, font size, font color, and font style of the title bar text.

➤ **Active Window Border**   The border surrounding the active window. You can set the border's width and color. Note that the width setting also controls the width of the taskbar when the Auto hide option is activated (right-click the taskbar, and then click **Properties**).

➤ **Application Background**   Sets the default color for the background of each application window.

➤ **Caption Buttons**   The buttons that appear in the upper-right corner of windows and dialog boxes. You can set the size of these buttons.

➤ **Desktop**   The desktop color. Note that this setting also controls the color of the backgrounds used with the desktop icons. You see this background color only if your desktop is covered with either a pattern or a wallpaper.

➤ **Icon**   The icons that appear on the desktop. You can set the icon size as well as the font attributes of the icon titles. Note that this font setting also controls the fonts displayed in Windows Explorer and all open folders (such as Control Panel and My Computer).

➤ **Icon Spacing (Horizontal)**   The distance allotted (in pixels) between desktop and folder icons on the left and right.

➤ **Icon Spacing (Vertical)**   The distance allotted (in pixels) between desktop and folder icons on the top and bottom.

➤ **Inactive Title Bar**   The title bars of the open inactive windows. You can set the size (height) and gradient colors of the bar, as well as the font, font size, and font color of the title bar text.

➤ **Inactive Window Border**   The borders surrounding the open inactive windows. You can set the border's width and color.

➤ **Menu**   The window menu bar. You can set the size (height) and background color of the menu bar, as well as the font attributes of the menu bar text.

➤ **Message Box**   Message boxes, such as error messages and information prompts. (Note that this setting doesn't apply to regular dialog boxes.) You can set the font attributes of the message text.

➤ **Palette Title**   The title bar of the "floating" toolbars (also known as *palettes*) used by many programs. (To see an example, drag the Quick Launch toolbar off the taskbar and drop it on the desktop.) You can set the size of the title bar and the font of the title text.

➤ **Scrollbar** The scrollbars that appear in windows and list boxes. You can set the width (or height, depending on the orientation) of the scrollbars.

➤ **Selected Items** The currently selected menu in a menu bar and the currently selected command in a menu. You can set the height and background color of the selection bar, as well as the font attributes of the item text.

➤ **ToolTip** The small banners that appear if you hover the mouse pointer over a toolbar button for a couple of seconds. You can set the background color and the font attributes of the ToolTip text. Note that the ToolTip font size also controls the size of a window's status bar text.

➤ **Window** The window background and text. You can set the color of these items.

You might have noticed that the Appearance tab's **Color** lists have an Other button. You can use this option to pick a different color from Windows 98's color palette, or you can create your own color. When you click the **Other** button, you see the Color dialog box, shown in the following figure.

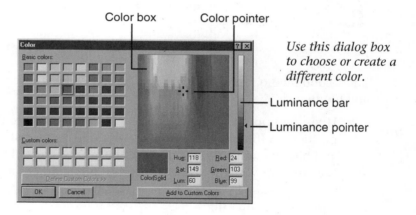

Color box   Color pointer

Use this dialog box to choose or create a different color.

Luminance bar

Luminance pointer

If you want to use one of the colors displayed in the **Basic colors** area, click it, and then click **OK**.

To create your own color, you can use one of two methods. The first method uses the fact that you can create any color in the spectrum by mixing the three primary colors: red, green, and blue. The Color dialog box lets you enter specific numbers between 0 and 255 for each of these colors by using the **Red**, **Green**, and **Blue** text boxes. A lower number means the color is less intense, and a higher number means the color is more intense.

To give you some idea of how this works, the following table lists eight common colors and their respective red, green, and blue numbers.

Color	Red	Green	Blue
Black	0	0	0
White	255	255	255
Red	255	0	0
Green	0	255	0
Blue	0	0	255
Yellow	255	255	0
Magenta	255	0	255
Cyan	0	255	255

Shades of Gray

Whenever the **Red**, **Green**, and **Blue** values are equal, you get a gray-scale color. Lower numbers produce darker grays, and higher numbers produce lighter grays.

The second method for selecting colors involves setting three attributes: hue, saturation, and luminance:

➤ **Hue**   This number (which is more or less equivalent to the term *color*) measures the position on the color spectrum. Lower numbers indicate a position near the red end, and higher numbers move through the yellow, green, blue, and violet parts of the spectrum. As you increase the hue, the color pointer moves from left to right.

➤ **Sat**   This number is a measure of the purity of a given hue. A saturation setting of 240 indicates that the hue is a pure color. Lower numbers indicate that more gray is mixed with the hue until, at 0, the color becomes part of the gray scale. As you increase the saturation, the color pointer moves toward the top of the color box.

➤ **Lum**   This number is a measure of the brightness of a color. Lower numbers are darker, and higher numbers are brighter. The luminance bar to the right of the color box shows the luminance scale for the selected color. As you increase the luminance, the pointer moves toward the top of the bar.

To create a custom color, you can either enter values in the text boxes, as just described, or you can use the mouse to click inside the color box and luminance bar. The **Color|Solid** box shows the selected color on the left and the nearest solid color on the right (if you're using a 16-color video driver). If you think you'll want to reuse the color down the road, click the **Add to Custom Colors** button to place the color in one of the boxes in the **Custom colors** area. When you're done, click **OK**.

Roll Your Own III: Creating a Custom Sound Scheme

As you work with Windows 98, you hear various sounds emanating from your speakers. Although it often seems like Windows 98 is simply talking to itself, these sounds always correspond to particular events. There's that relaxing (or annoying, depending on how many times you've had to listen to it), New Age–like music when you start Windows 98; there's the short, sharp shock of a sound when a warning dialog box pops up; and there's a happy little chime when you exit Windows 98.

If you're getting tired of the same old sounds, however, Windows 98 lets you customize what you hear by assigning different sound files to these various events. And if your ears enjoy a lot of stimulation, there also are a couple of dozen other events to which you can assign sounds. This section shows you how it's done.

The sounds assigned to various Windows 98 events comprise a *sound scheme*. To check out the current scheme, go to Control Panel and open the **Sounds** icon to display the Sounds Properties dialog box, as shown below.

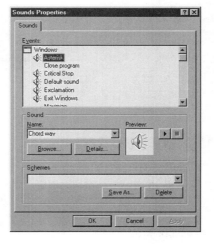

Use the Sounds Properties dialog box to change the current Windows 98 sound scheme.

Here's a rundown of the various doodads in this dialog box:

➤ **Events** This is a long list of the various Windows 98 events. Most of the events are self explanatory (for example, Close Program and Maximize). However, there are four that apply to the various types of dialog boxes displayed by Windows 98 and Windows applications: Asterisk, Critical Stop, Exclamation, and Question. If an event has a sound icon beside it, this means a sound file is currently assigned to that event.

➤ **Name** This drop-down list shows you the name of the sound file that's assigned to the currently highlighted event. You can use the **Browse** button to select a different sound file (or just use the **Name** drop-down list to select a sound file from Windows 98's Media subfolder).

➤ **Preview**   Click the **Play** button to hear how the sound file shown in the Name box will sound.

➤ **Schemes**   This drop-down list displays the currently selected sound scheme, if any.

You can use three methods to work with sound schemes:

➤ To change the current sound scheme, highlight items in the **Events** list and change the associated sound file.

➤ To use a different sound scheme, select it from the **Schemes** drop-down list.

➤ To create your own sound scheme, first associate sound files with the various system events you want to hear. Then click **Save As**, enter a name for the new scheme, and click **OK**.

Pre-Fab Sound Schemes

The Windows 98 CD-ROM ships with a few predefined sound schemes (such as Jungle, Musica, and Robotz). If you don't see these schemes in the Schemes box, you need to install them.

The Hopped-Up Keyboard

The Complete Idiot's Guide to Windows 98 showed you how to customize your mouse for comfy clicking and dragging. Keyboard connoisseurs can also horn in on the customization carousing. First, though, you need to learn a bit of ever-so-painless keyboard theory:

When you press and hold down a letter on your keyboard, you notice two things. First, there's a slight *delay* between the time you press the key and the time the second letter appears; second, the subsequent letters appear at a constant rate (called the *repeat rate*). Beginning keyboardists are usually better off with a longer delay and a slower repeat rate. More experienced typists, on the other hand, would probably prefer a short delay combined with a fast repeat rate.

Fortunately, Windows 98 allows you to change both of these settings. To see how, select **Start | Settings | Control Panel**. When the Control Panel window appears, open the **Keyboard** icon to display the Keyboard Properties dialog box shown in the following figure.

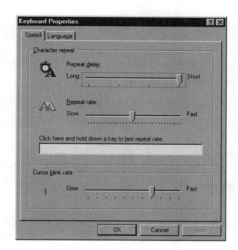

Use the Keyboard Properties dialog box to adjust your keyboard's delay and repeat rate.

You control the delay by using the **Repeat delay** slider. Move the slider bar (by dragging it with your mouse or by using the left and right arrow keys) to the left for a longer delay or to the right for a shorter delay.

As you've no doubt guessed by now, the **Repeat rate** slider controls the repeat rate. Move the slider bar to the left for a slower rate or to the right for a faster one.

To try out the new settings, head for the **Click here and hold down a key to test repeat rate** text box. Press and hold down any key to check out the delay and repeat rate.

Linguistic Leaps with the United States-International Keyboard Layout

While you've got the Keyboard Properties dialog box on the go, let's check out a little-used, but often handy setting. As you probably know, Windows 98 can deal with more than just the letters, numbers, and other symbols that you peck out on the keyboard. Symbols such as £ and ¢, and foreign letters such as ä and ç are all part of the so-called *Windows ANSI character set*.

How do you get at these extra characters? If you only need to use them once in a while, your best bet is to use one of the following techniques:

➤ Use the Character Map accessory (select **Start I Programs I Accessories I System Tools I Character Map**; see *The Complete Idiot's Guide to Windows 98* for more info).

➤ Hold down **Alt** and use your keyboard's numeric keypad to enter the character's two-, three-, or four-digit ANSI code. See Appendix C, "More Symbols: The Windows ANSI Character Set," for the complete list of these codes.

131

If you think you'll need such symbols regularly, however, Windows 98 provides a way to type them directly on the keyboard. The secret is that Windows 98 supports various *keyboard layouts*, which associate a keyboard key with a particular symbol. On the standard layout, pressing **y** gives you a *y* and pressing **1** gives you a *1*. With other layouts, however, some keys are mapped to different symbols.

In particular, a layout called United States-International augments the normal keys with many new symbols. To switch to this layout, follow these steps:

1. In the Keyboard Properties dialog box, select the **Language** tab.

2. In the **Language** list, highlight the **English (United States)** item.

3. Click the **Properties** button. Windows 98 displays the Language Properties dialog box.

4. In the **Keyboard layout** drop-down list, select **United States-International**, as shown in the following figure.

Use the Language Properties dialog box to choose the United States-International keyboard layout.

5. Click **OK** to return to the Keyboard Properties dialog box.

6. Click **OK** or **Apply**.

7. Follow the prompts when you're asked to insert your Windows 98 CD-ROM.

The table below summarizes the changes this new layout makes to your keyboard. The Ctrl+Alt column means that you hold down **Ctrl** and **Alt** and press the key; the Ctrl+Alt+Shift column means that you hold down **Ctrl**, **Alt**, and **Shift** and press the key.

Right Alt Is the Same as Ctrl Alt

Rather than holding down both Ctrl and Alt, you can use the right Alt key by itself.

Key	Ctrl+Alt	Ctrl+Alt+Shift	Key	Ctrl+Alt	Ctrl+Alt+Shift
1	¡	¹	U	ú	Ú
2	2	N/A	I	í	Í
3	3	N/A	O	ó	Ó
4	¤	£	P	ö	Ö
5	_	N/A	[	«	N/A
6	_	N/A	]	»	N/A
7	_	N/A	\	¬	¦
8	_	N/A	A	á	Á
9	'	N/A	S	ß	§
0	'	N/A	D		_
-	¥	N/A	L	ø	N/A
=	×	÷	;	¶	°
Q	ä	Ä	Z	æ	Æ
W	å	Å	C	©	¢
E	é	É	N	ñ	Ñ
R	®	N/A	M	µ	N/A
T	_	_	,	ç	Ç
Y	ü	Ü	/	¿	¿

Besides the layout changes shown in the table, Windows 98 also sets up several so-called "dead keys." These are keys that do nothing until you press another key. When you do, Windows 98 inserts the second key with an accent. The following table lists the dead keys. Note that, in each case, you press and release the dead key (such as ~), and then press and release the other key (such as N). If you want to type the symbol represented by a particular dead key, press the key and then press the **Spacebar**.

Dead Key	Accent Created	Example
~ (tilde) Tilde	Press ~ and then N to get ñ.	
' (back quote)	Grave accent	Press ' and then A to get à.
^ (caret) Circumflex	Press ^ and then E to get ê.	
" (quotation mark)	Diaeresis	Press " and then I to get ï.
' (apostrophe)	Acute accent	Press ' and then E to get é.

Foreign Tongues: Setting Up Keyboard Languages

If you need to write documents in different languages, or even if you need to use multiple languages in a single document, Windows 98 can make your life a lot easier. That's because no matter what kind of keyboard you have, Windows 98 supports keyboard layouts for various languages.

To add another keyboard language to Windows 98, follow these steps:

1. Display the **Language** tab in the Keyboard Properties dialog box.
2. Click the **Add** button. The Add Language dialog box, shown in the following figure, is displayed.

Use the Add Language dialog box to select the keyboard language you want to add.

3. Use the **Language** drop-down list to select the language you want to work with.
4. Click **OK** to return to the Keyboard Properties dialog box.
5. If you want to set the new language as the default for your applications, highlight the language, and then click **Set as Default**.
6. Use the **Switch languages** group to set the shortcut key for switching from one language to another.
7. If you leave the **Enable indicator on taskbar** check box activated, you can switch languages from the taskbar (explained after these steps).
8. Click **OK** or **Apply**.
7. Follow the prompts when you're asked to insert your Windows 98 CD-ROM.

After you add a second keyboard language, Windows 98 displays a language indicator in the taskbar's information area. Clicking this indicator displays a pop-up list of the available languages, as shown in the next figure. Click the language you want to use. (You can also cycle between languages by pressing the shortcut key you specified in the Keyboard Properties dialog box; the default is Left Alt+Shift.)

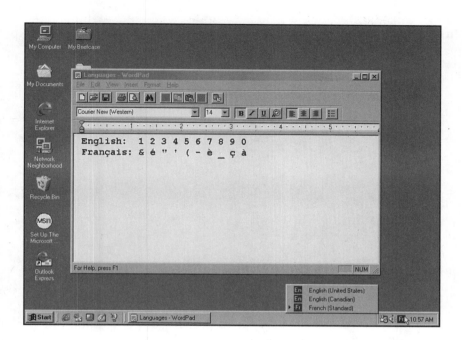

Use the taskbar's language indicator to choose the language in which you want to type.

Jumping for Joystick: Calibrating Your Game Controller

Nothing takes the joy out of playing certain kinds of games more than a joystick that's out of whack. If you use a joystick or other game controller for your Windows 98–based games, you want to calibrate it so that Windows 98 understands its features (range of motion, throttle, rudder, and so on). Here are the steps to follow to calibrate a game controller:

1. Select **Start | Settings | Control Panel**, and then open the **Game Controllers** icon. Windows 98 displays the Game Controllers dialog box, shown below.

2. If your game controller isn't listed, click **Add**, highlight the type of game controller you use, and then click **OK**.

3. If you have multiple game controllers, use the **Game Controllers** list to select the one you want to calibrate.

4. Click **Properties** to display the Game Controller Properties dialog box.

5. Click the **Calibrate** button. The Calibration dialog box for the selected game controller appears.

6. You now work through a series of dialog boxes that set various properties of the joystick, such as its center position (as shown in the following figure) and its range

of motion. In each, perform the requested action, press a joystick button, and click **Next**.

Use the Game Controllers dialog box to customize your joystick.

To calibrate your joystick, you run through a series of dialog boxes like this one.

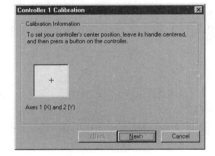

7. When the calibration is complete, click **Finish** to return to the Game Controller Properties dialog box.

8. To test your calibration, display the **Test** tab, as shown here.

9. Move the joystick and press its buttons to test the calibration, then click **OK**.

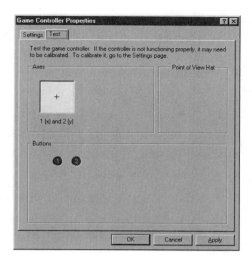

Use this dialog box to test your calibration.

Going Global: The Windows 98 Regional Settings

If you'll be writing documents to send to foreign countries, you need to tailor certain aspects of your writing for your readership. For example, if you'll be using foreign currency amounts, not only will you need to use the appropriate currency symbol, but you'll also want to place the symbol in the correct position relative to the amount. In Germany, for example, the deutsche mark symbol (DM) is placed after the amount (for example, 5,000 DM). Similarly, date formats are different around the world. In the United States, for example, 12/11/98 means December 11, 1998; in Great Britain and Spain, however, 12/11/98 is interpreted as the 12th of November, 1998.

To make your documents easier for foreign readers (and to avoid being embarrassingly late for some appointments!), Windows 98 supports different regional settings for various countries. These settings apply to all Windows applications, and they set the defaults for such things as number formats, currency symbols, and date and time formats.

To view these settings, select **Start | Settings | Control Panel**, and then open the **Regional Settings** icon from the Control Panel folder. Windows 98 displays the Regional Settings Properties dialog box, shown in the following figure. Use the drop-down list to select the country whose settings you want to work with and click **OK**. Windows 98 then prompts you to restart the computer.

If you need to change only a few settings, use the following tabs:

➤ **Number** The controls on this tab determine the default format for numeric values, including the number of decimal places, the negative number format, and the measurement system (Metric or U.S.).

Use this dialog box to set the default values for various regional settings used by your Windows applications.

➤ **Currency** The controls on this tab determine the default format for currency values, including the currency symbol and its position.

➤ **Time** The controls on this tab determine the default format for time values, including the time style and the time separator.

➤ **Date** The controls on this tab determine the default format for date values, including the short date style and separator and the long date style.

When you've made your selections, click **OK**.

Geek Chic: Customizing with TweakUI

Soon after Windows 95 was released, a few Microsoft programmers put together some small programs that extended the functionality of Windows. These utilities were called Power Toys, and some of them were quite handy. In fact, one of them—called QuickRes— is now part of Windows 98. (It's the on-the-fly color depth changer.) Another Power Toy is also available on the Windows 98 CD-ROM. It's called TweakUI, and it's crammed with options for changing and working with the Windows 98 user interface.

To install TweakUI, follow these steps:

1. Insert the Windows 98 CD-ROM. Hold down **Shift** while inserting the disc. This will bypass the AutoRun program on the CD.

2. Using Windows Explorer, display the **/tools/ResKit/Powertoy** folder.

3. Right-click the **tweakui.inf** file, and then click **Install** in the context menu.

To run TweakUI, open the Control Panel and click the **TweakUI** icon. You'll eventually see the Tweak UI window shown in the following figure. Unfortunately, I don't have the space to run through the myriad options in this jam-packed utility. If you're furrowing your brow over a particular setting, click the **?** button, and then click the control to get a brief explanation.

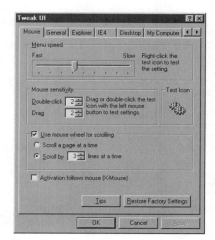

Tweak UI is loaded with useful customization options and settings.

From Here

This chapter shows you all kinds of new ways to customize Windows 98. I showed you how to create custom wallpapers, color schemes, and sound schemes, how to customize your keyboard and calibrate your joystick, how to work with the regional settings, and how to install and run the Tweak UI power toy.

You customization know-how gets a big boost as I introduce you to the Windows Registry in Chapter 10, "The Registry: The Soul of the Windows Machine."

The Registry: The Soul of the Windows Machine

In This Chapter

➤ Understanding the Registry

➤ How to work with the Registry Editor

➤ Keys, settings, and other Registry rigmarole

➤ Basic Registry editing techniques

➤ Your introduction to working safely with Windows' most crucial component

So far in Part 2 you've seen quite a few useful customization techniques. However, those techniques are mere tweaks compared to powerful things you can do using the Windows Registry. This chapter introduces you to the mysterious and often arcane world of the Registry. I'll show you that, with a little know-how and a healthy dose of caution, the Registry doesn't have to be the scary monster that most books make it out to be. Then, once you have a thorough grounding in the basics of the Registry, you'll put that knowledge to good use in Chapter 11, "Revving Up the Registry: A Few Handy Techniques."

Why "a healthy dose of caution"? Well, as you'll see, it's no stretch to call the Registry one of Windows 98's most crucial components. If the Registry isn't running on all cylinders, Windows itself probably won't run at all. Therefore, when working with the techniques in this chapter and particularly those in Chapter 11, please keep the following in mind:

➤ Always, always, *always* back up the Registry before changing even the smallest setting. I suggest using Microsoft Backup to create a backup job that does nothing else but back up the Registry's files. (I told you how to back up the Registry in Chapter 6, "A Few of My Favorite Windows Things.")

➤ The vast majority of the Registry's settings and options have nothing whatsoever to do with customizing Windows. Therefore, don't make changes to any setting if you're not sure what it does.

➤ The Registry has a weird layout and often uses long and obscure names for things. Therefore, always follow the instructions that I give you *very* carefully to make sure you get it right.

With these common-sense cautions at the fore, your Registry sessions should be pain-free and productive.

Check This Out...

Restoring the Registry

It's entirely possible that an imprudent edit can mess up the Registry to the point where you can't restart Windows 98 and, so, can't restore the Registry from your backup. If this happens, reboot your machine and use the Windows 98 Start Menu to get to the DOS prompt. (See "Taking Advantage of the Windows 98 Startup Menu" in Chapter 1.) At the DOS prompt, type the following command and press **Enter**:

```
scanreg /restore
```

This runs the Registry Checker and restores the Registry to the state it was in the last time you started Windows 98 successfully. For more on the Registry Checker, see Chapter 19, "For the Nerd in You: Higher-End System Tools."

What in Tarnation Is the Registry?

In the previous chapter, I showed you how to set up a custom Windows color scheme. After applying this new scheme, when you restart your computer, you notice that the colors are still displayed exactly as you had customized them. That's to be expected, but just how does Windows 98 "remember" the colors you selected?

Similarly, when you open Control Panel's Add/Remove Programs icon, you see a list of programs that can be removed automatically from your computer. How the heck does Windows 98 keep track of these "uninstallable" applications?

The secret to Windows 98's enormous memory is the Registry. The Registry is a kind of storehouse that holds anything and everything that relates to the configuration of your system. Change colors and Windows 98 makes a note about the new hues in the Registry; install an application and (usually) Windows 98 uses the Registry to jot down the appropriate uninstall information; modify your system's hardware configuration and the new device data is deposited in the Registry. Not only that, many Windows applications use the Registry to store their own setup and configuration morsels.

So now you see that the Registry's all-encompassing nature is what makes it all-important in the Windows world (and why you need to exercise caution when tinkering with the Registry's innards).

The Registry Editor: Your Royal Road to the Registry

The Registry actually consists of two files—called **SYSTEM.DAT** and **USER.DAT**—that dwell within your main Windows 98 folder (which is usually the **C:\Windows** folder). You never deal with these files directly, however. Instead, Windows 98 offers a special tool called the Registry Editor that's your ticket into the otherwise inaccessible world of the Registry.

As you can imagine, the Registry Editor is a powerful tool that's not to be wielded lightly. For that reason, the Windows 98 Setup program doesn't bother to install a shortcut for the Registry Editor on any of the Start menus. To run the Registry Editor, you must use either of the following techniques:

➤ Select **Start | Run**, type **regedit** in the Run dialog box, and then click **OK**.

➤ In Windows Explorer, highlight your main Windows 98 folder, and then open the file named **Regedit.exe**.

The following figure shows the Registry Editor window that shows up for work.

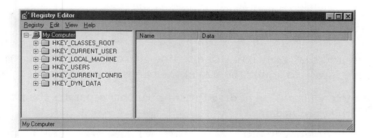

The Registry Editor, ready for action.

Understanding Keys and Other Registry Doodads

Except for those bizarre names (**HKEY_CLASSES_ROOT**, and so on), the Registry Editor looks pretty simple. In fact, it reminds me a lot of Windows Explorer. The left side of the Registry Editor window is arranged in "branches" just like Explorer's All Folders list. And the right side of the Registry Editor window shows two columns—Name and Data—which is reminiscent of Explorer's contents pane in Details view. As you'll see, the two programs *do* have many similarities, so you'll be able to put some of your hard-won Windows Explorer knowledge to good use here.

The Branches of the Tree: The Keys Pane

Those funny names on the left side of the Registry Editor window are called *keys*, and they serve to divide the Registry's contents into various categories. The left pane doesn't seem to have an official moniker so, for lack of anything better, I'll call the left pane the *Keys pane*.

The six keys you see when you first open the Registry Editor are special keys called *handles* (which is why their names all begin with **HKEY**). These keys are referred to collectively as the Registry's *root keys*. I'll tell you what to expect from them a bit later (see the section called "The Roots of the Tree: The Registry's Root Keys").

These keys all contain subkeys, and you navigate them just like you navigate folders in Windows Explorer:

➤ To open a key, click the plus sign (+) to the left of each key. You can also highlight a key and press the plus-sign (+) key on your keyboard's numeric keypad. When you open a key, the plus sign changes to a minus sign (–).

➤ To close a key, click the minus sign or highlight the key and press the minus-sign key on the numeric keypad.

It's not unusual to have to dig down several levels to get to the subkey you want. In the following figure, for example, I opened the **HKEY_CURRENT_USER** key, then I opened the **Control Panel** key, and then I highlighted the **Desktop** key. Notice how the status bar tells you the exact path to the current key.

Painless Pane Adjustments

If you find that a key name or a setting gets cut off at the edge of its pane, it's easy to adjust the size of the panes accordingly:

➤ Use your mouse to drag the split bar that separates the panes to the right or left.

➤ Select **View | Split**, use the left- and right-arrow keys to adjust the split bar's position, and press **Enter**.

The current key   Keys pane   The split bar   Settings pane

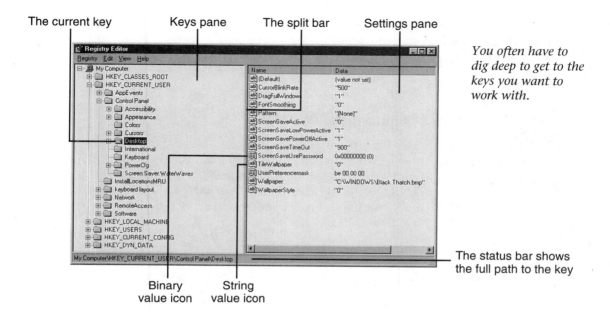

You often have to dig deep to get to the keys you want to work with.

The status bar shows the full path to the key

Binary value icon   String value icon

The Leaves of the Tree: The Settings Pane

The right side of the Registry Editor window displays the settings contained in each key. So, while I'm on a roll assigning wholly unimaginative names to things, I'll call the right side of the window the *Settings pane*.

The Settings pane shows two columns:

➤ **Name**   This column tells you the name of each setting in the currently selected key.

➤ **Data**   This column tells you the value of each setting.

In the previous figure, for example, the **Desktop** key has a setting called Wallpaper, and it stores the name of the current desktop wallpaper. (Or, more specifically, it stores the location of the BMP file used as the wallpaper.) As you can see in the Data column, on this system the current wallpaper is **C:\WINDOWS\Black Thatch.bmp**.

Registry key settings can be either of the following types:

➤ **String**   This is just a name or any value that combines letters and numbers. For these types of settings, the value is always surrounded by quotation marks.

➤ **Binary number**   This is a numeric value. (Technically, the value is a set of hexadecimal—base 16—digits.)

As pointed out in the previous figure, the Registry Editor differentiates between these two types by displaying a different icon to the left of the setting name. For example, the Wallpaper setting is a string value, and the **ScreenSaveUsePassword** setting is a binary value.

Another type of value: DWORD

In your Registry travels, you may come across a third type of setting that uses something called a *DWORD* value. These are 4-byte hexadecimal values arranged as eight digits. For example, 11 hex is 17 decimal, so this number would be represented in DWORD form as 0×00000011 (17). Why "DWORD"? Well, since a "word" in programming circles is 2 bytes, these 4-byte settings are "double word" values.

The Roots of the Tree: The Registry's Root Keys

The root keys are your Registry starting points, so you need to become familiar with what kinds of data each key holds. Fortunately, you won't have to deal with all of the root keys. In fact, there are only three you really need to worry about: **HKEY_CLASSES_ROOT**, **HKEY_CURRENT_USER**, and **HKEY_LOCAL_MACHINE**. This section gives you a summary of each of these root keys.

HKEY_CLASSES_ROOT

I've talked about file types in a few places so far in this book. (In Chapter 2, see "Figuring Out File Types," and in Chapter 6, check out "A Few of My Favorite Practical Windows Things.") All that file type flimflam is stored in the Registry in the HKEY_CLASSES_ROOT key.

The top part of this key contains subkeys for various file extensions. You see **.bmp** for BMP (Paint) files, **.doc** for DOC (WordPad) files, and so on. In each of these subkeys, the **Default** setting tells you the name of the registered file type associated with the extension. For example, in the following figure I've highlighted the **.bmp** subkey, which, as you can see, is associated with the **Paint.Picture** file type.

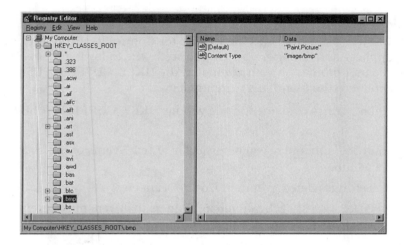

The first few subkeys in HKEY_CLASSES_ROOT are extensions that tell you their associated file type.

These registered file types appear as subkeys later in the **HKEY_CLASSES_ROOT** branch. For example, if you scroll down, you eventually come across the **Paint.Picture** subkey, which is shown in the following figure. The Registry keeps track of various settings for each registered file type. In particular, the shell subkey tells you the actions associated with this file type.

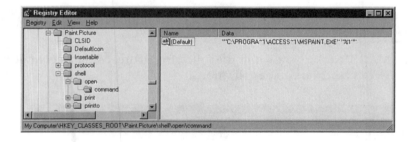

The registered file type subkeys specify various settings associated with each file type, including its defined actions.

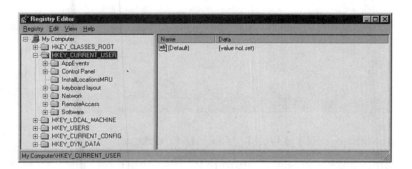

The HKEY_CURRENT_USER key controls settings for the current user.

147

HKEY_CURRENT_USER

HKEY_CURRENT_USER contains user-specific settings for Control Panel options, network connections, applications, and more, as you can see in the following figure. If you've set up multiple user profiles on your computer, the **HKEY_CURRENT_USER** key contains data that applies to the user that's currently logged on.

Here's a summary of the settings contained in the various **HKEY_CURRENT_USER** subkeys:

➤ **AppEvents** Sound files that play when particular system events occur (such as the maximizing of a window).

➤ **Control Panel** Settings related to certain Control Panel icons.

➤ **InstallLocationsMRU** A list of the drives and folders that were most recently used (MRU) to install software or device drivers.

➤ **keyboard layout** The keyboard layout as selected via Control Panel's Keyboard icon.

➤ **Network** Settings related to mapped network drives.

➤ **RemoteAccess** Settings related to Dial-Up Networking. (This branch only appears after you have created a Dial-Up Networking connection.)

➤ **Software** User-specific settings related to installed applications.

HKEY_LOCAL_MACHINE

The **HKEY_LOCAL_MACHINE** key, shown in the following figure, contains configuration data for your system's hardware and applications.

The HKEY_LOCAL_MACHINE key contains settings for devices and programs.

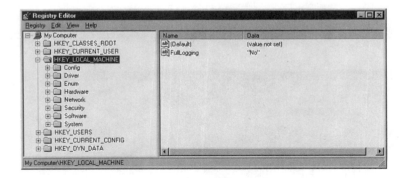

Let's run through the various **HKEY_LOCAL_MACHINE** subkeys:

➤ **Config** Contains subkeys for each hardware profile defined on your system. The subkey name is a unique identifier assigned to each profile (for example, 0001).

148

➤ **Enum**   Contains the hardware data gathered by the Windows 98 *bus enumerators* (small programs that poll the system hardware for info).

➤ **Hardware**   Contains subkeys related to serial ports and modems (used by HyperTerminal), as well as the floating-point processor.

➤ **Network**   Contains a **Logon** subkey with various settings related to the network logon, including the user name and whether the logon was validated by a network server.

➤ **Security**   Contains a Provider subkey that specifies the domain under which network security is administered.

➤ **Software**   Contains computer-specific settings related to installed applications. Many programs use this key to save their computer-specific settings. The settings related to Windows 98 can be found in the following subkey:

HKEY_LOCAL_MACHINE\Software\Microsoft\Windows\CurrentVersion

➤ **System**   Contains subkeys and settings related to Windows 98 startup.

How to Work with Registry Entries

The Registry is a bizarre little world, indeed, but I hope I've shown you that it's not hopelessly obscure. With a little practice and more than a little patience, you'll eventually become quite comfortable rooting around in the Registry's nooks and crannies.

You're now set to start working with the Registry's keys and settings. In this section, I'll give you the general procedures for basic tasks, such as modifying, adding, renaming, deleting, and searching for entries. These techniques will serve you well in Chapter 11 when you get to play with the Registry in earnest.

Editing a Registry Entry

Editing a Registry setting is the most fundamental of all Registry tasks. To illustrate how this process works, let's work through an example: changing the desktop wallpaper via the Registry. (As you'll see, it's much easier to change the wallpaper by using Control Panel. However, this simple example serves to illustrate the basic technique for altering Registry settings.) Here goes:

1. Use the Keys pane to display the key you want to work with, and then highlight it. The key's settings will appear in the Settings pane. For the example, select the following key:

   HKEY_CURRENT_USER\Control Panel\Desktop

2. Open the setting (in this example, the **wallpaper** setting) for editing by highlighting the setting name and selecting **Edit | Modify**. (Speedier alternatives include double-clicking the setting or highlighting the setting and pressing **Enter**.)

149

3. The dialog box that appears depends on the type of setting you're handling. For example, if the setting is a string value, you see the Edit String dialog box shown in the following figure. Use the **Value data** text box to enter a new string or modify the existing string. For the wallpaper example, enter the full pathname for the bitmap you want to use as the wallpaper (for example, **c:\windows\Carved Stone.bmp**).

Where's the Key?

The rub here is that finding the key you need isn't always a simple matter. Knowing the root keys and their main subkeys, as described earlier, will certainly help, and the Registry Editor also has a Find feature that's invaluable. I'll show you how to use it a bit later (see "Hunting Down Registry Entries").

You see the Edit String dialog box if you're modifying a string value.

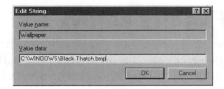

4. When you're finished editing the value, click **OK**.

Edited settings are written to the Registry right away, but the changes might not go into effect immediately. In many cases, you need to exit the Registry Editor, and then restart Windows 98. If you have user profiles activated on your machine, or if your machine is on a network, the easiest way to put Registry changes into effect is to select the **Start | Log Off** *User* command, where *User* is the name of the current user.

If you don't have user profiles activated or a network connection, you need to restart Windows 98 by selecting **Start | Shut Down** and activating the **Restart** option. Remember, however, that you can get a faster restart by holding down the **Shift** key when you click the **OK** button. This method bypasses the cold reboot and merely restarts Windows 98.

Some Other Useful Registry Techniques

Nearly all the modifications you make to Registry entries will involve modifying the value of an existing setting. You can also rename, add, and delete keys and settings. Here are the basic techniques:

➤ **Renaming a key or setting**   Highlight the key or setting and select **Edit | Rename** (or press **F2**). Make your changes in the text box and press **Enter**.

➤ **Adding a key or setting**   Highlight the key in which you want to add the subkey or setting. Select **File | New** and, in the cascade menu that appears, select **Key**, **String Value**, **Binary Value**, or **DWORD Value**.

➤ **Deleting a key or setting**   Highlight the key or setting and select **Edit | Delete** (or press **Delete**). When the Registry Editor asks you to confirm the deletion, click **Yes**.

Hunting Down Registry Entries

The Registry contains only six root keys, but these root keys contain hundreds of subkeys. If you know exactly where you're going, the Key pane's branches are a reasonable way to get there. However, if you're not sure where a particular subkey or setting resides, you could spend all day poking around in the Registry's labyrinthine lanes and alleyways.

To help you get where you want to go, the Registry Editor has a Find feature that helps you search for keys, settings, or values. Here's how it works:

1. In the Keys pane, highlight **My Computer** at the top of the pane (unless you're certain of which root key contains the value you want to find; in this case, you can highlight the appropriate root key instead).

2. Select **Edit | Find** or press **Ctrl+F**. The Registry Editor displays the Find dialog box shown in the following figure.

Use the Find dialog box to scope out hard-to-locate Registry items.

3. Use the **Find what** text box to enter your search string. You can enter partial words or phrases to increase your chances of finding a match.

4. You can use the check boxes in the **Look at** group to specify the Registry elements you want to search. For most searches, however, you'll want to leave all three check boxes activated.

5. If you want to find only those entries that exactly match your search text, activate the **Match whole string only** check box.

6. Click the **Find Next** button. The Registry Editor highlights the first match.

7. If this isn't the item you want, select **Edit | Find Next** (or press **F3**) until you find the setting or key you want.

When the Registry Editor finds a match, it displays the appropriate key or setting. Note that if the matched value is a setting name or data value, Find doesn't highlight the current key. This is a bit confusing, but just remember that the current key always appears at the bottom of the Keys pane.

From Here

This chapter introduced you to the wacky world of the Registry, the central storehouse for all things Windows. After giving you a mercifully brief explanation of the Registry, I showed you how to fire up the Registry Editor. From there, you learned some basic Registry flora and fauna, including keys, settings, and the root keys. The rest of the chapter dealt with basic Registry techniques such as renaming, deleting, and finding entries.

The real Registry action begins in Chapter 11, "Revving Up the Registry: A Few Handy Techniques," as I take you through some specific Registry modifications.

Revving Up the Registry: A Few Handy Techniques

In This Chapter

➤ Changing Setup information

➤ Redoing the desktop, Registry-style

➤ More ways to work with file types

➤ Reams of Registry routines for your customization pleasure

After all that Registry theory in Chapter 10, "The Registry: The Soul of the Windows Machine," you're probably hankering for some practical know-how. Well, you've come to the right place. This chapter takes the fundamentals you learned in Chapter 10 and puts them to work customizing Windows 98. I'll show you how to use the Registry to modify some of the information deposited there by the Windows 98 Setup program. You'll also learn how to customize certain aspects of the desktop (these are things you can't do from the Control Panel). I'll close with a look at yet another collection of file type techniques.

Editing Some Setup Info

When Windows 98 was installed on your system, the Setup program left behind a few tidbits—in the form of Registry settings—for Windows 98 to use. Most of these settings are highly technical and are of no use to the likes of you and me. However, a couple of them are highly useful, and I'll explain them in this section.

Editing Your Name and Company Name

Two of the Setup-related Registry items are your name and your company name (if you use Windows 98 at work). There are three ways that this information can get recorded:

➤ If you ran Setup yourself, the program may have asked you to enter your name and, optionally, your company name. (If you upgraded from Windows 95, this data was recorded when you ran the Windows 95 Setup program.)

➤ If you purchased a computer with Windows 98 already installed, your name will probably be something silly like "Preferred Customer," and the company name will likely be the name of the computer company.

➤ If Windows 98 was installed at work, the company name will be correct, but your name will either be missing or something generic.

These "registered names" appear in several places as you work with Windows 98:

➤ If you right-click **My Computer** and click **Properties** (or open the **System** icon in Control Panel), your registered names appear in the **General** tab of the System Properties dialog box.

➤ If you select **Help | About** in just about any Windows 98 accessory or folder, your registered names appear in the About dialog box.

➤ If you install a Windows 95 or Windows 98 application, the installation program uses your registered names for its own records (although you usually get a chance to make changes).

With these names popping up all over the place, what do you do if you want to change one or both of the names? Why, head for the Registry, of course. In particular, make tracks to the following key:

HKEY_LOCAL_MACHINE\SOFTWARE\Microsoft\Windows\CurrentVersion

This key has two settings that store your registered names: **RegisteredOrganization** and **RegisteredOwner**. Use these settings to tell Windows 98 that you want to use different registered names.

Changing Where Windows 98 Looks For Its Installation Files

When you install Windows 98, Setup makes a note of the disk drive you used for the source CD-ROM. Later, when you add new Windows 98 accessories or adjust your hardware, Windows 98 prompts you to insert the CD-ROM in the same drive so that it can install the necessary files.

If you have lots of hard disk space available (at least 130MB), you can save yourself the hassle of having to insert the Windows 98 CD-ROM every time Windows needs to install stuff. How? By copying the Windows 98 installation files to your hard disk. Not only does this save you from inserting the CD-ROM, but it's much quicker because your hard drive is *way* faster than your CD-ROM drive.

154

The following steps show you how to copy the Windows 98 installation files to your hard disk and how to make the necessary Registry adjustment for this to work:

1. Insert your Windows 98 CD-ROM.

2. Use Windows Explorer to open the CD-ROM drive. You should see a folder called Win98.

3. Copy the **Win98** folder to your hard drive. (The copy process will take quite a while, so this is a good time to take a break.)

4. Once the copy operation is complete, run the Registry Editor and highlight the following key:

   HKEY_LOCAL_MACHINE\SOFTWARE\Microsoft\Windows\CurrentVersion\Setup

5. Find the **SourcePath** setting and edit it so that it points to the new location on the hard drive. For example, if you installed Windows 98 originally from CD-ROM drive D, the **SourcePath** setting will be **D:**. If you copied the installation file to drive C, change **SourcePath** to **C:\Win98**.

6. Exit the Registry Editor to put the new setting into effect.

Doctoring the Desktop Icons

The default icons that populate the Windows 98 desktop are handy, but they can be annoyingly difficult to work with. For example, if you don't use My Computer, Network Neighborhood, or Recycle Bin, there's no way to delete them from the desktop. Also, you can rename all the desktop icons except for the Recycle Bin, which stubbornly refuses all renaming attempts.

Fortunately, all these problems are overcome easily with some simple Registry changes. The next few sections show you some tricks for modifying the desktop icons.

Substituting One Icon for Another

If you're getting a bit a tired of seeing the same old icons on your desktop, changing these icons is a nice way to give Windows 98 a quick facelift. In *The Complete Idiot's Guide to Windows 98* you learned that you can use the Icons tab of the Display Properties dialog box to change the icons for My Computer, Network Neighborhood, and the Recycle Bin. For the other desktop icons, you need to use the Registry.

Each desktop icon has a subkey in the following key:

HKEY_LOCAL_MACHINE\SOFTWARE\Classes\CLSID

CLSID is short for class ID, and each Windows 98 object has its own unique class ID. These values consist of no fewer than 32 hexadecimal digits arranged in an 8-4-4-4-12 pattern, surrounded by braces ({}), for good measure. For example, the **CLSID** for My

Computer is {20D04FE0-3AEA-1069-A2D8-08002B30309D}, so this is My Computer's Registry key:

HKEY_LOCAL_MACHINE\SOFTWARE\Classes\CLSID\{20D04FE0-3AEA-1069-A2D8-08002B30309D}

Ugly, or what? Unfortunately, if you want to deal with the desktop icons, you've got to deal with these geeky **CLSID** values. The following table lists the **CLSID** values for all the desktop icons (except those that are shortcuts).

Desktop Icon	CLSID
My Computer	{20D04FE0-3AEA-1069-A2D8-08002B30309D}
My Documents	{450D8FBA-AD25-11D0-98A8-0800361B1103}
Internet Explorer	{3DC7A020-0ACD-11CF-A9BB-00AA004AE837}
Network Neighborhood	{208D2C60-3AEA-1069-A2D7-08002B30309D}
Set Up The Microsoft Network	{4B876A40-4EE8-11D1-811E-00C04FB98EEC}
Recycle Bin	{645FF040-5081-101B-9F08-00AA002F954E}
My Briefcase	{85BBD920-42A0-1069-A2E4-08002B30309D}

Each desktop icon key contains various subkeys. In particular, you'll find a subkey named **DefaultIcon** that determines the icon used by each object. By changing the **Default** setting in the **DefaultIcon** subkey, you can define new icons for your desktop.

The **DefaultIcon** subkey's **Default** setting always uses the following general value:

```
IconFile,IconNumber
```

Here, *IconFile* is the name of a file (plus the drive and folder if the file isn't in the main Windows 98 folder or its **System** subfolder) that contains one or more icons. Most of the desktop icons use the file **Shell32.dll**.

IconNumber is an integer that specifies which icon to use in *IconFile*, in which the first icon is 0. For example, the Network Neighborhood's **DefaultIcon** setting is this:

shell32.dll,17

To change the icon, either specify a different icon number in the existing icon file or use a different icon file altogether.

How do you know which files contain which icons? Here's the best way:

1. If the desktop doesn't have any shortcuts on it, go ahead and create one. (See "Getting the Most Out of Shortcuts," in Chapter 1, "Beginning at the Beginning: Windows 98 Startup Techniques.")

2. Right-click the shortcut, and then click **Properties** to display the Properties dialog box for the shortcut.

3. In the **Shortcut** tab, click the **Change Icon** button. The Change Icon dialog box reports for duty, as shown in the following figure.

Use the Change Icon dialog box to browse the available icons in an icon file.

4. Use the **File name** text box to enter the name of an icon file and then press **Tab**. Here are a few suggested files to check out:

   C:\WINDOWS\SYSTEM\SHELL32.DLL

   C:\WINDOWS\SYSTEM\PIFMGR.DLL

   C:\WINDOWS\SYSTEM\USER.EXE

   C:\WINDOWS\EXPLORER.EXE

   C:\WINDOWS\MORICONS.DLL

   C:\WINDOWS\PROGMAN.EXE

5. After you've opened a file, use the **Current icon** box to browse the available icons.

6. If you see an icon you want to use, you can get its icon number by counting from the first icon, starting at 0, until you get to the icon. Note that you must count *down* each column and work your way across the columns.

7. Click **Cancel** to return to the Properties dialog box, and then click **Cancel** again to return to the desktop.

Renaming the Recycle Bin

Except for the Recycle Bin, you can rename all the desktop icons. If the name "Recycle Bin" just doesn't cut it for you, you can assign this icon a new name—Trash Can, Garbage Pail, Rubbish Heap, Last Stop Before Deletesville, or whatever—via the Registry. First, head for the Recycle Bin's CLSID key:

HKEY_CLASSES_ROOT\CLSID\{645FF040-5081-101B-9F08-00AA002F954E}

To change the name, edit the **Default** setting for this key. Note, too, that clearing the title from this setting will display the Recycle Bin with no name. To see the change, click the desktop, and then press **F5** to refresh it.

Recycling the Recycle Bin

You can delete most of the desktop icons by right-clicking an icon and then clicking **Delete**. (For the **My Documents** folder, right-click and then click the **Remove from Desktop** command.) Unfortunately, both the My Computer icon and the Network Neighborhood icon are permanent fixtures on the desktop, and so they can't be deleted.

That just leaves the Recycle Bin, which can only be deleted by using the Registry. What you have to do is delete the appropriate subkey in the **CLSID** key:

HKEY_LOCAL_MACHINE\SOFTWARE\Classes\CLSID\{645FF040-5081-101B-9F08-00AA002F954E}

Click the desktop and then press **F5** to refresh the icons. The Recycle Bin will turn into a folder icon, which you can then delete normally.

Playing with the Icon InfoTips

In Windows 98, when you point at many of the desktop icons, a banner called an InfoTip pops up with a brief description of the icon. For example, the following figure shows the InfoTip that appears when you point at the Internet Explorer icon.

Each desktop icon has an InfoTip setting that holds the InfoTip text.

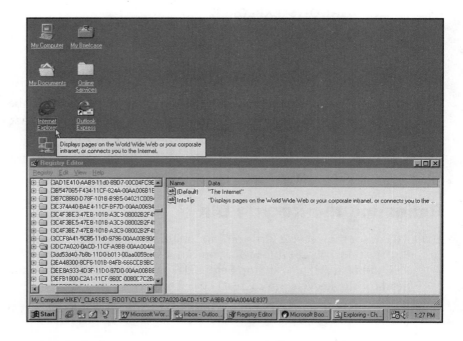

The InfoTip text is stored in the Registry, so you can edit the text to, for example, give further instructions to other folks who use your computer. To work with the InfoTip text, find the **CLSID** key for the desktop icon. As shown in the figure, you see an **InfoTip** setting. Just edit this string value to customize the InfoTip.

Customizing the System Icons

Most of the Windows 98 system icons—such as those that appear in the Start menu and the default icons that Explorer uses for unknown file types and DOS applications—can be customized. To understand how, let's run through an example. First, use the technique I showed you earlier to browse the icons in the file **Shell32.dll**. As you can see in the following figure, the third icon (icon 2) is the one Windows 98 uses in folder windows to display DOS applications. Suppose, instead, you want Windows 98 to display the computer icon, which is the one at the bottom of the fourth column (icon 15).

To accomplish this replacement, follow these steps:

1. Use the Registry Editor to display the following key:

   HKEY_LOCAL_MACHINE\SOFTWARE\Microsoft\Windows\CurrentVersion\explorer

2. Highlight the **Shell Icons** subkey.

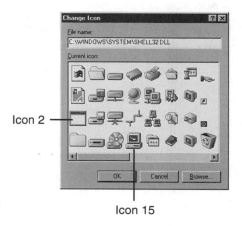

SHELL32.DLL contains most of the Windows 98 system icons.

3. Select **Edit | New | String Value** to create a new string value.

4. Now you need to name this new string value. The name you want to use is the number that corresponds to the position in **Shell32.dll** of the icon you want to replace. For the example, we're replacing the second icon, so type **2**, and then press **Enter**.

5. Double-click the new string value to display the Edit String dialog box.

6. In the **Value data** text box, change the value of the setting to **shell32.dll,n**, where n is the number of the replacement icon you want to use. For our example, you enter **shell32.dll,15** (see the next figure), and then click **OK**.

Here's the new setting to use for our example.

Putting this change into effect requires a bit more effort than usual. What you have to do is open the desktop's Properties dialog box (right-click the desktop, and then click **Properties**). In the **Appearance** tab, choose **Icon** from the **Item** drop-down list, modify the **Size** value (it doesn't matter what number you choose), and then click **Apply**. Return the **Icon** item to its original size and click **OK**.

As you might have guessed by now, you can use a similar technique to customize any of Windows 98's system icons. Use the Change Icon dialog box to get the appropriate number for the system icon in **Shell32.dll** (remember to start counting at 0) and create a string value setting for that number in the **Shell Icons** key. Change this setting to the icon file and icon number you want to use as a replacement.

To get you started, here are the setting names to use for the icons in the Start menu:

Command	Setting Name
Programs	19
Favorites	43
Documents	20
Settings	21
Find	22
Help	23
Run	24
Log Off	44
Suspend	25
Eject PC	26
Shut Down	27

More File Type Frivolity

File types seem to be cropping up all over the place in this book:

➤ In Chapter 1, the "Figuring Out File Types" section explained file types, and the "More File Flapdoodle: Understanding File Extensions," explained the relationship between file types and file extensions.

➤ In Chapter 6, "A Few of My Favorite Windows Things," the "File Type Tweak I: Modifying Actions" section showed you how to change the existing actions for a given file type. The "File Type Tweak II: Creating New Actions," section showed you how to create new things for a file type to do.

➤ In Chapter 10's "The Branches of the Tree: The Keys Pane," section, I told you that the **HKEY_CLASSES_ROOT** Registry key stores all of Windows 98's data about file extensions and their associated file types.

With all this file type stuff residing in the Registry, it makes sense that you can use the Registry to customize file types in interesting ways. The rest of this chapter shows you a few of them.

A New and Improved New Menu

One of Windows 98's handiest features is the New menu, which lets you create a new document without working within an application. There are two methods you can use in Windows Explorer:

➤ Select the **File | New** command.

➤ Right-click inside the Contents pane, and then click **New**.

Windows 98 then displays a menu similar to the one shown in the following figure. From here, select a command to create a new instance of that particular file type.

Windows 98 recognizes more than 100 file types, but the New menu lists only seven by default. (Applications that you install may add more.) What determines whether a file type appears on the New menu? The Registry, of course. Start the Registry Editor and open the **HKEY_CLASSES_ROOT** key. As I mentioned in the previous chapter, the first 150 or so subkeys of **HKEY_CLASSES_ROOT** are the file extensions that Windows 98 recognizes. Most of these keys contain only a **Default** setting that takes on either of the following values:

➤ If the extension is registered with Windows 98, the **Default** value is a string pointing to the file type associated with the extension. For example, the **Default** value for **.avi** is **avifile** (this is a video file type).

➤ If the extension isn't registered with Windows 98, the **Default** value isn't set.

161

The New menu lets you create new documents without opening an application.

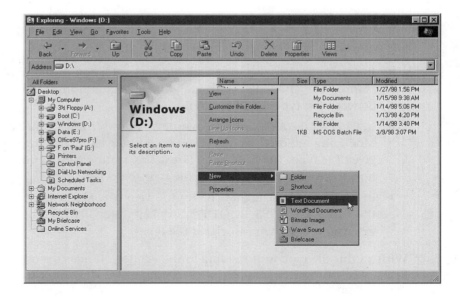

A few of these extension keys, however, also have subkeys. For example, open the **.bmp** key and you see that it has a subkey named **ShellNew**, as shown in the Registry below. This subkey is what determines whether a file type appears on the New menu. Specifically, if the extension is registered with Windows 98 and it has a **ShellNew** subkey, the New menu sprouts a command for the associated file type.

It's the ShellNew subkey that determines whether a file type shows up on the New menu.

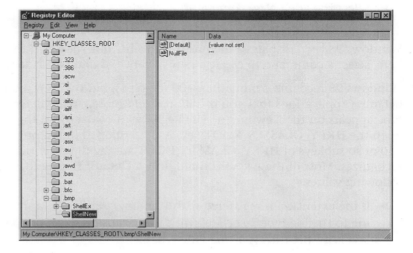

The **ShellNew** subkey always contains a setting that determines how Windows 98 creates the new file. Four settings are possible:

➤ **NullFile** This setting, the value of which is always set to a null string (""), tells Windows 98 to create an empty file of the associated type. Of the five file types (excluding Folder and Shortcut) that appear on the New menu, three use the **NullFile** setting: Text Document (**.txt**), Bitmap Image (**.bmp**), and Wave Sound (**.wav**).

➤ **FileName** This setting tells Windows 98 to create the new file by making a copy of another file. Windows 98 has a special folder to hold these "template" files. This folder, called **ShellNew** (see the next figure), is hidden, so you must activate Explorer's **Show all files** option to view it. On the New menu, only the WordPad Document (**.doc**) file type uses the **FileName** setting, and its value is **winword.doc**. To see this value, you need to open the following key:

HKEY_CLASSES_ROOT\.doc\Wordpad.Document.1\ShellNew

The ShellNew folder holds templates used by the New menu to create new documents.

➤ **Command** This setting tells Windows 98 to create the new file by executing a specific command. This command usually invokes an executable file with a few parameters. The New menu's Briefcase item uses this setting. If you check the **ShellNew** subkey for **.bfc** (Briefcase) in **HKEY_CLASSES_ROOT**, you see the following value for the **Command** setting:

C:\windows\rundll32.exe syncui.dll,Briefcase_Create %1!d! %2

➤ **Data** This setting contains a binary value, and when Windows 98 creates the new file, it copies this binary value into the file.

To make the New menu even more convenient, you can add new file types for documents that you work with regularly. For any file type that's registered with Windows 98, you follow a simple three-step process:

1. Add a **ShellNew** subkey to the appropriate extension key in **HKEY_CLASSES_ROOT**.

2. Add one of the four settings discussed in the preceding list (**NullFile**, **FileName**, **Command**, or **Data**).

3. Enter an appropriate value for the setting.

In most cases, the easiest way to go is to use **NullFile** to create an empty file. The **FileName** setting, however, can be quite powerful because you can set up a template file containing text and other data.

Let's try an example. **HKEY_CLASSES_ROOT** has a key for the **.htm** extension that's registered as a Microsoft HTML Document 4.0 file type. (There will also be a key for the HTML extension.) These are pages designed to appear on the World Wide Web. If you create your own Web pages, most of them will have the same basic structure. You could set up a template HTML file that uses this basic structure, and you could then assign this template to the New menu.

The first thing you must do is create the template. Using a text editor, word processor, or HTML editor, enter the basic HTML tags and text you want to use for the template, and save the file (using the **.htm** extension) in the **ShellNew** folder. For example, the following figure shows a template HTML file (**skeleton.htm**) that I use.

Create your template and save it in the ShellNew folder.

Start the Registry Editor and highlight the **.htm** key in **HKEY_CLASSES_ROOT**. Follow these steps to set up the **ShellNew** subkey:

1. Select **Edit | New | Key**. The Registry Editor adds a new subkey.

2. Type **ShellNew** and press **Enter**.

3. Select **Edit | New | String Value**. The Registry Editor adds a new setting.

4. Type **FileName** and press **Enter**.

5. Press **Enter** or double-click the **FileName** setting. The Edit String dialog box appears.

6. Type the name of your template file (for the example, type **skeleton.htm**, as shown in the next figure) and click **OK**.

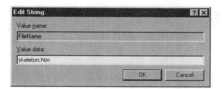

Enter the name of the template file.

7. Exit the Registry Editor.

The new setting goes into effect immediately, as you can see in the following figure, so you can try this without having to restart Windows 98.

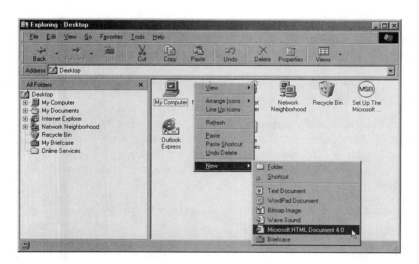

You can try out your new command without having to restart Windows 98.

Deleting File Types from the New Menu

Many Windows 98 applications like to add their file types to the New menu. (Microsoft Office alone adds five commands to the New menu.) If you find that your New menu is getting overcrowded, you can delete some commands to keep things manageable.

To do this, you need to find the appropriate extension in the Registry, and then rename the **ShellNew** subkey (to, say, **ShellNewOld**). If down the road you change your mind, you can always return to the extension and rename the subkey back to **ShellNew**.

What's the File Extension?

If you're not sure which extension is associated with the New menu command you want to delete, you could search the Registry all day looking for it. An easier way is to use the command to create a new document in any Windows Explorer folder and see the resulting extension.

Associating Multiple Extensions with One Application

In Chapter 2's "Opportunistic Opening: How to Open a File in Another Program" section, I showed you how to specify which program to use to open a document with a particular extension. What this does is register a new file type with Windows 98. For example, to handle the **Readme.1st** text files that come with some programs, you could associate the **.1st** extension with Notepad. This creates a new **.1st** file type.

The problem with this approach, however, is that it involves re-creating the wheel by having to set up certain actions—such as Open and Print—for the new file type. In the **.1st** file type, for example, the actions you'd want set up are identical to those that are already set up for the Text Document file type. It would be better if you could just augment an existing file type with a new extension, such as adding the **.1st** extension to the existing Text Document file type.

You know this is possible because if you look through the list of file types (in Windows Explorer, select **View | Folder Options** and activate the **File Types** tab), you see that several file types have multiple extensions. The Movie Clip file type, for example, has several extensions, including **.MPEG** and **.MPG**. Unfortunately, there's no way you can use the File Types tab to add an extension to an existing file type.

However, you can do this via the Registry. Here are the steps to follow:

1. In the Registry Editor, open **HKEY_CLASSES_ROOT**.

2. Find the extension subkey for the file type you want to work with. For the Text Document file type, for example, find the **.txt** subkey.

3. Make a note of the value of the extension subkey's **Default** setting. For example, the Default setting for the **.txt** subkey is **txtfile**.

4. Highlight **HKEY_CLASSES_ROOT** and add a key for the new extension. In the **.1st** extension example, you'd add a key named **.1st**.

5. For this new key, change the **Default** setting to the value you noted in step 3, as shown in the following figure.

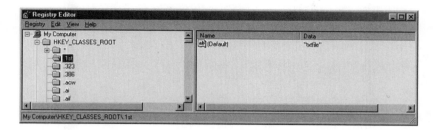

To associate an extension with an existing file type, you need to add the extension to the Registry.

After you've created this new key, it becomes available to Windows 98 immediately. To see for yourself, check out the file type in the File Types tab. You should see the new extension in the File type details group, as shown below.

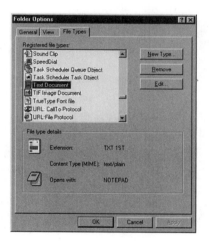

The new extension shows up in the File Types tab.

From Here

This chapter ran through some practical Registry editing techniques. You learned how to modify some Setup data, alter the desktop icons, and mess around yet again with file types.

This ends your tour of Windows 98's advanced customization options. From here, it's time to reach out and touch some Net in Part 3, "More Online Fun: Communications and the Internet."

Part 3
More Online Fun: Communications and the Internet

For many years, being online only meant using your modem to dial in to a bulletin board system (BBS, for short) to do some chatting and maybe download a file or two. Then along came the big online services—such as CompuServe and America Online—and suddenly there was a ton of content on the other end of our modems (as well as chatting and the downloading of a file or two). Nowadays, being online is synonymous with being on the Internet. Today's modern modem jockey has access to the World Wide Web, that ultimate collection of content, as well as to email, that most popular of all Internet services. (And, of course, people still chat and download a file or two. Some things never change.)

Whatever stage of "online-ness" you currently find yourself in, you're probably paying for it in some way (in time if not in money), so it pays to know what you're doing out there. Windows 98 has tons of tools for dealing with the online world, and the chapters here in Part 3 show you how to get the most out of those tools. You'll learn how to maximize your modem's potential, and how to configure Internet Explorer and Outlook Express to suit your online style. I'll also show you how to use Microsoft Chat (there's that chatting thing again) and Personal Web Server.

Chapter 12

Getting Your Modem's Mojo Working

In This Chapter

➤ How modems work

➤ Changing modem properties

➤ Testing your modem

➤ Setting up dialing locations

➤ Lots of useful theory and practice to help you max out your modem

Most folks find modems to be the most mysterious—in both word (or, I guess, sound) and deed—of all the computer components. After all, no other chunk of hardware makes quite the same racket that a modem in full squawk manages to inflict on our uncomprehending ears. And when you think about what a modem does—spitting data to and from remote locations using, of all things, a telephone line—well, the whole idea seems positively preposterous.

Granted, you don't need to penetrate this mystique to make basic connections to the online world. However, demystifying the modem will help you take charge of your online sessions, thus saving you both time and money. This chapter will help you do just that by offering you a brief modem communications primer and showing you a few useful techniques for controlling your modem.

Bits and Ports and Stuff: An Encyclopedic Primer

One of the reasons that modems remain a mystery is that the communications industry uses concepts and terms that developed and flourished in a geek-only world. The result is a mishmash of impenetrable terminology, inscrutable jargon, and unintelligible acronyms. To help you make sense of the insensible, this section presents a sort of encyclopedia of modemspeak. The following list of terms covers all the basic concepts you need to know, in the order that you need to know them.

Modem An electronic device that enables the transmission and reception of computer data over telephone lines. The word *modem* was coined by crashing the words *modulation* and *demodulation* (explained later in this list) together.

External modem This type of modem is a standalone box that you connect to a *serial port* on your computer with a special cable. External modems have several advantages over their *internal modem* cousins. For one, an external modem is easily shuffled between computers. For another, most external modems have a series of LED indicators on their front panel that tell you the current state of the modem. These lights are a useful troubleshooting tool. On the downside, external modems require a separate power source (which is usually a huge wall wart), and they tend to be more expensive than an equivalent internal modem.

Internal modem This type of modem is a circuit board that sits inside your computer. Many people prefer this type over *external modems* because no external power source is required, it's one less device taking up valuable desk space, no external serial port is used up, and they tend to be less expensive.

Bit This is the fundamental unit of computer information. Inside the computer, data is stored using tiny electronic devices called *gates*, which each hold one bit. Gates can be either on (electricity flows through the gate) or off (no electricity flows through). For human consumption, a gate that's on is represented by the number 1, and a gate that's off is represented by 0. These ones and zeros are the bits. Put eight of these bits together, and you get a byte, which holds a single character of data. For example, the letter "Z" is represented by the following 8-bit byte: 1011010.

Waves How sounds are transmitted across telephone lines. They're crucial for understanding how modems work. When you speak into a telephone, a diaphragm inside the mouthpiece vibrates. This vibration is converted into an electromagnetic wave that mirrors the original sound wave created by your voice. This wave travels along the telephone lines, and at the destination, electromagnets in the receiver vibrate another diaphragm that reproduces your voice.

Modulation The process used by a modem to convert the computer's digital data into a wave that's capable of being transmitted across a telephone line. In essence, bits—the ones and zeros that compose digital data—are converted into special signals that can be represented as tones that the phone system can transmit.

What's With All the Lights?

Wondering just what all those flashing LED lights on the front of your modem are for? Here's a summary:

LED	Name	Description
AA	Auto Answer	When this light is on, it tells you that the modem will answer incoming calls automatically.
CD	Carrier Detect	This light comes on when the modem receives the A-OK from the remote location to start transmitting data.
CS	Clear to Send	When this LED glows, it means that it's okay for your communications program to start shipping data to the remote location.
MR	Modem Ready	This one lights up when the modem's power is turned on.
OH	Off Hook	This light comes on when the modem takes control of the phone line (which is the modem equivalent of taking the telephone receiver off the hook).
RD	Receive Data	When you see this light turned on, it means your modem is busy receiving data.
RS	Request to Send	This light comes on when your computer asks the modem whether it's okay to start sending data.
SD	Send Data	When you see this light turned on, it means your modem is busy sending data.
TR	Terminal Ready	When this light is lit, it means the communications program is ready to start sending data.

Demodulation The process used by a modem to convert tones received over a phone line into digital data (bits) that the computer can understand. Now you know why modems make such a racket while they're communicating with each other: it's all those tones exchanged back and forth.

bps Bits per second. The rate at which the modem shouts data through a telephone line.

173

Data transfer rate   The fastest rate at which a modem can send data. The data transfer rate is measured in *bps*. The current standards for the data transfer rate are 28,000bps on the low end and 56,000bps on the high end.

Serial port   The link between your computer and your modem (also known as a "COM port" or "RS-232 port"). For an external modem, this link usually comes in the form of a serial cable that runs from the port to a plug in the back of the modem. For internal modems, the serial port is built right into the modem's circuitry. They're called "serial" ports because they transmit and receive data one bit at a time, in a series. (This is opposed to working with data in "parallel," in which multiple bits are transmitted simultaneously.)

Flow control   A routine that defines how the computer and the modem communicate with each other so that incoming data is received properly (or put off if the computer isn't quite ready to handle the data). There are two types of flow control: software and hardware (the latter is the one most commonly used these days).

Connection settings   A collection of settings that your modem uses in order to communicate successfully with a remote system. There are three types of connection settings: *data bits*, *stop bits*, and *parity*. When setting up a connection to a remote system, you need to make sure that these three settings match the parameters expected by the remote computer.

Data bits   The number of bits the remote system uses to define a character of information. Although your computer uses eight bits to define a character, as I said earlier, many remote systems are non-PC computers that use a different number of bits (seven is quite common).

Parity   A form of error checking that the modem uses to see if the data it just received was corrupted along the way.

Stop bit   An extra bit that's tacked on to the end of the *data bits*. Its job is to tell the remote system that it has reached the end of this particular chunk of data. Different systems look for stop bits with different lengths.

Terminal emulation   A method of translating computer input and output so that your computer acts as though it were a terminal connected to the remote system. When you use your modem to connect to a remote computer, you are, essentially, operating that computer from your keyboard and seeing the results onscreen. In other words, your computer has become a "terminal" attached to the remote machine. It's likely, however, that the remote computer is completely different from the one you're using. It could be a mainframe or a minicomputer, for example. In that case, it isn't likely that the codes produced by your keystrokes will correspond exactly with the codes used by the remote computer. Similarly, some of the return codes won't make sense to your machine. So for your computer to act like a true terminal, some kind of translation is needed between the two systems.

Common Connection Settings

All this monkeyshine about data bits, stop bits, and parity makes it sound as though setting up a remote connection is incredibly complex. In reality, however, there are two combinations used by the vast majority of remote systems:

➤ 7 data bits, even parity, 1 stop bit (usually written as 7-E-1). This combination is often used to connect to large online services that use mainframe computers (such as CompuServe)

➤ 8 data bits, no parity, 1 stop bit (8-N-1). This works for most bulletin board systems and PC-to-PC connections.

Download   To receive a file from a remote computer.

Upload   To send a file to a remote computer.

File transfer protocol   A method that two computers connected via a modem use to coordinate file *downloads* and *uploads*.

Setting Up a Modem from Scratch

Before you can use any communications software, you need to tell Windows 98 what kind of modem you have. After that, configure the modem to suit the types of online sessions you plan to run. To that end, this section takes you through the rigmarole of installing and configuring your modem.

Begin by cracking open the **Start** menu and selecting **Settings | Control Panel**. When the Control Panel window appears, launch the **Modems** icon. The Install New Modem Wizard appears. This wizard will attempt to detect your modem automatically. Activate the **Don't run the Hardware Installation Wizard** check box, and then click **Next**. Make sure your modem is attached and turned on, and then click **Next** to begin the detection process.

If the wizard finds your modem, you'll see a dialog box telling you so. Click **Next** to install the modem, and then click **Finish** when Windows 98 tells you that the modem has been set up.

If the wizard fails in its quest to find your modem, all is not lost. In this case, you need to follow these steps:

1. Click **Next** to get a list of all the modems that Windows 98 knows about.

2. Use the **Manufacturers** and **Models** lists to highlight your modem. If you don't see your modem, select **(Standard Modem Types)** in the **Manufacturers** list, and then choose the standard model that corresponds to your modem's speed.

3. Click **Next**. The next wizard dialog box asks you to select the port for your modem.

4. Highlight the port (if you're not sure, try COM1), and then click **Next**. Windows 98 installs your modem.

5. Click **Finish**.

When the Add New Modem wizard completes its labors, it displays the **Modems Properties** dialog box. This dialog box also appears the next time you launch the **Modems** icon in Control Panel. In this dialog box, you can do any of the following:

➤ To install a second modem, click **Add** to use the Add New Modem wizard once again.

➤ To delete a modem you don't use, highlight it and then click **Remove**.

➤ To change the way Windows 98 dials the modem, click **Dialing Properties**, and then, using the dialog box that shows up, make your changes. (See "Locations, Locations, Locations: Working with Dialing Locations," later in this chapter.)

When you're finished, click **OK** to return to Control Panel.

Changing Your Modem's Modus Operandi

Okay, with all that modem malarkey out of the way, you're ready to move on to more practical pursuits. This section takes you through the various Windows 98 options and settings that are available for your modem. (I'm assuming here that you have a modem installed in Windows 98. I showed you how to do this in *The Complete Idiot's Guide to Windows 98*.)

The General Properties

Your modem has all kinds of properties you can play with to alter how the device works and to troubleshoot problematic connections. To see these properties, follow these steps:

1. Select **Start | Settings | Control Panel**, and then open the **Modems** icon when the Control Panel window shows up. Windows 98 displays the Modem Properties dialog box.

2. If you have more than one modem installed, highlight the modem you want to work with.

3. Click the **Properties** button. Windows 98 tugs the modem's Properties dialog box onscreen, as shown in the following figure.

Use the General tab to control the modem's port, speaker volume, and maximum speed.

The General tab offers the following controls:

➤ **Port**   Use this drop-down list to specify the serial port you're using for the modem.

➤ **Speaker volume**   This slider determines how loud your modem sounds (although not all modems support this feature). Because modems can make quite a racket, you might consider setting the volume low or even off while using it in public or in a quiet office.

➤ **Maximum speed**   This setting determines the maximum data transfer rate (in bps) that the modem can handle. Your modem won't necessarily use this speed. Instead, it will determine the optimum speed based on the remote system and the line conditions. If, however, you prefer that your modem connect only at this speed, activate the **Only connect at this speed** check box (this feature isn't supported by all modems).

The Connection Properties

The settings in the **Connection** tab, shown in the following figure, enable you to control how your modem connects to the remote system. From our earlier discussion, you should recognize the controls in the **Connection preferences** group:

➤ **Data bits**   Use this drop-down list to specify the number of data bits the remote system expects.

➤ **Parity**   Use this list to pick out the type of parity checking that the remote system uses.

➤ **Stop bits**   Use this list to specify the length of the stop bits that the remote system expects.

Use the Connection tab to set up how the modem connects to remote computers.

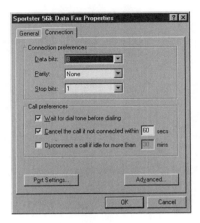

The **Call preferences** group has some useful settings:

➤ **Wait for dial tone before dialing**   When this check box is activated, the modem won't dial unless it can detect a dial tone, which is usually what you want. If your modem doesn't seem to recognize the dial tone in your current location (if you're in a different country, for example), or if you need to dial manually, deactivate this check box.

➤ **Cancel the call if not connected within *x* secs**   When this check box is activated, the modem stops trying to connect to the remote system after the specified number of seconds.

➤ **Disconnect a call if idle for more than *x* mins**   When this check box is turned on, the modem bails out of the call if there has been no activity for the specified number of minutes. This is useful if you forget to hang up the connection (particularly if long-distance charges apply).

Clicking the **Port Settings** button displays the Advanced Port Settings dialog box, shown in the next figure. A UART is a Universal Asynchronous Receiver/Transmitter, and its operation is as complex and unwieldy as its name. Suffice it to say that the UART resides inside your computer's serial port and controls the flow of data between the serial port and your computer's microprocessor. The two sliders in this dialog box operate as follows:

➤ For best performance, move the sliders to the right (towards High).

➤ If you're having communications problems, move the sliders to the left (towards Low).

When you're done, click **OK** to return to the modem's Properties dialog box.

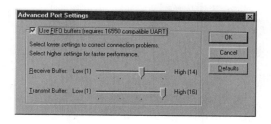

The Advanced Port Settings dialog box controls how the UART thingy operates.

Clicking the **Advanced** button displays the Advanced Connection Settings dialog box, shown in the following figure. Here's the summary:

➤ **Use error control** The latest modems come with built-in error checking to help ensure accurate data transfers. Activating this check box tells the modem to use this error checking.

➤ **Required to connect** If you activate this check box, the modem uses its error-checking routine to establish a connection. If a reliable connection can't be established, the modem bails out of the call.

➤ **Compress data** Thoroughly modern modems also have built-in data compression, which temporarily shrinks the data before transmission for faster data transfers. Activating this check box tells the modem to use data compression.

➤ **Use cellular protocol** Activate this option to enable the cellular error-correction feature found in most PC Card modems. If you have such a modem, you should activate this check box if you plan to connect via a cellular phone.

➤ **Use flow control** Activate this check box to enable flow control. Select either **Hardware (RTS/CTS)** (this is by far the most common type) or **Software (XON/OFF)**.

➤ **Modulation type** This drop-down list determines the type of modulation to use with the modem. Don't worry about this.

➤ **Extra settings** Use this text box to enter extra dialing strings to customize the modem's setup. See your modem's manual to determine the string formats to use.

➤ **Append to log** If you activate this check box, Windows 98 creates a file named *Modem*.log (where *Modem* is the name of your modem) in your main Windows 98 folder. The system monitors the calls and uses the log to keep track of connection events, status messages, and other items that might be useful during troubleshooting. Click **View Log** to open the log file in Notepad.

When you're done, click **OK** to return to the modem's Properties dialog box.

The Advanced Connection Settings dialog box has options that will warm the cockles of only the nerdiest hearts.

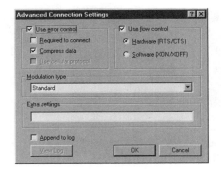

It's Alive! Or Is It? Modem Diagnostics

After you configure your modem, you should test it to make sure that everything is on the up-and-up. To do this, follow these simple steps:

1. In the modem's Properties dialog box, display the **Diagnostics** tab.
2. Click inside the **Port** column beside your modem.
3. If you have an external modem, make sure that it's powered up and attached to the serial port.
4. Click the **More Info** button. If there's a problem with your modem, a dialog box lets you know. Otherwise, after a minute or two, you see a dialog box that tells you lots of ignorable gobbledygook about your modem.

Locations, Locations, Locations: Working with Dialing Locations

Modems can deal with different dialing locations, which tell Windows 98 whether you use a calling card, the number to dial to get an outside line, and more. Locations are particularly useful for Dial-Up Networking (see Chapter 24, "Keeping In Touch: Mobile Computing with Dial-Up Networking") because notebook computer users often have to connect to their networks from different places:

➤ You may need to connect from home, where you have call waiting (which needs to be disabled).

➤ You may need to connect from a client's office where you have to dial 9 for an outside line.

➤ You may need to connect from out of town, dialing the number as long distance and using your corporate calling card.

For such situations, you can change these and other location parameters by clicking the **Dialing Properties** button in the **General** tab of the modem's Properties dialog box. The following figure shows the dialog box that sashays your way.

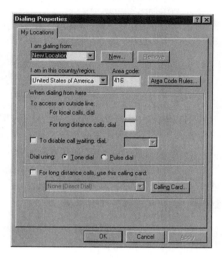

Use this dialog box to adjust the settings that Windows 98 uses to dial your modem.

Here's a rundown of the controls in this dialog box:

➤ **I am dialing from** This list contains all the dialing locations you've defined. To set up another location, click **New**, enter a name in the Create New Location dialog box, and then click **OK**. You then customize the rest of the dialog box fields to set up the dialing properties for the new location.

➤ **I am in this country/region** Use this list to set the country from which you'll be dialing. Why the country? Because that determines the country code the modem must dial to initiate the call (such as the 1 you have to first dial when calling long-distance within the U.S. or Canada).

➤ **Area code** Use this text box to set the area code from which you'll be dialing.

➤ **Area Code Rules** This button enables you to set up 10-digit dialing and other area code customizations. See "Figuring Out Area Code Weirdness," later in this chapter.

➤ **To access an outside line** Use the **For local calls, dial** text box to enter the code that must be dialed to get an outside line for local calls (such as 9). Use the **For long distance calls, dial** text box to enter the code that must be dialed to get an outside line for long distance calls (such as 8).

➤ **To disable call waiting, dial** To deactivate call waiting before making the call, activate this check box and then either enter the appropriate code in the text box or select one of the existing codes from the list.

181

Disabling Call Waiting is a Must!

Because the extra beeps that call waiting uses to indicate an incoming call can wreak havoc on modem communications, you should always disable call waiting before initiating a data call. The sequences *70, 70#, or 1170 (which are the ones listed in the **To disable call waiting**, **dial** drop-down list) usually disable call waiting, but you should check with your local phone company to make sure.

➤ **Dial using**   Select **Tone dial** or **Pulse dial**, as appropriate for your telephone line.

➤ **For long distance calls, use this calling card**   These controls enable you to set up a calling card or long-distance carrier. This procedure is explained in the section "That Long Distance Feeling: Setting Up a Calling Card," later in this chapter.

Figuring Out Area Code Weirdness

Clicking the **Area Code Rules** button displays the Area Code Rules dialog box (shown in the next figure), which has two groups:

➤ **When calling within my area code**   In some cases, the phone company requires that you dial the area code even if you're calling another number in the same area code. If the call isn't a long-distance number, activate the **Always dial the area code (10-digit dialing)** check box. If some of the phone number prefixes in your area code are long distance calls (and thus require the country code), click **New** to add the prefixes to the list.

➤ **When calling to other area codes**   In some larger cities, the telephone company has run out of phone numbers in the main area code. To overcome this problem, the phone company usually splits off part of the existing customer base into a new area code and requires that calls between the two areas be prefaced with the appropriate area code. Because these aren't long-distance calls, however, no country code is required. In this case, click **New** to add the area codes for which Windows 98 shouldn't dial a 1.

That Long Distance Feeling: Setting Up a Calling Card

Although most of your phone calls are likely to be free, at times this might not be the case, and you'll want to make some other arrangements for charging the call. Two situations, in particular, might crop up from time to time:

➤ You're dialing from a hotel and want to charge the call to your calling card.

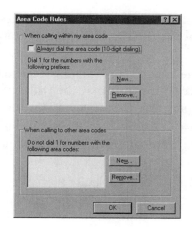

Use this dialog box to set up 10-digit dialing.

➤ You need to make a long-distance connection, in which case you might want to first dial the number of a long-distance carrier.

Windows 98 can handle both situations. To specify either a calling card number or a long-distance carrier phone number, follow these steps:

1. Activate the **For long distance calls, use this calling card** check box in the Dialing Properties dialog box.

2. Click the **Calling Card** button to display the Calling Card dialog box.

3. Use the list box to choose the type of calling card or long-distance carrier you have (see the following figure).

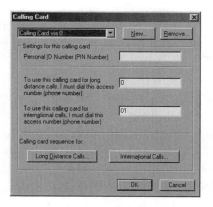

Use the Calling Card dialog box to enter a calling card number or select a long-distance carrier.

4. For a calling card, use the **Personal ID Number (PIN Number)** text box to enter your PIN.

183

5. Fill in the next two text boxes with the access numbers required by your calling card or carrier. The first text box is for long-distance calls, and the second is for international calls.

6. To change the long-distance dialing sequence for the calling card or carrier, click **Long Distance Calls** to display the Calling Card Sequence dialog box. In each step, select the appropriate **Dial** code and use the **then wait for** list to specify which signal Windows 98 must wait for before continuing. Click **OK** when you're finished.

7. To change the international call long distance dialing sequence, click **International Calls** and fill in the dialog box that appears.

8. Click **OK** to return to the Dialing Properties dialog box.

If your calling card or long-distance carrier doesn't appear in the list, follow these steps to add it:

1. In the Calling Card dialog box, click the **New** button to display the Create New Calling Card dialog box.

2. Enter a descriptive name for the calling card or carrier, and then click **OK**. Windows 98 tells you that you must now enter the dialing rules for the card or carrier.

3. Click **OK** to return to the Calling Card dialog box.

4. Follow steps 4 through 8 in the preceding series to specify the dialing rules for your new card or carrier.

Fast Fax Facts: Using Microsoft Fax

Nowadays, faxing is just another humdrum part of the workaday world, and any business worth its salt has a fax machine on standby. Increasingly, however, dedicated fax machines are giving way to *fax modems*—modems that have the capability to send and receive faxes in addition to their regular communications duties.

If you're looking to get into the fax fast lane, look no farther than the Microsoft Fax service. This section shows you how to install and configure Microsoft Fax, and how to use it to send and receive faxes.

For starters, you can only use Microsoft Fax if it's installed on your computer. If you used Microsoft Fax with Windows 95, it will still work with Windows 98. If you have a new Windows 98 installation, however, you first need to make sure that one of the following programs is installed on your machine

➤ Microsoft Exchange (this program shipped with the original version of Windows 95).

➤ Windows Messaging (this program replaced Microsoft Exchange in later versions of Window 95). If you don't have this program, you can install it from the Windows

98 CD-ROM. Insert the disc and display it in Windows Explorer or My Computer. Open the folder named **\tools\oldwin95\message\us**. In this folder, launch the file named **wms.exe** to install Windows Messaging on your system.

➤ Microsoft Outlook (not the Outlook Express program that comes with Windows 98).

With that out of the way, you now need to install Microsoft Fax (assuming that it's not already on your system from your old version of Windows 95). Here are the steps to follow:

1. Insert the Windows 98 CD-ROM and display the disc in Windows Explorer or My Computer.

2. Open the **\tools\oldwin95\message\us** folder once again. In this folder, launch the file named **awfax.exe** to start the installation.

3. The license agreement appears. Read it and click **Yes**. Windows 98 then busies itself installing some stuff on your computer.

4. When the appropriate fax files have been installed, Windows 98 will ask if you want to restart your system. Click **Yes**.

Once your system restarts, you'll see a new desktop icon called **Inbox**. There are two methods you can use to start Windows Messaging:

➤ Open the desktop's **Inbox** icon.

➤ Select **Start | Programs | Windows Messaging**.

Windows Messaging gives you two ways to add Microsoft Fax to your profile and get it configured:

From the Inbox Setup wizard   When you first start Windows Messaging, the Inbox Setup wizard appears and displays a list of the information services it can install (see the following figure). Be sure to activate the **Microsoft Fax** check box and then click **Next**. The Inbox Setup wizard then runs through a few dialog boxes that configure the basic faxing properties. You'll be asked to select the fax modem you want to use with Microsoft Fax, whether you want Microsoft Fax to answer incoming calls, and your name, country, and fax phone number (the fax number is required).

From within Windows Messaging   If Windows Messaging is already installed, it's no sweat adding the Microsoft Fax service from within Windows Messaging. What you need to do is select the **Tools | Services** command and then click **Add**. In the **Add Service to Profile** dialog box, shown in the next figure, highlight **Microsoft Fax**, click **OK**, and then click **Yes** in the dialog box that appears. You'll then see the **Microsoft Fax Properties** dialog box. All you need to do is fill in your fax number in the **User** tab and select your fax modem in the **Modem** tab.

Make sure that you activate Microsoft Fax in the initial Inbox Setup wizard dialog box.

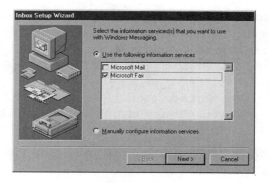

You can add the Microsoft Fax service if Windows Messaging is already installed.

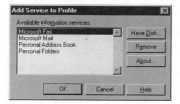

Sending a Fax

Microsoft Fax offers the Compose New Fax wizard that leads you step-by-step through the entire fax-creation process. Here's how it works:

1. To start the wizard, use either of the following techniques:

   ➤ Select **Start** | **Programs** | **Accessories** | **Fax** | **Compose New Fax**.

   ➤ In Windows Messaging, select **Compose** | **New Fax**.

2. The first wizard dialog box asks you which dialing location you want to use. You can click the **Dialing Properties** button either to select a different location (as described earlier in this chapter) or to adjust the properties of the current location. Otherwise, click **Next**.

3. In the next wizard dialog box, shown in the following figure, either enter a fax number or use the **Address Book** button to choose a fax recipient from your Personal Address Book. Then click **Next**.

4. The next wizard dialog box asks whether you want a cover page. Click **No** if you don't want one. If you want a cover page, click **Yes** and highlight the cover page you want to use. You can also click the **Options** button to display some settings that relate to when you want the fax sent. Click **Next** to continue.

5. The wizard now prompts you to enter the **Subject** line and **Note** for the fax (see the following figure). If you're using a cover page, activating the **Start note on cover**

page check box tells Microsoft Fax to begin your note on the cover page. If you deactivate this check box, the note begins on a fresh page. Click **Next** when you're finished.

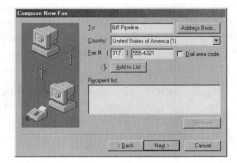

Use this wizard dialog box to enter the fax number of the recipient.

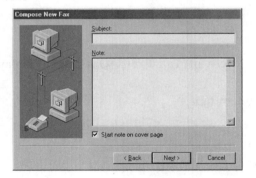

Use this wizard dialog box to enter the subject line and note for the fax.

6. Your next chore is to specify any files you want to include with the fax transmission. Click the **Add File** button, highlight the file in the **Open a File to Attach** dialog box that appears, and click **Open**. Click **Next** when you've added all the files you need.

7. In the last wizard dialog box, click **Finish** to send your fax.

Receiving and Viewing an Incoming Fax

Shipping out faxes to all and sundry is, of course, only half the fax battle because you'll also receive faxes from time to time. This section explains how Microsoft Fax handles incoming faxes and shows you how to view those faxes when they're sitting in your Inbox.

First off, you have to decide how you want Microsoft Fax to handle incoming calls. To do this, follow these steps:

Faxing from an Application

You can bypass Windows Messaging altogether and send a document directly from an application. You don't need applications with special features to do this because when you install Microsoft Fax, it adds a new printer to Windows 98. *Printer*? Yeah. You see, this "printer" doesn't send a document to your real printer. Instead, it renders the document as a fax and then sends it to your modem.

To try this, open the document in your application and select the **File | Print** command. When the Print dialog box appears, use the **Name** drop-down list to select the Microsoft Fax printer driver. When you click **OK**, the Compose New Fax wizard starts so that you can specify a recipient, a cover page, and other fax options.

Even better, if you have a particular document you want to fax, you don't have to open its application to fax it. Instead, just right-click the document, click **Send To** in the menu that appears, and then click **Fax Recipient**.

1. Select **Tools | Microsoft Fax Tools | Options** to display the **Fax Modem Properties** dialog box.

2. Select the **Modem** tab.

3. Highlight your fax modem and then click **Properties**. You'll then see the dialog box shown here.

Use this dialog box to specify what you want Microsoft Fax to do when a call comes in.

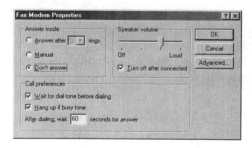

4. The **Answer mode** group boasts three options that determine how Microsoft Fax deals with incoming calls:

   ➤ **Answer after *x* rings** Tells Microsoft Fax to answer incoming calls automatically. This is the easiest way to handle incoming calls. In this mode, Microsoft Fax constantly checks your computer for calls. When it detects an incoming call, it waits for whatever number of rings you specified (which can be as few as two or as many as 10) and then leaps into action. Without any prodding from you, it answers the phone and immediately starts conversing with the remote fax machine. The **Microsoft Fax Status** window appears onscreen so that you can see the progress of the transfer.

➤ **Manual**   Lets you answer incoming calls manually. When you work with Microsoft Fax in manual mode, you'll see the **Receive Fax Now?** dialog box whenever the program detects an incoming call. To have Microsoft Fax field the call, click **Yes**. If you know that it's a voice call, click **No** and answer the call yourself.

Handling Voice and Fax Calls on the Same Line

Manual mode is ideal if you receive both voice calls and fax calls on the same phone line. Here's the basic procedure you'll need to follow for incoming calls:

1. When the phone rings, pick up the receiver.
2. If you hear a series of annoying tones, you know that a fax is on its way. In this case, click the **Yes** button in the **Receive Fax Now?** dialog box. If it's a voice call, click **No** instead.
3. After you click **Yes**, Microsoft Fax initializes the modem to handle the call. Wait until Microsoft Fax reports **Answering call** in the **Microsoft Fax Status** window, and then hang up the receiver. (If you hang up before this, you'll disconnect the call.)

Don't answer   Tells Microsoft Fax to ignore any incoming calls. If you know you have a fax coming in (if, say, you pick up the receiver and hear the tones from the remote fax machine), click the **Microsoft Fax** icon in the toolbar's information area. This opens the **Microsoft Fax Status** window. Now click the **Answer Now** button (or select the **Options | Answer Now** command).

Depending on the size of the fax transmission and the type of fax you're getting, Microsoft Fax takes anywhere from a few seconds to a few minutes to process the data. Eventually, though, your fax appears in the Windows Messaging Inbox.

Double-click the fax message to open it. (Depending on how the fax was sent, you may see a message window with a Fax icon. In this case, double-click the Fax icon.) Windows Messaging displays the image of the fax in the **Imaging** window, as shown in the following figure. (If your **Imaging** window looks different, select the **File | Open Image for Editing** command, and then click **Yes** to have Microsoft Fax always open faxes in the **Imaging** window shown here.)

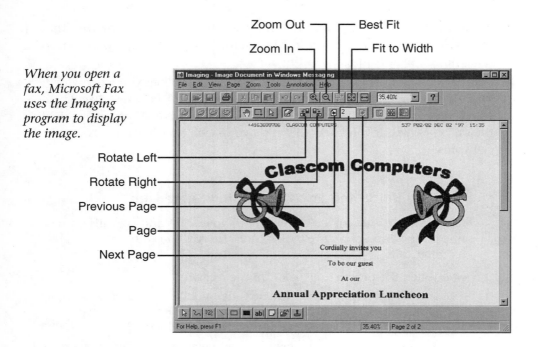

When you open a fax, Microsoft Fax uses the Imaging program to display the image.

Imaging is basically a graphics viewer with a few extra features that let you navigate multipage faxes. Here's a quick summary of the Imaging techniques you can use to examine your faxes:

Zooming the image   The **Zoom** menu contains commands (such as **Zoom In** and **Zoom Out**) that let you zoom into or out of the image. You can also choose specific magnifications: **25%**, **50%**, or **100%**. To fit the image to the window, select **Fit to Width**, **Fit to Height**, or **Best Fit**. Some of these commands are also available as toolbar buttons (see the previous figure).

Rotating the image   For faxes that come with the wrong orientation, the commands on the **Page | Rotate Page** menu let you turn the image so that you can read the fax. Select either **Right** or **Left** to rotate the image 90 degrees, or select **180°** to rotate the image 180 degrees.

Navigating multiple pages   Imaging has a few more tricks up its sleeve for moving between pages. On the **Page** menu, select **Next**, **Previous**, **First**, or **Last**. You can also select the **Go To** command to head toward a specific page number.

From Here

This chapter showed you how to perform various modem machinations. After explaining some important modem and communications concepts, I then showed you how to configure your modem for optimum service. You then learned how to test your modem. I closed by showing you how to set up dialing locations.

If you use your modem to connect to the Internet, you'll enjoy Chapter 13, "The Savvy Surfer: Extending Internet Explorer." In that chapter, I show you all kinds of ways to get the most out the Internet Explorer Web browser.

The Savvy Surfer: Extending Internet Explorer

Like electrons passing in the night, World Wide Web users never see each other as they surf sites. If they could, however, there might be a mutual flash of recognition between them because most Web users seem to fall into one of three categories:

Clickstreamers   Users who spend their online time wandering aimlessly from site to site, hoping for serendipitous finds (a new word: surfendipity!). By the way, *clickstream* is Web jargon for the "path" a person takes as they navigate through the Web by clicking links.

Nooksurfers   People who keep going to the same sites over and over and rarely check out new sites.

Researchers   People who use the Web exclusively for gathering information.

Whatever kind of Web user you are, your online time will be vastly more fun and/or productive if you can play your browser like a virtuoso. To that end, this chapter presents a master class for Internet Explorer. (For basic surfing techniques, please see *The Complete Idiot's Guide to Windows 98*.) You'll learn how to manage favorites and subscriptions, how to customize the Links bar, how to set up security, how to work with Internet Explorer's options, and lots more.

Saving Sites for Subsequent Surfs

The Web is so staggeringly huge—there are now hundreds of millions of pages—that it's almost impossible to retrace your steps and find a site you visited on a previous Web-surfing safari. Happily, both Internet Explorer and Windows 98 offer lots of methods for saving sites for later use. This section tells you about three of them: the Favorites folder, URL shortcuts, and the Links bar.

Taming the Favorites Folder

As you learned in *The Complete Idiot's Guide to Windows 98*, you use Internet Explorer's Favorites feature to save the name and address of Web sites that you deem worthy of a second surf. Here's a quick recap of the basics:

➤ To add the currently displayed page to the Favorites list, select Internet Explorer's **Favorites | Add to Favorites** command.

➤ To go to a saved site, pull down the **Favorites** menu and click the name of the page in the list at the bottom of the menu. Note that the Favorites menu is also available in Windows Explorer and on the Windows 98 Start menu.

If you spend even a moderate amount of time on the Web, you'll soon end up with a Favorites list that's overflowing with saved sites. If you find that it takes longer to track down a site on your Favorites list than it would to find the site on the Web, then you know it's time to get your Favorites affairs in order.

The good news is that the Favorites list you see in Internet Explorer is nothing more or less than the contents of the Favorites folder, which resides within your main Windows 98 folder (see the following figure). Each time you add a site to the Favorites list, Windows 98 creates an "Internet shortcut" within the **Favorites** folder. An Internet shortcut is just like a regular file or folder shortcut, except that its target is a Web address.

The upshot of this is that you can manage your Favorites list by accessing the **Favorites** folder with Windows Explorer and using the usual gang of file and folder techniques that I'm sure you're wearily familiar with by now:

➤ **Renaming a favorite** Highlight the shortcut file, press **F2**, enter the new name, and then press **Enter**.

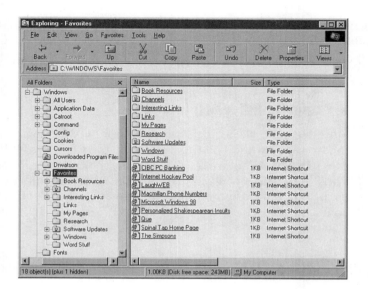

*Windows 98 stores your Favorites list inside the **Favorites** folder.*

➤ **Changing the address of a favorite**   To point an Internet shortcut at a different Web page, highlight it and select **File | Properties** to display a Properties dialog box like the one shown in the following figure. Use the **Target URL** text box to enter the new address, and then click **OK**.

Use the Properties dialog box to change the target address for an Internet shortcut.

➤ **Creating a new subfolder**   The best way to get your Favorites list organized in a hurry is to create new subfolders to hold related links. For example, you could create a folder for search sites, another for "what's new" sites, and another for the home pages of your favorite computer book authors. You create a new subfolder by selecting **File | New | Folder**.

➤ **Moving favorites**   Use the usual drag-and-drop techniques to move Internet shortcuts from one folder to another.

➤ **Deleting a favorite**   Highlight the shortcut file and then press **Delete**.

Quick Favorites Folder Maintenance

If you just need to make a quick adjustment or two, Internet Explorer offers a fast way to work with the stuff inside the **Favorites** folder: select **Favorites | Organize Favorites**. This displays the Organize Favorites dialog box from which you can play with the **Favorites** folder's shortcuts and subfolders. It's not quite as powerful as working with the **Favorites** folder directly, but it'll do in a pinch.

Creating a Shortcut to a URL

Since the Favorites list is nothing but a bunch of Internet shortcuts, you might think that you could create your own Internet shortcuts anywhere. You're right, you can. Here's how:

➤ Select **File | New | Shortcut** (or right-click the folder and then click **New | Shortcut**). In the Create Shortcut dialog box that appears, enter the Web page address in the **Command line** text box.

➤ To create an Internet shortcut for the currently displayed page, use the page icon that appears in the Address bar (to the left of the address). Drag this icon and drop it on the desktop (or whatever folder you want to use to store the shortcut).

➤ To create a shortcut for any hypertext link, drag the link text from the page and drop it on the desktop or inside a folder.

After your shortcut is in place, launching the shortcut's icon starts Internet Explorer and loads the Web page.

Customizing the Links Bar

I like Internet Explorer's Links bar because, in my never-ending quest to minimize mouse clicks and keystrokes, it gives me one-click access to a few sites. The problem, however, is that I don't use the Links bar's predefined sites all that often. The solution? I just gave the default links the heave-ho and replaced them with my most frequently accessed sites. Here's a rundown of some of the things you can do to remake the Links bar:

➤ **Changing a button's address**   If you right-click a button and then click **Properties**, Internet Explorer displays the Properties dialog box for an Internet shortcut. Use the **Target URL** text box to edit the button's address.

➤ **Creating a button for the current page**   To add a new Links bar button for the current page, drag the page icon from the Address bar and drop it on the Links bar.

➤ **Creating a button from a hypertext link**   If a page has a hypertext link, you can create a button for that link by dragging the link text into the Links bar.

➤ **Deleting a button**   To blow away a button from the Links bar, drag the button and then drop it in the Windows 98 Recycle Bin. (You can also right-click the button and then click **Delete**.)

Besides adding and deleting buttons, here are a few other ways you can work with the Links bar layout:

➤ **Moving the Links bar**   By default, the Links bar appears to the right of the Address bar. This is fine if you're running Windows 98 on a large screen or with a high resolution because the entire Links bar will be visible. If horizontal screen space is limited, however, you can still view the full Links bar by moving it so that it's flush with the left edge of the screen. To do this, move your mouse over the **Links** label and then drag the bar to the left side of the screen.

➤ **Sizing the Links bar**   Rather than moving the Links bar, you may only need to change its size. To give it a whirl, position the mouse pointer over the vertical bar on the left side of the Links bar, then drag the bar left or right.

➤ **Scrolling the Links bar**   If the Links bar is cut off on the right side of the screen, you can still get to the other buttons by clicking the arrow that appears on the right side of the Links bar. This will scroll the buttons to the left. To scroll back to the right, click the arrow that now appears on the left side of the Links bar.

➤ **Changing button positions**   The positions of the Links bar buttons are not set in stone. To move any button, use your mouse to drag the button left or right along the Links bar.

Managing Your Subscriptions

In World Wide Web lingo, a *cobweb page* is a page that hasn't been updated in a while. Many Web pages suffer this ignominious fate, but there are plenty that provide fresh information regularly. The problem, however, is how do you know when this new info is in place? The brute force method is to just click over to the sites you care about and eyeball them for new content. Fortunately for those of us with lives to lead, Internet Explorer offers an easier solution: subscriptions. Setting up a subscription to a Web page tells Internet Explorer to check the page at regular intervals and then let you know when the page content changes. Nothing could be finer.

In *The Complete Idiot's Guide to Windows 98*, I showed you how to set up a basic subscription. Here's a more detailed technique that enables you to set up a custom subscription:

1. Start by doing one of the following:

   ➤ If the page is one of your Favorites, open the Favorites folder, right-click the page, and then click **Subscribe**. Internet Explorer displays the **Subscribe Favorite** dialog box.

   ➤ Otherwise, use Internet Explorer to display the page, and then select the **Favorites | Add to Favorites** command to display the Add Favorite dialog box.

2. Select one of the following options (depending on the dialog box, the wording of each option varies slightly):

   ➤ **Only tell me when this page is updated**   Activating this option tells Internet Explorer to ship you an email message when it sees that the page has new or changed content.

   ➤ **Notify me of updates and download the page for offline viewing**   Activating this option tells Internet Explorer not only to fire off an email message to you when it sees the page is changed, but it also downloads the new page so that you can view the revised page without having to connect to the Internet.

3. Click **Customize** to launch the Subscription Wizard, shown in the following figure.

Use the Subscription Wizard to set up a customized subscription.

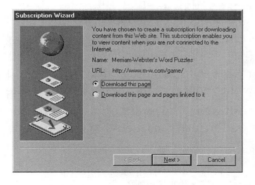

4. In the initial Wizard dialog box, choose one of the following options and then click **Next**:

   ➤ **Download this page**   If you activate this option, Internet Explorer downloads the page specified by the subscription.

   ➤ **Download this page and pages linked to it**   Activating this option tells Internet Explorer to download not only the subscribed page, but also any pages that are referred to in links on the subscribed page. If you select this option, the next dialog box asks how many linked pages deep you want to go. You should probably stick with going just 1 page deep. Any deeper and you might end up with hundreds of downloaded pages (and the need for a bank loan to pay for your connection charges).

5. Now the Wizard wonders whether you want to receive an email message letting you know that the subscribed page has been updated (click **Next** when you're ready to move on):

   ➤ **No**   Activate this option to leave email out of this.

   ➤ **Yes, send an email message to the following address**   Activate this option to sign up for email notifications. If no email address is displayed, or if you want to change the address, click **Change Address** to display the Mail Options dialog box. Enter your email address and the name of your email server, then click **OK** to return to the Wizard.

6. The next item on the Wizard's agenda (see the following figure) is to set up a schedule for updating the subscription. You have the following choices (click **Next** when you're done):

   ➤ **Scheduled**   If you activate this option, Internet Explorer will automatically check for changes. To set the frequency of those checks, use the drop-down list to choose Daily, Weekly, or Monthly.

   ➤ **New**   Click this button to set up a custom schedule.

   ➤ **Edit**   Click this button to customize the selected frequency.

   ➤ **Dial as needed if connected through a modem**   If you activate this check box, Internet Explorer does all the dirty work of dialing your modem to connect to the Internet in order to check the subscriptions.

   ➤ **Manually**   If you choose this option, Internet Explorer doesn't check for changes automatically. Instead, you have to run the Update All Subscriptions command, as described a bit later.

Turning On Automatic Dialing

For this automatic dialing feature to work, you have to set up Internet Explorer properly. Open Control Panel and launch the **Internet** icon. Select the **Connection** tab and click **Settings**. In the Dial-Up Settings dialog box, activate the **Connect automatically to update subscriptions** check box. Click **OK** until you're back in Control Panel.

Use this wizard dialog box to set up a schedule for the subscription update.

7. The final wizard dialog box asks if the site requires a password. If it does, activate **Yes** and then enter the appropriate **User name** and **Password**. Click **Finish** to return to the Subscribe Favorite (or Add Favorite) dialog box.

8. Click **OK**.

Now, each night (at whatever time you specified), Internet Explorer will connect to the Internet, check out your subscriptions, and then notify you about the updates. Note, too, that you can force Internet Explorer to update all your subscriptions at any time by selecting the **Favorites | Update All Subscriptions** command.

If you want to customize the way Internet Explorer deals with your subscriptions, select the **Favorites | Manage Subscriptions** command. In the Subscriptions window that appears, highlight a subscription, and then select **File | Properties**. The dialog box that pops up contains three tabs:

➤ **Subscription** This tab gives you a summary of the subscription settings. If you no longer want to subscribe to the Web page, click the **Unsubscribe** button.

➤ **Receiving** Use this tab to specify a **Subscription type** (notification only or notification plus download). You can also use the **Notification** group to specify the email address used by Internet Explorer to notify you of updates.

➤ **Schedule** Use this tab to set up a schedule for the subscription update. If you activate **Manually**, Internet Explorer doesn't automatically check for changes. Instead, you have to run the Update All Subscriptions command, as described earlier. If you activate the **Scheduled** option instead, Internet Explorer will automatically check for changes. To set the frequency of those checks, click **Edit** and use the Custom Schedule dialog box to choose the frequency of the updates and the time of day they occur.

Caveat Surfer: Internet Explorer and Security

Tons of people are flocking to the Web, and tons of content providers are waiting for them there. Still, the Web is by no means in the mainstream. Although millions of people surf the Web, it's still only a small percentage of the hundreds of millions of potential Web denizens that remain resolutely unwired. There are many reasons for this, but one of the biggest is the security issue. There are two issues, actually:

➤ **Protecting the data that you send to the Web**   Many Web page forms ask you to supply sensitive data, such as your credit card number. You wouldn't leave credit card receipts lying in the street, but that's more or less what you're doing if you submit a normal Web form that has your Visa number on it. The solution here is to only enter sensitive data on Web pages that are secure (more on this in a sec).

➤ **Being protected from the data that the Web sends to you**   The nature of the Web means that all kinds of items—text, graphics, sounds, Java applets (a kind of mini-program), ActiveX controls (another mini-program), and more—get deposited on your computer, at least temporarily. How do you know all that stuff is safe? And if you're not sure about something, how do you refuse delivery?

Internet Explorer offers a number of features that tackle these issues directly. For example, the Internet Explorer window gives you visual cues that tell whether a particular document is secure. For example, the following figure shows Internet Explorer displaying a secure Web page. Notice how a lock icon appears in the lower-right corner, and the address of a secure page uses **https** rather than **http**. Both of these features tell you that the Web page has a security certificate that passed muster with Internet Explorer.

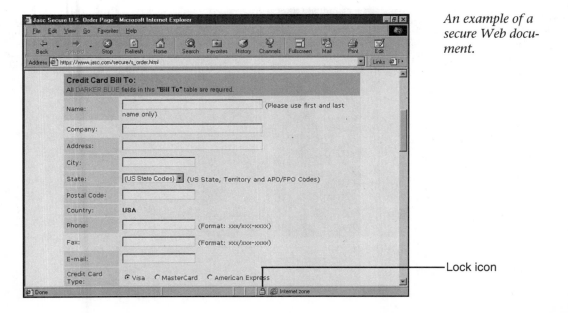

An example of a secure Web document.

Lock icon

Internet Explorer also displays security warning dialog boxes (see the following figure). These seemingly paranoid notes are actually quite useful most of the time. They warn about all kinds of potentially sinister activities:

➤ Entering a secure Web site.

➤ Browsing allegedly secure Web sites that don't have a valid security certificate.

➤ Leaving a secure Web site (see the next figure).

➤ Being redirected to a page other than the one you specified.

➤ Downloading and running objects, including files, ActiveX controls, Java applets, and scripts.

➤ Submitting a form unsecurely.

Internet Explorer warns you when you're about to send data from an unsecure form.

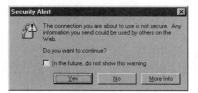

Note that these dialog boxes contain a check box that enables you to turn the warning off. You can also use the Security tab in the Internet Options dialog box (shown in the following figure; select **View** | **Internet Properties**) to toggle these warnings on and off and customize the level of security used by Internet Explorer.

Use the Security tab to set the level of security you're comfortable with.

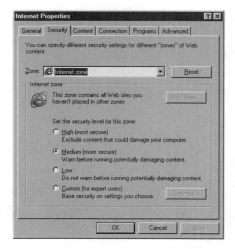

The way Internet Explorer handles security is to classify Web pages according to different security *zones*. Each zone is a collection of Web pages that implements a common security level. There are four zones:

➤ **Local intranet zone**   This zone covers Web pages on your local hard drives and on your local area network (intranet). The default security level is Medium.

➤ **Trusted sites zone**   You use this zone to specify Web sites that you trust. In these sites, you're certain that any objects you download and run are safe. The default security level is Low.

➤ **Internet zone**   This is a catch-all zone that includes all Web pages that aren't in any of the other zones. The default security level is Medium.

➤ **Restricted sites zone**   You use this zone to specify Web sites that you don't trust, and, therefore, want to implement the tightest possible security. The default security level is High.

You can add sites to three of Internet Explorer's security zones: Local intranet, Trusted sites, and Restricted sites. Here's how you do it:

1. In the Security tab, use the **Zone** drop-down list to choose the zone you want to work with.

2. Click the **Add Sites** button.

3. If you're working with the Local intranet zone, you'll see a dialog box with check boxes that determine the sites that are part of the default settings for this zone. Leave these as is and click **Advanced**.

4. Use the dialog box shown in the following figure to add individual sites to a zone. (The exact layout of this dialog box varies from zone to zone.) To add a site, enter the address in the **Add this Web site to the zone** text box, and then click **Add**.

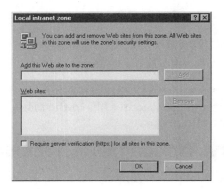

Use this dialog box to add and remove Web sites to the security zone.

5. To remove a site from the zone, highlight it in the **Web sites** list, then click **Remove**.

6. If you want Internet Explorer to make sure each site's Web server is using the HTTPS security protocol, activate the **Require server verification (https:) for all sites in this zone** check box.

7. Click **OK.**

Internet Explorer has three predefined security levels: **High** (most secure), **Low** (least secure), and **Medium** (in between). You can assign any of these levels within the Security tab by first using the **Zone** list to choose the security zone, and then activating the appropriate option button for the security level you want.

Internet Explorer also has a **Custom** level that you can use to set specific security settings. After you activate this option, click **Settings** to display the Security Settings dialog box. This dialog box lists various Web site objects and actions and offers several settings for each. In most cases, you have three choices:

➤ **Enable**   Internet Explorer accepts the content or action automatically.

➤ **Prompt**   Internet Explorer displays a Security Alert dialog box that enables you to accept or reject the content or action.

➤ **Disable**   Internet Explorer rejects the content or action automatically.

A Few More Useful Internet Explorer Options

It's probably safe to crown Internet Explorer the undisputed heavyweight customization champion of the Windows world. This baby is bursting at the seams with settings, options, dials, and widgets for changing the way the program works. The secret to the prodigious customizability is the Internet Options dialog box, part of which you saw in the previous section. To shove this dialog box into the fray, use either of the following techniques:

➤ In Internet Explorer, select **View | Internet Options.**

➤ In Control Panel, launch the **Internet** icon.

I covered many of the settings in this dialog box in *The Complete Idiot's Guide to Windows 98.* The rest of this chapter fills in the blanks by covering all the settings that I missed in the other book.

Cache and Carry: Working with Temporary Internet Files

I mentioned earlier that when you dial up a Web page, the remote server immediately starts bombarding your browser with files: the Web page, its graphics, and any other goodies embedded within the page. This can take quite a while, particularly if you have a slow Internet connection. To help speed things up, Internet Explorer assumes you're going to revisit the page sometime soon, and it saves all those files in a special folder called **Temporary Internet Files** (that sits inside your main Windows 98 folder). The idea here is that if you do return to the page, Internet Explorer grabs the necessary files from your hard disk, which means the page displays lickety-split. In geek circles, this type of folder is known as a *disk cache*.

If you display the **General** tab in the Internet Options dialog box, you'll see a **Temporary Internet files** group. The options in this group enable you to work with and control the cache:

➤ **Delete Files**   Click this button to remove all the files from the cache. This is useful if you're getting low on disk space.

➤ **Settings**   Click this button to display the Settings dialog box shown in the following figure. Here's a quick review of the controls in the Settings dialog box:

> **Check for newer versions of stored pages**   These options determine what Internet Explorer does when you visit a site that's already in the cache. If you select the **Every visit to the page** option, Internet Explorer updates each page as you visit it. To update all pages in the cache, activate the **Every time you start Internet Explorer** option. To bypass these checks, activate the **Never** option.

> **Amount of disk space to use**   This slider determines the maximum size of the cache as a percentage of the total disk space on the hard disk where the cache folder resides. If you have a lot of free space available, specifying a larger cache size speeds up your browsing.

> **Move Folder**   If you have another hard disk that has more free space available, you'd be better off moving the cache to that drive. To do so, click the **Move Folder** button and use the dialog box that pops up to specify the new folder to use. (Note that you'll lose all your subscriptions if you do this.)

> **View Files**   If you're curious about what's being dumped on your disk, or if you're trying to track down a particular file from a Web page you visited, click this button to view the cache files.

> **View Objects**   Click this button to view a list of the Java applets, ActiveX controls, and other objects that have been foisted on your system during your Web sessions.

The Settings dialog box lets you configure Internet Explorer's disk cache.

Have It Your Way: Using Your Own Web Page Settings

Web page designers work long and hard setting up their pages for what they think is the optimum viewing experience. If you want, you can throw all of that careful planning to the wind by telling Internet Explorer to display Web pages to your own specifications. For example, if your eyesight isn't what it used to be, you can tell Internet Explorer to display Web pages in a bigger-than-usual font.

To customize how Internet Explorer displays Web pages, use the following four buttons at the bottom of the **General** tab in the Internet Options dialog box:

➤ **Colors**   Click this button to display the Colors dialog box shown in the following figure. From here, you can deactivate the **Use Windows colors** check box to set the default **Text** and **Background** colors used in the Internet Explorer window. (If you leave this check box activated, Internet Explorer uses the colors defined in the Display Properties dialog box.) You can also use the **Visited** and **Unvisited** buttons to set the default link colors. Finally, activate the **Use hover color** check box to have Internet Explorer change the color of a link when you position the mouse pointer over the link. (Use the **Hover** button to set the color.)

Use the Colors dialog box to specify the Web page colors Internet Explorer should use.

➤ **Fonts**   Click this button to display the Fonts dialog box, which lets you determine how Web page fonts appear within Internet Explorer.

On-the-Fly Font Changes

To change the size of the Web page font, select **View** | **Fonts**, and then choose a relative font size from the cascade menu (for example, Large or Small). Later on (see the "Internet Explorer's Advanced Options" section), I'll show you how to add a Fonts button to the toolbar, which enables you to easily cycle through the font sizes.

➤ **Languages** Click this button to display the Language Preferences dialog box, which enables you to add one or more languages to Internet Explorer. This enables Internet Explorer to handle foreign language pages. You can also use this dialog box to set up relative priorities for the designated languages.

➤ **Accessibility** Click this button to display the Accessibility dialog box. From here, you can tell Internet Explorer to ignore the colors, font styles, and font sizes specified on any Web page. You can also specify your own style sheet for formatting Web pages.

Internet Explorer's Advanced Options

The Internet Options dialog box has an **Advanced** tab (shown in the next figure) that boasts an impressive list of settings. These range from the downright indispensable to the hopelessly technical, so let's see if we can sort through them.

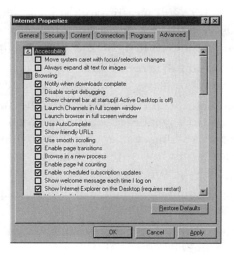

The Advanced tab contains dozens of settings for customizing Internet Explorer.

I'll start with the **Accessibility** settings:

➤ **Move system caret with focus/selection changes**   The system caret monitors where the current focus is on the screen. If you activate this check box, Internet Explorer moves the system caret whenever the focus or selected control changes. This is handy if you use a screen reader that uses the position of the system caret to determine which portion of the screen to magnify.

➤ **Always expand alt text for images**   If you clear the **Show pictures** check box, as described below, Internet Explorer displays a text description of the picture, instead. This is known as the *alt text* ("alt" is short for "alternate"; this text is defined by the Web page designer). If you activate this check box, Internet Explorer expands the size of the image icon so that the entire alt text can be seen.

The **Browsing** branch has over a dozen settings that help you customize your browsing experience:

➤ **Notify when downloads complete**   When Internet Explorer finishes downloading a file, it displays a dialog box telling you the download is complete. To avoid seeing this dialog box, deactivate this check box.

➤ **Disable script debugging**   If you have a script debugger installed, activate this check box to disable the debugger.

➤ **Show Channel bar at startup (if Active Desktop is off)**   If you've turned off the Active Desktop, activating this check box tells Windows 98 to display the Channel bar on the desktop at startup.

➤ **Launch channels in full screen window**   This check box determines whether active channel Web sites are displayed in full screen mode (that's the view where Internet Explorer hides its title bar, menu bar, toolbars, and status bar).

➤ **Launch browser in full screen window**   This check box determines whether Internet Explorer is displayed in full screen mode at startup.

➤ **Use AutoComplete**   This check box toggles the AutoComplete feature on and off. AutoComplete works by monitoring the text you type in the Address bar. If the text matches a previous address you entered, Internet Explorer completes the address for you automatically, just in case that's the one you want.

➤ **Show friendly URLs**   When this check box is turned on, the URLs displayed in the status bar contain only the filename of the Web page. Deactivate this check box if you prefer to see the full URL.

➤ **Use smooth scrolling**   This check box toggles Internet Explorer's "smooth scrolling" feature on and off. When this feature is on, page scrolling occurs at a preset speed.

➤ **Enable page transitions** This check box toggles support for page transitions (such as the current page fading out and the next page fading in). These transitions are supported only by certain Web sites (particularly those that use Microsoft Internet Information Server with FrontPage extensions).

➤ **Browse in a new process** If you activate this check box, a new version of Internet Explorer is launched whenever you open an HTML file.

➤ **Enable page hit counting** When this check box is activated, Internet Explorer lets Web sites track which pages you visit, even those pages that are downloaded and read offline. If you deactivate this check box, your page visits will not be logged.

➤ **Enable scheduled subscription updates** When this check box is activated, Internet Explorer updates your subscriptions at the specified times. If you don't want your subscriptions updated (if you're going on vacation, for example), deactivate this check box.

➤ **Show welcome message each time I log on** This check box toggles the Internet Explorer startup welcome message on and off.

➤ **Show Internet Explorer on the desktop (requires restart)** If you deactivate this check box, Windows 98 no longer displays the Internet Explorer icon on the desktop. You need to restart Windows 98 to put this setting into effect.

➤ **Underline links** These options determine when Internet Explorer displays link text with an underline **Always**, **Never**, or **Hover** (that is, when you position the mouse pointer over a link).

The stuff in the **Multimedia** branch controls how Internet Explorer gets along with various multimedia files:

➤ **Show pictures** When this check box is activated, Internet Explorer loads and displays whatever images are part of the Web page. If you're on a slow connection, you can speed up your Web work by turning off this option and preventing Web graphics from being displayed. Instead, you'll see an icon that represents the image. If you then want to see a particular graphic, right-click the icon and then click **Show Picture** from the menu.

➤ **Play animations** This check box toggles the display of animated GIF images on and off. Again, when this option is off you can display an animated GIF image by right-clicking the icon and clicking **Show Picture**.

➤ **Play videos** Internet Explorer also supports Web page-based video files. Turning off this check box prevents Internet Explorer from downloading and playing these files.

➤ **Play sounds** When this check box is activated, Internet Explorer plays any sounds embedded in a Web page. Again, it can take quite a while to download sound files

209

on a slow link, so you can turn off this option for faster loading (and to save your ears from the execrable MIDI files that most Webmasters seem to feature).

➤ **Smart image dithering** When this check box is activated, Internet Explorer "dithers" images in an attempt to smooth jagged edges.

The **Security** branch contains quite a few options for fine-tuning Internet Explorer security:

➤ **Enable Profile Assistant** This check box toggles the Profile Assistant on and off.

➤ **PCT 1.0** This check box toggles support for Microsoft's Private Communications Technology security protocol.

➤ **SSL 2.0** This check box toggles support for the Secure Sockets Layer Level 2 security protocol. This is the standard security protocol used on the Web.

➤ **SSL 3.0** This check box toggles support for the Secure Sockets Layer Level 3 security protocol. SSL 3.0 is more secure than SSL 2.0, but it doesn't yet have the broad support enjoyed by SSL 2.0.

➤ **Delete saved pages when browser closed** If you activate this check box, Internet Explorer clears out the Temporary Internet Files folder each time you shut down the program.

➤ **Do not save encrypted pages to disk** If you activate this check box, Internet Explorer will not cache any Web pages accessed via a secure server. This is a good idea if you share your computer and don't want other people to see these secure pages.

➤ **Warn if forms submit is being redirected** When this check box is activated, Internet Explorer warns you if the form data you submit is going to be sent to a server other than the one used to display the form page.

➤ **Warn if changing between secure and not secure mode** Activating this check box tells Internet Explorer to warn you when you switch between a secure document and an unsecure document.

➤ **Check for certificate revocation** If you activate this check box, Internet Explorer checks security certificates to see if they have been revoked.

➤ **Warn about invalid site certificates** When this option is turned on, Internet Explorer displays a warning if a site provides a certificate that appears to be invalid.

➤ **Cookies** These options determine how Internet Explorer reacts when a Web page attempts to write a cookie to your computer. A cookie is a small text file that Web sites store on your computer to save information about you, such as selections you've made in a Web "shopping cart." Cookies are benign creatures so, for best surfing, you'll probably want to leave the **Always accept cookies** option activated. If you're concerned about privacy, however, activate **Prompt before accepting**

cookies to have Internet Explorer ask if you want to receive each cookie. If you detest cookies with every fiber of your being, go ahead and activate the **Disable all cookie use** option.

The **Java VM** branch controls various behaviors for Internet Explorer's Java Virtual Machine:

➤ **Java console enabled (requires restart)**   Toggles whether or not Internet Explorer uses a separate console window for Java applet output and error messages. When this option is activated (you need to restart Windows 98 to put the new setting into effect), select **View | Java Console** to open the console window.

➤ **Java JIT compiler enabled**   Toggles whether or not Internet Explorer uses its internal "just-in-time" Java compiler to compile and run Java applets.

➤ **Java logging enabled**   Toggles whether or not Internet Explorer keeps a log of all Java applet activity on your system.

The **Printing** branch contains a single option: **Print background colors and images**. If you activate this check box, Internet Explorer includes the page's background when you print the page. If the page has a busy background, you'll speed up your printing considerably if you turn off this setting.

The **Searching** branch allegedly controls what Internet Explorer does when you enter an incorrect URL. (I say "allegedly" because these options don't actually seem to do anything). However, for the sake of completeness, I'll run through them anyway:

➤ **Autoscan common root domains**   When this check box is activated and a URL you entered cannot be found, Internet Explorer is supposed to run through all the root domains (**.com**, **.edu**, **.gov**, **.mil**, **.net**, and **.org**) in an attempt to find the correct URL. For example, if Internet Explorer can't find **www.microsoft.org**, it will try the other roots—**www.microsoft.gov**, **www.microsoft.edu**, and so on—until it finds one that works (**www.microsoft.com**, in this case).

➤ **Search when URL fails**   These options offer another searching alternative for those times when Internet Explorer can't find an address. In this case, the program can search for URLs that are similar to the one you entered.

The **Toolbar** branch has two check boxes that enable you to customize the Standard Buttons toolbar:

➤ **Show Font button**   This check box toggles the Fonts toolbar button on and off. Clicking the Fonts toolbar button produces a menu of font and language options.

➤ **Small icons**   This check box toggles the toolbar between small icons and large icons. Note that the small icons are only marginally smaller, so you don't gain that much extra screen space by activating this setting.

Finally, the **HTTP 1.1 settings** branch has check boxes that control whether Internet Explorer uses the HTTP 1.1 protocol. However, you can safely ignore these options.

From Here

This chapter took you through a host of advanced-but-practical Internet Explorer features. I showed you how to work with the Favorites folder, Internet shortcuts, the Links bar, and subscriptions. You also learned about Internet Explorer's options for security, the disk cache, and Web page display. I closed by running through all of the advanced settings.

Next up is Chapter 14, "The Ins and Outs of Outlook Express," where you'll learn some powerful techniques and useful customizations that should serve to put the "express" in Outlook Express.

The Ins and Outs of Outlook Express

As I mentioned in the introduction to Part 3, email is by far the most popular of Internet pastimes. Every day, tens of millions of e-scribes barrage the Internet with hundreds of millions of e-notes, e-memos, and e-tirades. Microsoft recognized not only the popularity of Internet email, but also the crucial fact that Internet email requires specialized tools, and not just a Jack-of-all-email-trades program. The result was Outlook Express, an email program built from the ground up to handle the rigors of Internet email.

I showed you the basics of Outlook Express in *The Complete Idiot's Guide to Windows 98*. In this chapter, you go beyond the basics and learn many of the more advanced features and options. I'll show you how to manage message folders, work with stationery and signatures, filter incoming messages, search for Internet email addresses, and customize all kinds of Outlook Express options.

Taking Charge of Your Message Folders

Right out of the box, Outlook Express comes with five pre-fab folders: **Inbox** (incoming messages), **Outbox** (messages waiting to be sent), **Sent Items** (messages that you've sent), **Deleted Items** (messages that you've blown away), and **Drafts** (saved messages that you're still working on). Surely that's enough folders for everyone, right?

Maybe not. Even if you're good at deleting the detritus from your **Inbox** folder, it still won't take long before it becomes bloated with messages, and finding the missive you need becomes a real needle-in-a-haystack exercise. What you really need is a way to organize your mail. For example, suppose you and your boss exchange a lot of email. Rather than storing all her messages in your **Inbox** folder, you could create a separate folder just for her messages. You could also create folders for each of the Internet mailing lists you subscribe to, for current projects on the go, or for each of your regular email correspondents. There are, in short, a thousand-and-one uses for folders, and this section tells you everything you need to know.

To create a new folder, follow these steps:

1. Select the **File | Folder | New Folder** command to display the Create New Folder dialog box, shown in the following figure.

Use this dialog box to create your new folder.

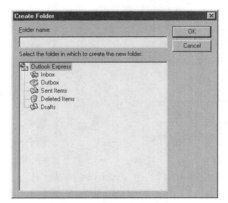

2. In the **Folder** list, select the folder within which you want the new folder to appear.
3. Use the **Folder name** text box to enter the name of the new folder.
4. Click **OK**.

Here's a quick look at a few other folder maintenance chores you may need from time to time:

➤ **Renaming a folder** The names of the five predefined Outlook Express folders are set in stone, but it's easy to rename any folder that you create yourself. To do so, highlight the folder, and then select **File | Folder | Rename** (or press **F2**). In the Rename Folder dialog box, enter the new name, and then click **OK**.

➤ **Compacting a folder**   To help minimize the size of the files that Outlook Express uses to store messages, you should *compact* the files regularly. To do this, select **File | Folder**, and then select either **Compact** (to compact just the currently highlighted folder) or **Compact All Folders** (to compact the whole shooting match).

➤ **Moving a folder**   If you want to move a folder to a different location, the easiest method is to use your mouse to drag the folder and drop it on the new location. (The harder method is to highlight the folder and select **File | Folder | Move To**. In the Move dialog box, use the folder tree to highlight the new location for the folder, and then click **OK**.)

➤ **Deleting a folder**   To get rid of a folder you no longer need, highlight the folder and select **File | Folder | Delete**. Outlook Express then warns you that the deletion can't be reversed and asks if you want to proceed. Ponder this warning carefully and, if you still want to go ahead, click **Yes** to delete the folder. (Click **No** if you get cold feet and decide not to destroy the folder.)

Some Handy Message Maneuvers

You'll spend the bulk of your Outlook Express time shipping out messages to far-flung folks and reading messages that those folks fire back at you. To help you get the most out of these sending and reading tasks, this section looks at the wide range of message options that Outlook Express offers.

Options for Sending Messages

Let's begin by examining the various options that Outlook Express provides for sending email. Select **Tools | Options**, and in the Options dialog box that appears, display the **Send** tab. You'll see the controls shown in the following figure.

The **Mail sending format** group contains two option buttons that determine whether your messages contain formatting: **HTML** and **Plain Text**.

If you activate the **HTML** button, Outlook Express enables you to waste all kinds of time by applying a number of formatting options to your messages. In effect, your message becomes a tiny little Web page that can be formatted in much the same way that a Web page can. Note, however, that this formatting will be visible only to recipients who use email software that understands HTML (such as Netscape Mail, Outlook, and of course, Outlook Express). In addition, you can click the **Settings** button beside the **HTML** option to display the HTML Settings dialog box. However, I don't recommend changing any of these settings.

The Outlook Express options for sending email.

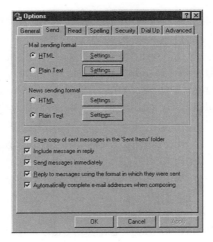

If you activate the **Plain** option, instead, Outlook Express sends your message as regular text, without any formatting doodads. Clicking the **Settings** button displays the Plain Text Settings dialog box, shown in the following figure. Here's what you get:

➤ **MIME** MIME stands for Multipurpose Internet Mail Extensions, and it's the standard encoding technique. Why is encoding required? Internet email supports only text, so messages that contain attachments (such as pictures) or foreign characters, must be encoded. This list determines how (or whether) Outlook Express encodes message text:

> **None** Tells Outlook Express not to encode the text.

> **Quoted Printable** Use this encoding if your messages have foreign characters or ANSI characters 128 and up (see Appendix C, " More Symbols: The Windows ANSI Character Set").

> **Base 64** Use this encoding if your message contains pictures or other binary data.

➤ **Allow 8-bit characters in headers** When this check box is activated, characters that require 8 bits—that's ANSI 128 or higher—will be allowed within the message header without being encoded. If you leave this check box deactivated, these characters are encoded.

➤ **Uuencode** This is an older encoding format that is primarily used when sending binary files to Usenet newsgroups.

➤ **Automatically wrap text at *x* characters, when sending** This spinner determines the point at which Outlook Express wraps text onto a new line. Many Internet systems can't read lines longer than 80 characters, so you shouldn't select a value higher than that. A value less than 80 is best because it allows for bonus greater than signs (>), which are placed at the beginning of each line to indicate the original message in a reply.

➤ **Indent the original text with > when replying or forwarding**   It's standard on the Internet that original message text in a reply be indicated with a greater-than sign (>) at the beginning of each line. (Colons are also sometimes used.) When this check box is activated, Outlook Express prefaces each line of the original message with whatever character you specify in the list.

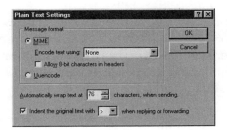

Use this dialog box to work with settings associated with the Plain Text sending format.

Here's a quick rundown of the rest of the options in the Send tab:

➤ **Save copy of sent messages in the 'Sent Items' folder**   When this check box is activated, Outlook Express saves a copy of your message in the Sent Items folder. It's a good idea to leave this option checked because it gives you a record of the messages you send.

➤ **Include message in reply**   If you activate this check box, Outlook Express includes the original message text as part of the new message when you reply to or forward a message.

➤ **Send messages immediately**   When this check box is activated, Outlook Express ships out your message as soon as you click the Send button. If you deactivate this option, clicking the Send button when composing a message only stores that message in the Outbox folder. This is useful if you have a number of messages to compose, and you use a dial-up connection to the Internet. That is, you could compose all your messages offline and store them in the Outbox folder. You could then connect to the Internet and send all your messages at once.

➤ **Reply to messages using the format in which they were sent**   When this check box is activated, Outlook Express automatically selects either the HTML or Plain Text sending format depending on the format used in the original message. If you'd prefer to always use your default sending format, deactivate this check box.

➤ **Automatically complete email addresses when composing**   When this check box is activated, Outlook Express monitors the email addresses you enter while composing a message. If you've entered a similar address before, the program will complete the rest of the address automatically.

Working with Stationery and Signatures

In the real world, stationery is paper that includes predefined text, colors, and images. Outlook Express lets you set up the electronic equivalent. That is, you can define email stationery that includes a background image and predefined text. This is essentially a Web page to which you can also add your own text.

You can also customize the default look of a message as follows:

➤ You can specify a message font.

➤ You can add a signature. (In Internet email circles, a *signature* is text that appears at the bottom of all your messages. Most people use a signature to provide their email and Web addresses, their company contact information, and perhaps a snappy quote or epigram that reflects their personality.)

➤ You can attach a vCard (electronic business card).

The rest of this section shows you how to work with these options.

To set a message font, follow these steps:

1. Select **Tools | Stationery** to display the Stationery dialog box, shown in the following figure.

Use this dialog box to set up a default font and stationery.

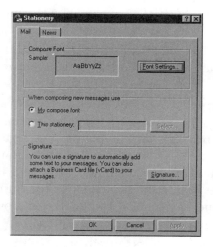

2. To set the message font, click **Font Settings**, use the standard Font dialog box to pick your font options, and then click **OK**.

3. To use this font, head for the **When composing new messages use** and make sure the **My compose font** option button is selected.

4. Click **OK**.

If you'd prefer to use stationery, try this:

1. Select **Tools | Stationery** to display the Stationery dialog box once again.

2. In the **When composing new messages use** group, activate the **This stationery** option.

3. Click **Select** to display the Select Stationery dialog box shown in the following figure. You have four choices here:

   ➤ To use one of the stationery samples that comes with Outlook Express, high-light it in the **Stationery** list.

   ➤ To choose another Web page, click **Browse**, and then use the Stationery dialog box to pick the Web page you want to use.

   ➤ To make changes to an existing stationery, highlight it, and then click **Edit**. This loads the stationery into FrontPage Express so that you can edit the page.

   ➤ You can download other stationery samples by clicking the **Get More** button, which takes you to the Microsoft Greetings Workshop on the Web.

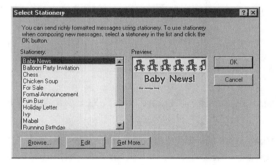

Use the Select Stationery dialog box to pick out the Web page pattern you want to use with your messages.

4. When you're done, click **OK** to return to the Stationery dialog box.

5. Click **OK**.

Rather than setting a default stationery, you may prefer to select a stationery to use only in a single message. Outlook Express gives you two ways to do this:

➤ To start a new message using a specific stationery, select **Compose | New Message using** (you can also click the downward-pointing arrow in the Compose Message toolbar button). When Outlook Express displays its menu of stationery options, click the one you want to use.

➤ If you've already started a message, you can choose a stationery by selecting the **Format | Apply Stationery** command, and then picking out the stationery you want from the submenu that appears.

As I mentioned earlier, a signature is a few lines of text that provide contact information and other data. Outlook Express lets you define a signature and have it appended to the bottom of every outgoing message (or you can insert it by hand in individual messages). Outlook Express also supports the vCard electronic business card format and lets you create and add a vCard to your messages.

To do this, you must first follow these steps to define a signature or vCard:

1. Select **Tools | Stationery**.
2. Click the **Signature** button to display the Signature dialog box shown in the following figure.

Use the Signature dialog box to define a signature and vCard.

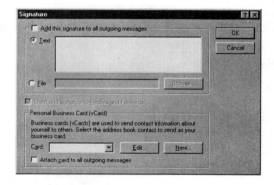

3. To define a text signature, activate the **Text** option and enter your signature in the box provided.
4. If your signature text resides in a text file, activate the **File** option, and then enter the location and name of the file in the box provided. (Or click **Browse** to choose the file from a dialog box.)
5. If you want Outlook Express to add the signature to all of your messages, activate the **Add this signature to all outgoing messages** check box.
6. If you'd rather use the signature only on original messages, leave the **Don't add signature to Replies and Forwards** check box activated.
7. If you have an Address Book entry for yourself, use the **Card** list to select that entry. Otherwise, click **New** to create a contact for yourself.
8. To send the vCard as an attachment with all your messages, activate the **Attach card to all outgoing messages** check box.
9. Click **OK** to put the signature options into effect.

If you choose not to have your signature and vCard added automatically, you can insert them manually by using either of the following techniques in the New Message window:

➤ Select **Insert | Signature** or click the Insert Signature button on the toolbar.

➤ Select **Insert | Business Card** to your messages.

Options for Reading Messages

Outlook Express has quite a few options related to reading the messages that come your way. To check them out, select **Tools | Options**, and then display the **Read** tab in the Options dialog box, as shown in the following figure. Many of these settings are related to reading Usenet newsgroups, so I'll skip them. Here's a review of the mail-related controls:

➤ **Message is read after being previewed for *x* second(s)**   Deactivate this check box to prevent Outlook Express from removing the bold while you're reading a message. Alternatively, you can use the spinner to adjust how long it takes Outlook Express to remove the bold.

➤ **Automatically show picture attachments in messages**   When this check box is activated, Outlook Express displays attached picture files after the message text.

➤ **Show multiple pictures as a slide show**   If you activate this check box, Outlook Express handles multiple picture attachments as a "slide show." That is, the first picture is displayed at the bottom of the message, and controls are added for viewing the other images. If you leave this check box deactivated, Outlook Express displays all the attached pictures at the bottom of the message.

➤ **Fonts**   Click this button to display the Fonts dialog box, which enables you to choose the fonts Outlook Express should use when displaying messages.

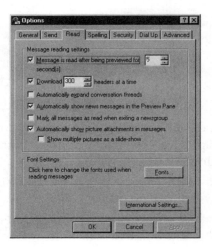

Use the Read tab to set various properties related to reading messages.

Dealing with the Onslaught: Filtering Messages

As email becomes a ubiquitous feature on the business (and even home) landscape, you'll find that email chores take up more and more of your time. And I'm not just talking about the three R's of email: reading, 'riting, and responding. Basic email maintenance—moving, deleting, and so on—also takes up large chunks of otherwise-productive time.

To help ease the email time crunch, Outlook lets you set up "rules" that allow Outlook Express to automatically move an incoming message to a specific folder if the message contains a particular keyword in the subject or body, or if it's from a particular person.

Outlook Express comes with an Inbox Assistant that makes it easy to set up and define these rules. Here's how it works:

1. Select **Tools | Inbox Assistant**. The Inbox Assistant dialog box appears.

2. Click the **Add** button. You'll see the Properties dialog box shown in the following figure.

Use this dialog box to define a rule.

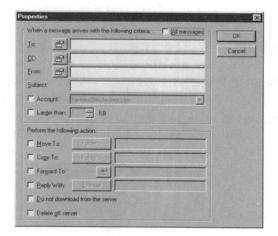

3. Now you must define the criteria that will cause Outlook Express to invoke this rule. Specify what conditions an incoming message must meet for the rule to be applied to that message. That's the purpose of the controls in the **When a message arrives with the following criteria** group:

   ➤ **All messages**   Activate this check box to invoke the rule on all incoming messages.

   ➤ **To**   Use this text box to specify the addresses or names of the direct message recipients that will invoke the rule.

   ➤ **CC**   Use this text box to specify the addresses or names of the CC message recipients that will invoke the rule.

➤ **From**   Use this text box to specify one or more email addresses or names. In this case, Outlook Express will invoke the rule for any message sent from one of these addresses.

➤ **Subject**   Use this text box to enter a word or phrase that must appear in the **Subject** line to invoke the rule.

➤ **Account**   Activate this check box and choose the mail account that will invoke the rule.

➤ **Larger than *x* KB**   Activate this check box and send the message size that will invoke the rule.

4. Now you need to specify the action Outlook Express should take with any message that satisfies these criteria:

➤ **Move To**   Moves the message to the folder selected by clicking the Folder button.

➤ **Copy To**   Copies the message to the folder selected by clicking the Folder button.

➤ **Forward To**   Forwards the message to the recipient selected by clicking the Select Recipients button.

➤ **Reply With**   Replies to the message using the file specified by clicking the Browse button. You can select a file that uses one of the following formats: Mail (**.eml**), News (**.nws**), HTML, or Text.

➤ **Do not download from server**   Activate this check box to leave the message on the server.

➤ **Delete off server**   Activate this check box to delete the message from the server. In this case, you'll never see the message (although Outlook Express does tell you that the message was deleted from the server).

5. Click **OK** to add the new rule to the Inbox Assistant.

You can use the Inbox Assistant dialog box to maintain your rules:

➤ Each rule you've defined has a check box beside it that toggles the rule on and off.

➤ You can change a rule by highlighting it and clicking **Properties**.

➤ the Inbox Assistant processes the rules in the order they appear in the list. You can use the **Move Up** and **Move Down** buttons to change this order.

➤ The rules apply to the Inbox folder. If you'd like the rules to also apply to another folder, click **Apply To** and choose a folder in the Select Folder dialog box.

➤ To get rid of a rule, highlight it and click **Remove**.

Finding Folks on the Internet

When you need to call a person or company, and you don't know the phone number, you probably head for the white or yellow pages directory and look them up there. What if you need to track down an email address? One way to go would be to search for the person's or company's Web site, and then snoop around the site for contact info.

If that's a no go, try using a *directory service*. A directory service is a database of names and email addresses that you can use to search for people you know (or would like to know). Conveniently, Outlook Express offers predefined accounts for several of the most popular directory services, including Bigfoot, Yahoo! People Search, Verisign, and WhoWhere. (You can see a complete list of these accounts by selecting **Tools | Accounts** to display the Internet Accounts dialog box. Activate the **Directory Service** tab. Note, too, that you can also use this dialog box to add your own directory service accounts.)

To use one of the directory services to find someone on the Internet, follow these steps:

1. Select **Edit | Find People** to display the Find People dialog box.

2. Use the **Look in** list to select the directory service you want to use, as shown in the following figure. (You can also look for people in the Address Book.) If you want to find out more about a service before using it, click the **Web Site** button to load Internet Explorer and display the Web site for the selected directory service.

Use this dialog box to find a person on the Internet by using a directory service.

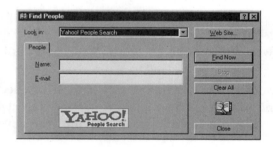

3. Use the **Name** text box to enter some or all of the name of the person you want to find.

4. Use the **Email** text box to enter the full email address of the person you want to find.

5. Click **Find Now**. Outlook Express connects to the directory service. If it finds any matches, it displays them at the bottom of the dialog box.

Customizing Outlook Express

You've seen quite a few Outlook Express customization options so far. However, Outlook Express is quite a flexible program, so we've only scratched the surface of what it can do. The rest of this chapter digs below that surface and runs through a few more customization options that should come in handy.

Rearranging the Message Columns

The Outlook Express folders display your messages using a number of columns that supply you with the info you need for gleaning the basics of any message. (Who sent it, when you received it, the Subject line, whether the message has attachments, and so on.) There's more data available, however. For example, you might want to know the date and time the message was sent, the size of the message, and to whom the message was sent. All this stuff and more can be displayed as columns in the message list. If you think Outlook Express is already displaying too much data, you can get rid of columns you don't care about.

Here are the steps to follow to customize the Outlook Express columns:

1. Select **View | Columns**. Outlook Express displays the Columns dialog box shown in the following figure.

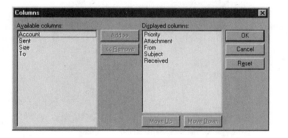

Use the Columns dialog box to customize the columns displayed in the message list.

2. To add a column, highlight it in the **Available columns** list and click **Add>>**.

3. To remove a column, highlight it in the **Displayed columns** list and click **<<Remove**.

4. To change the order of the columns, highlight a column in the **Displayed columns** list, and then use the **Move Up** and **Move Down** buttons to position the column where you want it. (Columns listed top to bottom are displayed left to right in the message list.)

5. When you're done, click **OK**.

225

Here are a few more column customization tricks:

➤ To change the width of a displayed column, use your mouse to drag the right edge of the column's header to the left or right.

➤ To change the width of a displayed column to fit its widest entry, double-click the right edge of the column's header.

➤ To change the position of a column, use your mouse to drag the column's header left or right.

➤ To change the size of the message list, use your mouse to drag the bar that separates the message list and the list of folders.

Renovating the Outlook Express Layout

You can give the Outlook Express interface a facelift by selecting the **View | Layout** command to display the Window Layout Properties dialog box shown in the following figure.

Use this dialog box to customize the layout of the Outlook Express window.

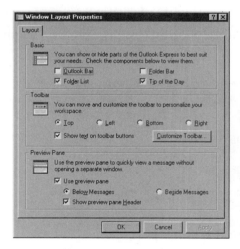

The **Basic** group contains four check boxes that toggle the following features on and off:

➤ **Outlook Bar**   This is a strip that runs down the left side of the window (to the left of the Folder List). It contains icons for the various Outlook Express folders.

➤ **Folder Bar**   This is a strip that runs across the window, just below the toolbar. It tells you the name of the current folder.

➤ **Folder List**   This is the folder tree that appears to the left of the messages list.

➤ **Tip of the Day**   This is a short tip that appears in the Outlook Express folder. When this feature is activated, a new tip appears each time you start Outlook Express.

No Folder List? No Problem!

If you decide to junk the Folder List, you can still navigate the folders by selecting the **Go | Go To Folder** command (or by pressing **Ctrl+Y**). In the Go To Folder dialog box that appears, use the folder tree to select the folder you want to work with, and then click **OK**.

The **Toolbar** group gives you four options—**Top**, **Left**, **Bottom**, and **Right**—that determine the position of the toolbar within the Outlook Express window. You can also use the **Show text on toolbar buttons** check box to toggle the toolbar text on and off. To customize the toolbar buttons, follow these steps:

1. Click the Customize Toolbar button to display the Customize Toolbar dialog box shown in the following figure.

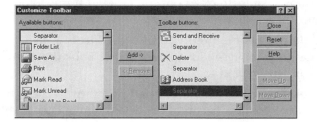

Use this dialog box to customize the Outlook Express toolbar.

2. To add a button, highlight it in the **Available buttons** list and click **Add+>**. (The Separator "button" adds a vertical separator bar.)

3. To remove a button, highlight it in the **Toolbar buttons** list and click **<-Remove**.

4. To change the order of the buttons, highlight a button in the **Toolbar buttons** list, and then click **Move Up** and **Move Down** to position the button where you want it. (Buttons listed top to bottom are displayed left to right in the toolbar.)

5. When you're done, click **Close**.

The controls in the **Preview Pane** group set several options related to the Preview pane:

➤ **Use Preview pane**   This check box toggles the Preview pane on and off.

➤ **Below Messages** or **Beside Messages**   These options determine where the Preview pane sits in relation to the messages list.

➤ **Show Preview pane header**   This check box toggles the header at the top of the Preview pane on and off.

Setting Some Outlook Express Options

Earlier in this chapter, I told you about the settings available in the Options dialog box, particularly the Send and Read tabs. There are tons more mail-related options in this dialog box, so I'll end this look at Outlook Express customization by taking you through those settings. Select **Tools | Options** to get the Options dialog box out of bed, and then make sure the **General** tab is displayed (see the following figure). Here's the rundown of the mail-related settings:

➤ **Check for new messages every *x* minute(s)**   Activate this check box to have Outlook Express automatically check for new messages using the interval specified in the spinner.

➤ **Play sound when new messages arrive**   Outlook Express plays a sound whenever a new message arrives. If you'd prefer the sounds of silence, deactivate this check box.

➤ **Empty messages from the 'Deleted Items' folder on exit**   Activate this check box to force Outlook Express to clean out the **Deleted Items** folder each time you exit the program.

➤ **Automatically put people I reply to in my Address Book**   If you activate this check box, Outlook Express adds to the Address Book the name and email address of the people you send replies to.

➤ **Make Outlook Express my default email program**   When this check box is activated, Outlook Express becomes the default email client. This means that Outlook Express is invoked if you click a "mailto" link in a Web page, select any mail-related commands in your Web browser, or select **Send To | Mail Recipient** in Windows 98.

➤ **Make Outlook Express my default Simple MAPI client**   When this check box is activated, Outlook Express is invoked when you select the **File | Send** command in an application that supports email operations (such as the Microsoft Office suite).

➤ **When starting, go directly to my 'Inbox' folder**   Activate this check box to force Outlook Express to open the **Inbox** folder at startup. When this option is deactivated, the top-level **Outlook Express** folder is displayed at startup.

➤ **Automatically display folders with unread messages**   When this check box is activated, Outlook Express looks for folders that have unread messages at startup. If it finds any, it opens the appropriate branches in the Folder List tree so that you can see which folders have unread messages. This is a useful option if you're using the Inbox Assistant to filter incoming messages to different folders.

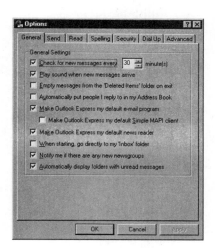

The General tab is chock-a-block with mail-related options.

I'll close by looking at what's available on the **Dial Up** tab, which is shown in the next figure. These options control how and when Outlook Express invokes your Internet dial-up connection. Here's a quick look at each control:

➤ **When Outlook Express starts**   These options determine whether Outlook Express connects to the Internet at startup. Select **Do not dial a connection** to work offline, or **Dial this connection** to connect using whatever Dial-Up Networking connection you select in the list. If you want to have a choice, activate **Ask me if I would like to dial a connection.**

➤ **Warn me before switching dial-up connections**   When this check box is activated, Outlook Express warns you if your connection is no longer working and offers to try another one (assuming you have multiple Dial-Up Networking connections defined).

➤ **Hang up when finished sending, receiving, or downloading**   When this check box is activated, Outlook Express automatically severs your Internet connection as soon as it has finished with the server. This is a handy way to prevent your online time (and, possibly, your connection and long-distance charges) from mounting unnecessarily.

➤ **Automatically dial when checking for new messages**   When you turn on this option, Outlook Express connects to the Internet automatically whenever it checks for new messages. This is useful if you've set up the program to check for new messages at regular intervals.

Use the Dial Up tab to configure the Outlook Express dial-up options.

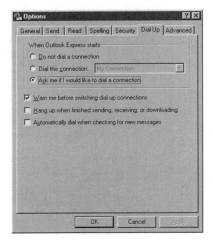

From Here

This chapter took you through a few advanced Outlook Express email chores. You learned how to work with message folders, how to specify a signature and stationery, how to filter incoming messages, and how to find people on the Internet. I also showed you several ways to customize Outlook Express, including how to wield many of the settings in the Options dialog box.

Speaking of Internet-based conversations, Chapter 15, "Becoming a Member of the Chattering Classes: Microsoft Chat," shows you how to use Microsoft Chat to have real-time conversations with complete strangers.

SURE I'M A WOMAN...

Joining the Chattering Classes with Microsoft Chat

In This Chapter

➤ Creating your Microsoft Chat persona

➤ Getting online with a chat server

➤ The basics of chat room conversations

➤ How to create your own chat room

➤ Everything you need to know to chew the chat fat

Windows 98 has no shortage of conversational tools. Taken together, these features form a kind of "hierarchy of intimacy." The least intimate of these talk tools is the Usenet newsgroup support in Outlook Express. You send a message to a newsgroup and then, a day or two later, some stranger responds. Email is a bit better because the turnaround time is usually shorter, and you're usually "conversing" with someone you know. The most intimate tool is certainly NetMeeting with its support of realtime audio (or even video!) conversations.

If you like the give-and-take and immediacy of a real one-on-one conversation, but you don't have the proper gadgetry to get a NetMeeting connection going, fear not. Windows 98 comes with a program called Microsoft Chat that enables you to access various *chat rooms*. These are meeting places where any number of people can join and converse with each other in realtime by typing messages. It's usually more than a little chaotic, but they're very popular spots, and most people have a lot of fun as long as they get in with a good crowd. This chit-chatty chapter shows you how to work with Microsoft Chat.

Opening Lines: Getting Started with Microsoft Chat

Before you start chatting, there are a few options and some personal info to set up. Follow these steps:

1. Select **Start | Programs | Internet Explorer | Microsoft Chat**. Microsoft Chat loads and tosses the Chat Connection dialog box your way.

2. The options in the **Connect** tab specify which chat server you want to use (the chat server is the place that has all the chat rooms) and the chat room you want to start in. You should leave these settings as is for now.

3. Display the **Personal Info** tab. The only field you have to fill in here is **Nickname**, which is the name that the other chatterers will see when you enter the chat room. If you like, you can also enter your **Real name, Email address, WWW Home Page**, and a **Brief description of yourself** (see the following figure).

Use the Personal Info tab to provide more information on yourself.

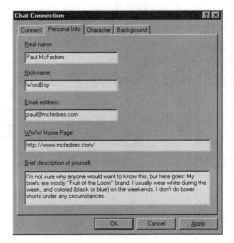

4. Display the **Character** tab. You use this tab (see the following figure) to choose the character that will represent you in the chat room. (Chat types call this character an *avatar*.) The little faces below the character are the various expressions (laugh, shout, and so on) the character can be made to make.

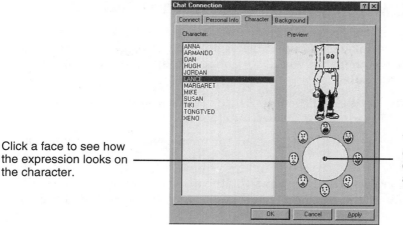

Use the Character tab to choose which Chat character will be your chat room representative.

Click a face to see how the expression looks on the character.

You can also get an expression by dragging this dot around the circle.

5. Display the **Background** tab (see the following figure). Use this tab to select a background image upon which all the chat room characters will be displayed.

6. Click **OK**. Microsoft Chat displays a Message of the Day dialog box.

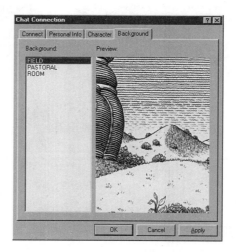

Use the Background tab to set the chat room backdrop.

7. If you don't want to be pestered with this message in the future, deactivate the **Show this whenever connecting** check box.

8. Click **OK** to get to the Microsoft Chat window.

If you want to change one of the options you set, select the **View | Options** command and use the tabs in the Microsoft Chat Options dialog box to make your adjustments.

Rat-a-Tat Chat: Connecting to a Chat Server

With all that out of the way, you're ready to chat your face off. Select the **Room | Connect** command to display the Connect dialog box, and then click **OK**. Microsoft Chat connects you to the Internet (if you're not online already), and then connects to Microsoft's chat computer.

When the connection is established, you'll see a window similar to the one shown in the following figure. This window is divided into four areas:

The comic strip panel This is where the members' messages appear as a series of comic strip panels.

The member list This box shows you the names of all the people in this chat room. To toggle this list between text and icons, select **View | Member List**, and then activate either **List** or **Icon**.

Your character This box shows the character you chose. Use the faces below to select an expression.

Message box: Use this text box to type your messages.

The Chat habitat: A typical chat room.

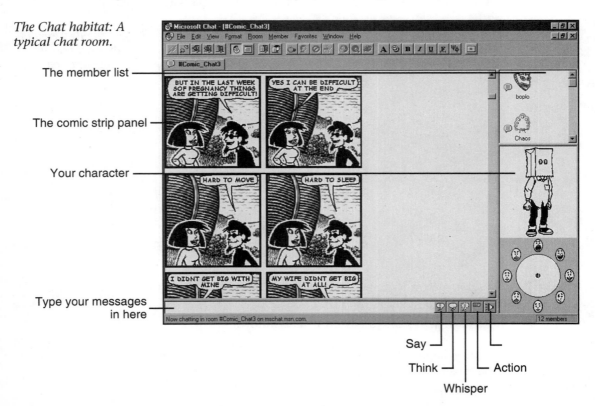

234

If you'd prefer to see the messages in text rather than images, activate the **View | Plain Text** command. The following figure shows how the window looks with plain text messages. Notice how this view gives you much more information: who enters and leaves the conversation, the name of the person who sent the message, and so on.

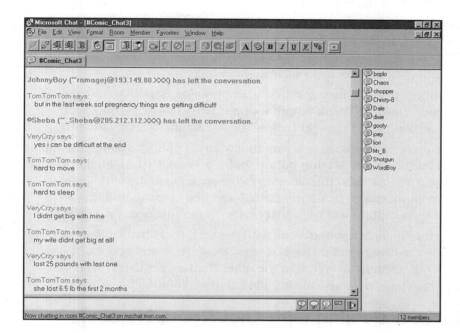

Microsoft Chat in text view.

Chat Chinwagging: Holding Up Your End of the Conversation

I should warn you here that most of what goes on inside a typical chat room is juvenile, nonsensical, and often profane. Chat rooms tend to be dominated by sex-obsessed teenagers with *way* too much time on their hands. I'll show you later on how to ignore messages sent by individual members and how to check out different chat rooms. In most cases, you'll need to look around a bit to find a reasonable group to interact with.

For now, though, let's see how this chat thing works. Once you've got a feel for the ongoing conversations (if that's at all possible), it's time to toss in your two cents worth. To send a message into the fray, follow these steps:

1. Type your message in the message box at the bottom of the screen.

2. To format the color or font of the message text, pull down the **Format** menu and use the commands (such as Color and Bold) to format the text.

3. To change the expression your character displays, click one of the expression icons shown below your character.

4. To send the message, use any of the following techniques:

   ➤ Press **Enter** or click the **Say** button.

   ➤ If you'd prefer that only a particular member receive your message, click the member's name in the member list, and then click the **Whisper** button (or press **Ctrl+W**). If you want to whisper to multiple members, hold down the **Ctrl** key and click each member's name.

   ➤ If you want to "think" a message (that is, display a message that isn't directed at the group), click the **Think** button (or press **Ctrl+T**). The message will appear in a comic strip "thought bubble" over your character's head.

   ➤ Rather than saying anything, you can display an "action" caption at the top of the panel by clicking the **Action** button (or by pressing **Ctrl+J**). Microsoft Chat prefixes your nickname to this caption, so use an active statement. For example, if your nickname is "Chatty Cathy" and you enter "is mulling over your offer," the caption will be "Chatty Cathy is mulling over your offer."

   ➤ If you want to include a sound along with the text, click the **Play Sound** button, use the Play Sound dialog box to pick out the sound you want, and then click **OK**. (Note, however, that the other chatterers will only hear the sound if they have the sound file installed on their computer.)

Working the Room I: Dealing with Chat Room Members

It probably goes without saying, but chat room quality rises and falls depending on who's doing the chatting. If you get a few people who are truly interested in learning about each other and discussing the issues of the day in a civilized manner, it can be a pleasant way to waste an hour or three. (Some folks find chat rooms totally addictive.) On the other hand, even one bad apple can spoil the whole member bunch.

Whether you're dealing with good apples or rotten ones, it still pays to know how to work with the members of the chat room. Here's a quick review of the member-related techniques that Microsoft Chat offers:

➤ To see a list of all the people currently using Microsoft Chat, select **Member | User List**, and then click **Update List** in the User List dialog box that appears.

➤ To invite one of these users to join your chat room, display the User List dialog box again, highlight the user, and then click **Invite**. (You can also select **Member | Invite**, enter the user's nickname, and then click **OK**.)

➤ If you want to know more about a participating member, click his or her name in the member list, and then select **Member | Get Profile**. (Note, too, that most member commands are also available by right-clicking a member.)

➤ If you think a particular member is a bit of a bozo (there's no shortage of them in these chat rooms), you can tell Microsoft Chat not to show you any of that person's messages. Click their name in the member list and select **Member | Ignore**.

➤ To send an email to a member, highlight his or her name in the member list and select **Member | Send Email**.

➤ To send a file to a highlighted member, select **Member | Send File**, and then use the dialog box that shows up to pick out the file you want to send. Note that the member must agree to accept the file before the transfer will take place.

➤ To visit a member's Web home page, highlight his or her name in the member list and select **Member | Visit Home Page**.

➤ To offer to connect with a member using NetMeeting, select **Member | NetMeeting**.

➤ If you want to know how long it takes messages to reach a member, highlight the member and select **Member | Lag Time**. Select the **Member | Local Time** command to find out the current time in the member's location.

Working the Room II: Dealing with Chat Rooms

Despite your best efforts with the Ignore command, you may find that a particular chat room is just too busy or too populated with morons to be an even remotely pleasant diversion. In this case, you have no choice but to try another chat room. Here are a few techniques you can use to manipulate chat rooms:

➤ To leave the current chat room, select **Room | Leave Room**.

➤ To see a list of other chat rooms, select **Room | Room List**. In the Chat Room List dialog box (shown in the following figure), activate the **Show only registered rooms** check box (this separates the room wheat from the room chaff). Now highlight the room you want to visit and click **Go To**.

➤ To enter a specific room, select **Room | Enter Room**, type the name of the room in the dialog box (with the room's password, if necessary), and then click **OK**.

A Room of One's Own: Creating a Chat Room

If you like, you can create and host your own chat room. Here's how it's done:

1. Select the **Room | Create Room** command. Microsoft Chat displays the Create Chat Room dialog box.

2. Use the **Chat room name** text box to enter a catchy name for your room.

3. Use the **Topic** box to enter a description of what kinds of conversations you expect in your room.

4. Activate any of the following options as you see fit:

Use this dialog box to pick out a chat room to crash.

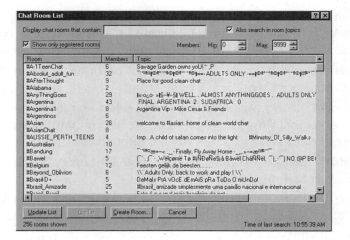

➤ **Moderated** If you activate this check box, the only people who can send messages in the room are you and whatever other members you designate. Everyone else in the room is relegated to mere spectator status.

➤ **Set Topic anyone** When this check box is turned on, any member of the room can change the room's topic.

➤ **Invite only** If you activate this option, people can join your room only if you invite them to.

➤ **Hidden** With this check box on, your chat room won't appear in the Chat Room List dialog box. (More specifically, only members of your chat room can see it on the list.)

➤ **Private** Activate this check box to prevent people outside of your chat room from seeing information about your room.

➤ **Set Maximum Users** If you activate this check box, you can use the text box beside it to set the maximum number of members that can be inside the room at any time.

➤ **Optional password** If you activate this check box, you can use the text box beside it to enter a password that users must enter before they can join the room.

5. When you're done (the following figure shows a completed dialog box), click **OK**.

Note that you can change the setup of your room at any time by selecting the **Room | Room Properties** command.

*Use this dialog box
to construct your
very own chat room.*

As the host of your chat room, you're free to exercise whatever megalomaniac power fantasies you've harbored over the years. Select the **Member | Host** command, and you get a submenu with the following commands:

➤ **Kick**   If a member is being particularly annoying, highlight their nickname and select this command to toss them out the door. In the Kick dialog box, enter a reason you're kicking them out, and then click **OK**.

➤ **Ban / Unban**   If a member is downright loathsome, highlight their nickname and choose this command to ban them from your room for good. In the dialog box that drops in, click **Ban**. If you have a change of heart down the road, select this command, highlight the user, and then click **Unban**.

➤ **Sync Backgrounds**   Select this command if you want each member to use the same background as the one you've specified on your system.

➤ **Host**   For a moderated room, highlight a member and activate this command to designate that user as a host.

➤ **Speaker**   If your room is moderated, highlight a member and activate this command to enable that user to send messages.

➤ **Spectator**   For a moderated room, highlight a member and activate this command to prevent that user from sending messages.

Disconnecting from the Chat Server

Given an engrossing conversation, it's easy to forget about time while you're chatting away. However, don't forget that while you're connected to the chat server, you're also connected to the Internet, so you're running up your connection time (and possibly your connection charges, too!). So when you've had just about enough of the inane chatter, you can disconnect by selecting the **Room | Disconnect** command.

Dis and Dat Chat: Some Microsoft Chat Options

As you work with Microsoft Chat, certain irksome behaviors will crop up and mar your confabs. For example, lots of folks seem to think that it's a cool idea to have some sort of sound accompaniment with their messages. However, having your machine booping and beeping every couple of minutes is hair-pullingly, teeth-gnashingly, bothersome. So are people who get their jollies by "flooding" a chat room with tons of messages over a short period of time.

Microsoft Chat offers quite a few options to help you overcome these and other irritants. On the positive side of the ledger, they also enable you to do some interesting and handy things. For example, you can set up a "macro" that fires off a specified message when you press a particular keystroke.

The source of these and many other settings is the Microsoft Chat Options dialog box, which you can get onscreen by selecting **View** | **Options** (or by pressing **Ctrl+Q**). The **Personal Info**, **Character**, and **Background** tabs are the same as those you saw when you first started Microsoft Chat. This section looks at the other tabs that are available.

The **Settings** tab, shown in the following figure, is loaded with useful options:

➤ **Don't send Microsoft Chat specific information**   Most chat software supports only text messages. So if you're talking to someone who isn't using Microsoft Chat, it's a waste of time for them to receive non-text info such as your character and the fonts you choose. In this case, activate this check box to avoid sending this extraneous Microsoft Chat-specific data.

➤ **Content Advisor**   Enables you to restrict usage of Microsoft Chat to those who have a password. I explained the Content Advisor in detail in *The Complete Idiot's Guide to Windows 98*.

➤ **Allow whispers**   Leave this check box checked to receive whispered messages from other users. If you think whispering is impolite, deactivate this check box.

➤ **Play sounds**   If you prefer the sounds of silence to the relentless noise some members inflict on a room, deactivate this check box.

➤ **Show arrivals/departures**   You saw earlier that the text view shows arrival and departure messages when members join and leave. To suppress these messages, deactivate this check box.

➤ **Get identity on arrival**   In text view, deactivate this check box to tell Microsoft Chat not to display the full identity of users who enter the room.

➤ **Receive chat invitations**   If you don't want to receive any invitations to join other rooms (the majority of these invitations are sexual in nature, unfortunately), deactivate this option.

➤ **Receive file transfer requests** If you don't want to receive any requests to transfer a file to you, deactivate this check box.

➤ **Receive NetMeeting calls** Deactivate this check box to avoid getting any invitations to connect via NetMeeting.

➤ **Prompt to save on exit** Microsoft Chat normally tosses your chat sessions in the electronic garbage pail when you close up shop. If you'd like Microsoft Chat to ask you if you'd like to save the chat conversation, activate this check box.

➤ **Sound search path** This text box specifies the location on your hard drive that Microsoft Chat uses to display the list of sound files when you click the Play Sound button.

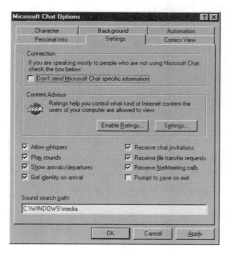

The Settings tab is crammed with useful Chat options.

If you're working in text view, the Microsoft Chat Options dialog box will have a **Text View** tab instead of the **Character** and **Background** tabs (see the next figure). Here's a look at the settings on this tab:

➤ **Place blank lines between** These options determine how Microsoft Chat separates messages in text view. Select **all messages** to separate every message with a blank line; select **different message types** to put a blank line between messages only if they are of a different type (Say, Think, Whisper, and so on); select **no blank lines** to scrunch all the messages together.

➤ **Headers and messages on different lines** The "header" is the text that tells you who sent the message and what type of message it is (for example, "Chatty Cathy says:"). When this check box is activated, Microsoft Chat puts the header on one line and the message text on the next line.

➤ **Text Fonts**   Click **Change Font** to specify the font and color that Microsoft Chat should use to display the various message types. Click **Reset Defaults** to use Microsoft Chat's default fonts.

➤ **Highlight host messages**   These check boxes determine whether headers and messages from the chat room's host are displayed in bold.

Use the Text View tab to set up how Microsoft Chat works when you select the Plain Text command.

Finally, the **Automation** tab, shown in the following figure, continues some interesting settings for automating a few Microsoft Chat chores:

➤ **Automatic Greeting**   If you're hosting a chat room, use these controls to send new members a hearty welcome as soon as they join. You can have the greeting **Whispered** or **Said**, and you use the box to edit the greeting text. (Note that **%name** displays to the new member's nickname, and **%room** displays the name of your chat room.)

➤ **Auto Ignore Flooders**   A *flooder* is a person who sends a whack of messages in a short period of time. To thwart these pinheads, leave the **Auto ignore enabled** check box activated. This tells Microsoft Chat to automatically ignore any member who sends a certain number of messages (given by the **Message Count** spinner) within a certain number of seconds (specified by the **Interval (sec)** spinner).

➤ **Macros**   If you find yourself sending the same messages over and over, you'll love Microsoft Chat's macros feature. A *macro* is a text message that's associated with a particular key combination. Pressing that key combo automatically sends the message, which can save tons of wear-and-tear on your typing fingers. To define a macro, select a **Key combination**, enter a **Name**, and then use the larger box to spell out your message. When you're done, click **Add Macro**.

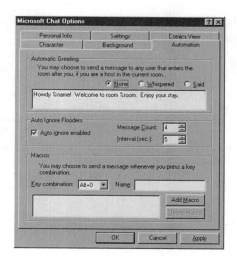

The Automation tab lets you automate a few routine Chat tasks.

From Here

This chapter showed you how to get your conversational ya-yas out by using Microsoft Chat. I began by showing you how to start Microsoft Chat and how to configure your chat persona. From there, I told you how to connect to a chat server, and I gave you a tour of the Microsoft Chat window. You then learned how to send messages and how to work with members and chat rooms (including how to create your own room). I finished by running through quite a few useful Microsoft Chat options and settings.

Chapter 16, "The Self-Serve Web: Running Personal Web Server," finishes Part 3 by showing you how to become your own Webmaster with Windows 98's Personal Web Server program.

The Self-Serve Web: Running Personal Web Server

In This Chapter

➤ Installing Personal Web Server

➤ Configuring Personal Web Server to your liking

➤ Setting up directories and other options

➤ Publishing pages to your Web site

➤ Everything you need to know to serve up Web pages piping hot

In *The Complete Idiot's Guide to Windows 98*, I showed you how to use FrontPage Express to build Web pages, and how to use the Web Publishing Wizard to deliver your pages safe and sound to their home on your Web hosting provider. You can then advertise your Web address to all and sundry, and those surfing dudes and dudettes can browse your pages and marvel at your unmatched talents.

You may be wondering why you have to bother shipping out your pages to a Web hosting provider. If you have an Internet connection on the go, can't people just access your pages right from your computer? No, I'm afraid not. To display any page over the Internet, a browser has to have a conversation with a *Web server* program. In short, the browser sends a request for a page to the server, the server gathers all the necessary files, and then sends them back to the browser in a format that the browser can understand.

For most Webmeisters, this server stuff is best left in the competently geeky hands of a Web hosting provider. This simplifies things considerably, but the trade-off is that you either have to pay to use their server, or face restrictions such as the amount of disk space you can use or the number of megabytes you can ship out to Web surfers.

If you have a large number of pages, and if you want complete control over how they're served to the Web community, you might consider serving yourself.

Run my own Web server!? Those things are complex and expensive, and I'm not a nerd or a nabob.

While it's true that there are plenty of Web servers available that require both a Ph.D. and Gatesian riches, there's one that requires neither: Personal Web Server. It runs on any garden-variety Windows 98 machine, it's easy to set up and maintain, and it costs exactly nothing! This chapter shows you how it works.

Getting Personal Web Server Ready for Action

Before installing the program, understand that there are a few prerequisites associated with not only Personal Web Server, but any server:

You must be connected to the Internet. Web wanderers won't be able to connect to your server unless your computer is connected to the Internet. Ideally, you should have a permanent connection so that people can access your pages any time of day or night. However, many Webmasters make their servers available only during certain hours.

Your computer must have a "host address." Even if you're connected to the Internet, surfers won't be able to find your server if they don't know the proper address. That address is known as the *host address* and usually takes the following form:

user.domain

Here, *user* is the user name you use to log onto your service provider, and *domain* is the domain name of your service provider. If you're not sure about this, contact your service provider's systems administrator. For this chapter, I'll use a temporary account as an example. The user name is **test** and my domain is **mcfedries.com**, so my host address is **test.mcfedries.com**. This means my Web server will use the following URL:

http://test.mcfedries.com/

Note, however, that these conditions don't apply if you're setting up Personal Web Server for use on a corporate intranet. (An intranet is a network that uses Internet technologies.)

My Real Web Server Address

The test.mcfedries.com address is a temporary server setup for the purposes of this chapter. My full-time Web server can be found at the following URL:

http://www.mcfedries.com/

Personal Web Server is an add-on program that comes on the Windows 98 CD-ROM. It's a scaled-down version of Microsoft's high-end Internet Information Server, and it supports fancy-schmancy features such as Active Server Pages, FrontPage server extensions, and other high falutin' stuff. Unfortunately, Personal Web Server does have its limitations:

➤ Connections are limited to 10 users

➤ There's no support for passwords

➤ There's no FTP service

To get started, you have to install Personal Web Server from your Windows 98 CD-ROM. Here are the steps to plow through:

1. Insert the Windows 98 CD-ROM.

2. Use Windows Explorer to open the CD-ROM drive, open the **add-ons** folder, and then display the **pws** folder. Launch **setup.exe** to fire up the Personal Web Server Setup program.

3. In the first Personal Web Server Setup dialog box, click **Next**.

   PWS Setup now gives you a choice of three different setup routes, which you select by clicking one of the following buttons:

   ➤ **Minimum**   This option installs a bare-bones system. Only choose this option if disk space is at a premium.

   ➤ **Typical**   This option installs everything you need to serve Web pages, including the Personal Web Server documentation pages. This is the option I recommend.

   ➤ **Custom**   This option displays a dialog box that you use to pick out the configuration you want to install. If you choose this path, a dialog box will appear with a list of the various components you can install. Use the check boxes to toggle the Personal Web Server pieces on and off, and then click **Next** when you're done.

4. As you can see in the following figure, Personal Web Server Setup now asks you to select a home directory for your Web site files. The default home directory is

247

C:\InetPub\wwwroot. If you want to change this, either edit the directory or click the Browse button to choose the new directory using the Select Directory dialog box. Click **Next** when you're done.

Use this Setup dialog box to choose the home of your Web files.

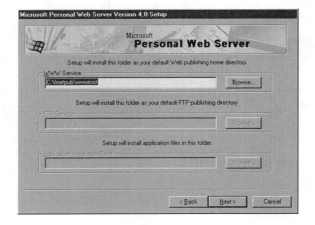

5. If you chose the Custom installation earlier, the next few dialog boxes you see will depend on the components you installed. Complete these dialog boxes as necessary.

6. Setup now busies itself copying files to your computer. When it's done, click **Finish** to complete the installation.

7. When Windows 98 asks if you want to restart your computer, click **Yes**.

When your computer resurfaces, you'll see that Personal Web Server has redecorated your system:

➤ There's a new **Publish** icon sitting on the desktop. This icon launches the Personal Web Manager, which enables you to maintain your site, publish pages to your site, and more. I'll show how this works in a second.

➤ There's a Personal Web Server icon lurking in the system tray (the area on the right side of the taskbar). This icon tells you whether Personal Web Server is running, stopped, or paused. By default, Personal Web Server is set up to run automatically when you start Windows 98.

➤ Select **Start | Programs** and you'll see that there's a new Microsoft Personal Web Server menu.

Before you start serving pages, though, you need to understand some of the defaults that are set for Personal Web Server. To do this, display the Personal Web Manager by using any of the following methods:

➤ Launch the desktop's **Publish** icon.

➤ Double-click the Personal Web Server icon in the system tray.

➤ Select **Start | Programs | Internet Explorer | Microsoft Personal Web Server | Personal Web Manager**.

Whichever method you use, Windows 98 opens the Personal Web Manager window shown in the following figure. (If you see a Tip of the Day window, read the tip and then click **Close**.)

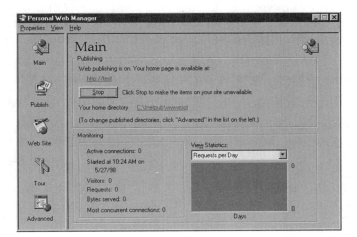

Use the Personal Web Manager to configure Personal Web Server.

Easing System Tray Crunch

It seems that just about every Tom, Disk, and Harry of a program adds an icon to the taskbar's system tray. If your system tray is getting overpopulated, you can ease the congestion by telling Personal Web Server not to display its icon, thank you very much. To do this, deactivate the **Properties | Show Tray Icon** command in Personal Web Manager.

The left side of the Personal Web Manager window shows five icons that represent the various views available.

The Main view shows you, among other things, the address of your Web server. (This is the address that appears under the **Your home page is available at** label.) This address always takes the following form:

http://*host*

As I mentioned earlier, Internet addresses take the following form:

host.domain

Here, *host* is the Internet name of your computer, and *domain* is the Internet service provider. When you're not on the Internet, only the *host* part is used, so that's what Personal Web Manager shows. For example, my computer has the host name **test**, so my Personal Web Server address is the following:

http://test

This works fine if you only browse your site from the comfort of your own computer. However, if you want others to access your site via either a corporate intranet or the World Wide Web, the simple **http://***host* format won't work. Instead, the root address depends on how you want other people to access your site:

> **Via a corporate intranet** In this case, the root address takes the following form:
>
> **http://***name*
>
> Here, *name* is your computer's network name. For example, if the computer name is **hermes**, your intranet root address is as follows:
>
> **http://hermes**
>
> **Via the World Wide Web** In this situation, your site's root address takes the following form:
>
> **http://***host.domain*
>
> For this address, *host* is your computer's host name, and *domain* is the domain name of your TCP/IP network. For example, if the host name is **test** and the domain name is **mcfedries.com**, the WWW root address is the following:
>
> **http://test.mcfedries.com**

The **Your home directory** item shows you the folder on your computer that corresponds to the server's main directory. The location of this folder is associated with (*mapped* to) the server's home (or *root*) directory. So the default folder of **C:\Inetpub\wwwroot** corresponds to the root (/) of your Web site.

In my example, the server's root directory is **http://test.mcfedries.com/**, which is the same thing as **C:\Inetpub\wwwroot**.

Personal Web Server Startup and Shutdown

So far so good. Now you need to understand the difference between a "server" and a "service." A service is an operation that runs behind the scenes and generally just waits for something to happen. For example, Personal Web Server installs the HTTP (*Hypertext Transfer Protocol* in geek lingo) service, which monitors your Internet (or network) connection and waits for Web page requests. If a request comes along, the HTTP service passes it along to the Web server. The server then locates the appropriate file (or files) and tells the HTTP service to pass them back to the browser.

As I mentioned earlier, this service is launched automatically each time you start Windows 98. You can pause or stop the service by using the following methods:

To stop the service In Personal Web Manager, either click **Stop** in the Main view, or select **Properties | Stop Service**. (Another way to do this is to right-click the Personal Web Server icon in the system tray, and then click **Stop Service**.)

To pause the service When you stop the service, Personal Web Server disables the items in the **Monitoring** group (which give you data about the current server connections). If you prefer to leave these items enabled while the server is unavailable, *pause* the service, instead. To do this in Personal Web Manager, select the **Properties | Pause Service** command. (You can also right-click the Personal Web Server icon in the system tray, and then click **Pause Service**.)

To get Personal Web Server back on its feet, you have the following choices:

To start the service If you stopped the service, you can start it again in Personal Web Manager either by clicking **Start** in the Main view, or by selecting **Properties | Start Service**. (Alternatively, right-click the Personal Web Server icon in the system tray, and then click **Start Service**.)

To continue the service If you paused the service, you can resume by selecting the **Properties | Continue Service** command. (And, yes, you can also right-click the Personal Web Server icon in the system tray, and then click **Resume Service**.)

Taking the Web Server for a Test Drive

With the service started, you should now check to make sure that the server works properly before moving on to more serious administration issues. This section shows you how to test the server on both an Internet and an intranet connection.

If you want to use Personal Web Server to hand out Web pages to Internet-based surfers, first test your server using the basic host address (that is, the address shown in the Personal Web Manager's Main view). You should see a page like the one shown in the following figure. (If you don't see this page, double-check that you have the service started.)

As you can see from this figure, the **welcome.htm** page supplied with Personal Web Server isn't very welcoming, so you'll need to make changes before inviting guests to your Web home. Here are a couple of ways to proceed:

The default home page displayed by Personal Web Server.

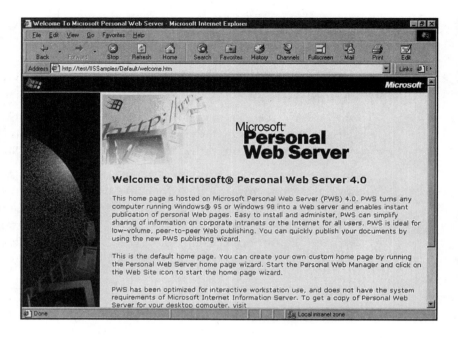

Use the Home Page Wizard   If you just need a quick-and-dirty home page for testing, the Home Page Wizard that comes with Personal Web Server might be all you need. To try it, click the **Web Site** icon in Personal Web Manager, or select **View | Web Site**. You'll see the Home Page Wizard view, shown in the following figure, which will take you step-by-step through the process of creating a page.

Create the page yourself   For greater control over your page, use either HTML or FrontPage Express (FrontPage Express is the Web page editor that comes with Windows 98).

Run the Home Page Wizard Anyway

Even if you won't use the finished product, it's a good idea to run through the Home Page Wizard anyway. That's because you can't access the Personal Web Server publishing features until you've dealt with the Home Page Wizard.

It's now time to try out some honest-to-goodness Internet Web serving. First, establish a connection to your Internet service provider (ISP), if necessary. Now load your Web browser and enter the root address of your server. What is your root address? It's **http://** followed by the host name assigned to your computer, as in this example:

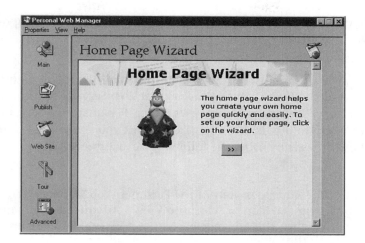

Use the Home Page Wizard to create a quick home page.

http://test.mcfedries.com/

Again, you should see the default home page previously shown.

If you'll be using Personal Web Server on an intranet, you need to do two things before trying out the Web server:

➤ Establish a connection to the network.

➤ Enable "WINS resolution" so that other computers on the intranet can find your server. See your system administrator.

To test the connection, start a Web browser and enter an URL of the following form:

http://*name*/

Here, ***name*** is the network name of the computer running the Web server (for example, **http://hermes/**).

Configuring Your Web Site Folders

Assuming that Personal Web Server is serving up Web pages without a complaint, it's now time to get your site ready for external access. This task involves a number of administrative details, not the least of which is creating the pages that people will see when they access your site. Before you get to that, however, you need to know how to create and edit the folders that will comprise your site.

PWS handles folders in two different ways:

➤ If a folder is a subfolder of the root (**C:\Inetpub\wwwroot**), browsers can access the folder directly. For example, if you add a **home** subfolder

(**C:\Inetpub\wwwroot\home**), users can access this folder by adding **home/** to the root address:

http://*server*/home/

➤ For all other folders, you must set up an alias that maps the folder path to a *virtual directory* on the server. For example, the Personal Web Server documentation pages are located in the **C:\Windows\Help\pws** folder. Personal Web Server maps **C:\Windows\Help** to the **iishelp** alias. This means you access the documentation folder in a Web browser by using the following virtual directory:

http://*server*/iishelp/pws/

These aliases are set in the Advanced view of the Personal Web Manager. (To display this view, either click the **Advanced** icon or select the **View | Advanced** command.) As you can see in the following figure, the Advanced view has a **Virtual Directories** group that displays a list showing all the folders that are mapped to your root folder.

Use the Advanced view to set up virtual directories for the folders on your computer.

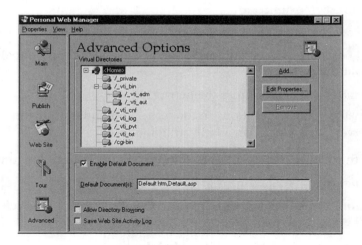

Here's how you add a new virtual directory:

1. Click the **Add** button. Personal Web Manager displays the Add Directory dialog box shown in the next figure.

2. Use the **Directory** text box to enter the location of the folder you want to work with (or click **Browse** to use another dialog box to choose the folder).

3. Use the **Alias** text box to enter an alias for the folder. (Remember: this is the name Web surfers will use to access this directory.)

Use the **Access** options to determine the type of access allowed in this folder:

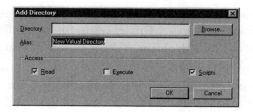

Use this dialog box to add a new virtual directory to your Web site.

➤ **Read**   Activate this check box to enable the user to read and download files in the directory. If you'll be placing executable files in this directory (see the **Execute** option, next), deactivate this check box.

➤ **Execute**   Activate this check box if you'll be placing applications in this directory (such as CGI files).

➤ **Scripts**   Activate this check box if you'll be placing ASP or IDC (Internet Database Connector) scripts within the directory.

4. Click **OK** to add the alias and return to the Personal Web Manager.

Alias Maintenance Chores

To make changes to an existing alias, highlight it in the **Virtual Directories** list and click **Edit**. If you no longer need an alias, highlight it and click **Remove**.

All Web servers define a default document for every directory. If a user doesn't specify the name of an HTML document in the URL, the server displays the default document. Personal Web Server defines two default documents: **Default.htm** and **Default.asp**. If your root contains a file named **Default.htm**, this means the following URLs will display the same document:

http://*server*/

http://*server*/default.htm

The Advanced view contains the following controls that are related to the default document:

➤ **Enable Default Document**   When this check box is activated, users who don't specify a document when entering a URL will be shown the default document (assuming that one exists in the folder).

➤ **Default Document(s)**   Use this text box to specify the name of the default document used in each folder. The most common names for default documents are **default.htm**, **default.html**, **index.htm**, and **index.html**.

➤ **Allow Directory Browsing**   When this check box is activated and no default document exists in a folder (or if you deactivate the **Enable Default Document** check box), the user sees a list of all the files in the folder.

Logging Site Activity

After your Web server is chugging along and serving pages to all and sundry, you might start to wonder which pages are popular with surfers and which ones are languishing. You might also want to know if users are getting errors when they try to access your site.

You can tell all of this and more by working with Personal Web Server's logs. A *log* is a text file that records all the activity on your Web site, including the Internet address and computer name (if applicable) of the surfer, the file that was served, the date and time the file was shipped to the browser, and the server return code (see the next Techno Talk box). For each server request, the log file writes a sequence of comma-separated values, which makes it easy to import the file into a database or spreadsheet program for analysis.

To customize the Web server's logging, display the Advanced view in Personal Web Manager and make sure the **Save Web Site Activity Log** check box is activated.

The log files are stored in the **\System\LogFiles\W3svc1** subfolder of your main Windows 98 folder. Each filename takes the form **Nc***yymm***.log**, where *yy* is the two-digit year and *mm* is the two-digit month. For example, the log for August 1998 would be stored in **Nc9808.log**.

Publishing Pages to Your Web Site

Putting up pages on your Web site isn't hard. In fact, the easiest route is simply to use Windows Explorer to copy the necessary files to either your home directory or one of your virtual directories.

If you'd rather not worry about gathering the necessary support files (such as graphics files), Personal Web Server offers the Publishing Wizard, which will copy a Web page into your home directory and adjust the locations of links and graphics within that page so they point to the appropriate files. Here's how it works:

1. In Personal Web Manager, click the **Publish** icon or select **View | Publish**. The Publishing Wizard appears.

2. Click the wizard image or the >> button. (If you see a Security Alert, click **Yes**.) Personal Web Manager displays the controls shown in the next figure.

3. Use the **Path** text box to enter the full path and filename of the Web page you want to publish. (Or click **Browse** to select the file using the Server File System window.)

Serverspeak: The Server Return Codes

When Personal Web Server handles a request, it also returns a code that summarizes the result of the request. A return code of 200 means the document was sent successfully to the browser. For unsuccessful operations, here's a summary of some of the return codes you'll find in the log:

Return Code	What It Means
204	File contains no content
301	File moved permanently
302	File moved temporarily
304	File not modified
400	Bad request
401	Unauthorized access
402	Payment required
403	Access forbidden
404	File not found
500	Internal server error
501	Service not implemented
502	Bad gateway
503	Service unavailable

Easier Page Publishing

You can launch the Publishing Wizard and fill in the **Path** text box automatically by using either of the following methods:

➤ Drag the Web page file from Windows Explorer and drop it on the desktop's **Publish** icon.

➤ Right-click the Web page file, and then select **Send To | Personal Web Server**.

Use the Publishing Wizard to copy Web pages to the server's home directory.

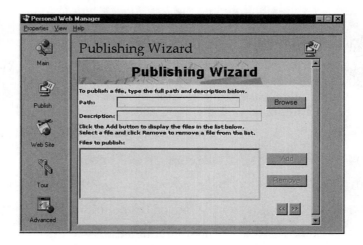

4. Use the **Description** text box to enter a description for the Web page.

5. Click **Add** to add the page to the **Files to publish** list.

6. Repeat steps 3–5 to add other pages.

7. Click >>. The wizard publishes the files.

From Here

This chapter showed you how to set up a Web server on a Windows 98 machine. You learned how to install and set up Personal Web Server, and then how to test the server. From there, you learned how to set up virtual directories and default documents, log Web site activity, and publish pages on your site.

This ends your advanced look at Windows 98's communications and Internet features. Next up is Part 4, "Swifter, Higher, Stronger: More Windows 98 System Tools," where you'll learn how to use Windows 98's system tools to make your machine faster and more reliable.

Part 4
Swifter, Higher, Stronger: More Windows 98 System Tools

The Windows 98 box contains countless new bells, whistles, and other noisemakers. There's the famous (or infamous, depending on which side you support in the Microsoft vs. DOJ debate) Web integration, a ton of useful Internet programs, and support for some nifty new hardware gadgetry. For my money, however, one of the best things about Windows 98 is the massive number of system tools—programs and utilities designed to help make your system faster and more efficient, and to correct any problems that may crop up.

I told you about many of these tools in The Complete Idiot's Guide to Windows 98. *The three chapters here in Part 4 continue the system tools tutorial by looking at the rest of Windows 98's utilities and by showing you how they can make your computer a better place to work and play.*

THIS BABY PURRS...

Chapter 17

From Slowpoke to Speed Demon: Making Windows Fly

In This Chapter

➤ Getting the most out of your computer's memory

➤ Making your hard drive howl

➤ Getting your video up to speed

➤ A fistful of ways to avoid the dreaded hourglass icon

Your applications have all the zip of a wet sponge, but hey, that's the reality of working in Windows, right? Wrong! Unless your system is extremely old, or has extremely slow hardware (especially the hard disk and video card), there's plenty you can do to rev up Windows to a respectable pace. And I'm not talking about upgrading to blazing Pentium II machines with humungous hard disks and scads of memory. This chapter shows you how to soup up your machine using only the programs and features that come built right into Windows 98. It all comes free of charge, and you'll be surprised at what a difference it makes.

Thanks for the Memory: Maximizing Your System's Memory

Entire books can be (and have been) written about the relationship between Windows and memory. What it all boils down to, though, is quite simple: the more memory you have, the happier Windows is. However, not all of us can afford to throw dozens of megabytes of memory at our problems. We have to make do with less and that, in essence, is what this section is all about. I'll show you some ways to fight back if a lack of memory is causing your applications to run slowly (or not at all).

Your computer's memory is arguably its most important component, yet few people seem to understand what it is or what it does. So I'll begin with a brief, non-technical explanation of some basic memory concepts.

To begin with, let's talk about the difference between your *hard disk* and your *memory*. Many people confuse these two terms because the storage capacity of both is measured in megabytes. There's a big difference, however, and to see it, try thinking of your computer as a carpenter's workshop. A typical workshop is divided in two basic areas: storage space and work space. During a project, the carpenter will take materials and tools from the storage area and manipulate them in the work area. This is exactly what happens in your computer. Your applications and data files are stored on your hard disk and when you need to work with them, they're copied into memory.

The problem is that most hard disks can store hundreds of megabytes of data, whereas the memory capacity of a typical computer is limited to only 16 megabytes or so. This means that your computer's "work space" is much smaller than its "storage space." For a carpenter, a small work space limits the number of tools and materials he can use at any one time. For a computer, it limits the number of programs and data files that you can load.

Tracking System Resources with the Resource Meter

System resources are small memory areas that Windows 98 uses to keep track of things like the position and size of open windows, dialog boxes, and your desktop configuration (wallpaper, and so on). You can have scads of free memory and still get **Insufficient Memory** errors if you run out of system resources!

To make sure this doesn't happen, and to prevent the problems that occur when the system resources get too low, use Windows 98's Resource Meter utility. To try out Resource Meter, select **Start | Programs | Accessories | System Tools | Resource Meter**. If this is the first time you're starting Resource Meter, you see a dialog box that just states the obvious: that Resource Meter itself will use up a few system resources. To avoid this dialog box in the future, activate the **Don't display this message again** check box and click **OK**.

When the Resource Meter loads, it adds an icon to the taskbar's system tray that gives you a visual representation of the system resource status. The green bars indicate free system resources, and the "level" goes up and down as you open and close applications and windows. Resource Meter actually tracks three values: System, User, and GDI. However, the System value is the only one to worry about. To see the current level, use either of the following techniques:

➤ Hover the mouse pointer over the Resource Meter icon for a second or two to display a banner showing the individual resource percentages.

➤ Double-click the Resource Meter icon to display the Resource Meter dialog box, which shows a bar chart for each resource percentage (see the following figure).

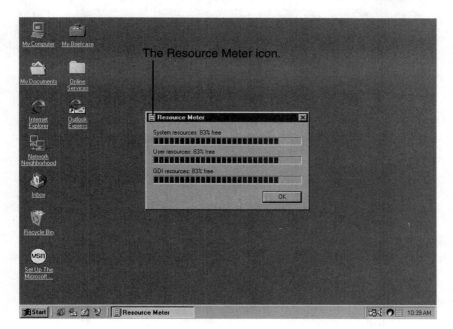

Double-click the Resource Meter icon in the toolbar to display a graphical representation of your free system resources.

So what do these numbers mean in the real world? Well, as long as the bars in the Resource Meter icon are green, you're fine: This means that Windows 98 has plenty of resources available. As the bar inches downward, however, keep an eye out for a color change:

➤ When the bars change to yellow, the free resources have dropped below about 34 percent. You should exercise caution at this point and avoid opening more applications or windows. Run through some of the techniques discussed below for saving system resources.

➤ When the bars change to red, the free resources have dropped to 15 percent or less. This is very dangerous territory, and you should immediately start shutting down applications.

When the free resources drop to 10 percent or less, you see the dialog box shown in the next figure. (Note that this dialog box appears whether or not you have the Resource Meter running.) Your system is in imminent danger of hanging, so you must start closing applications to avoid losing data.

263

Windows 98 warns you when your free system resources drop to 10 percent or less.

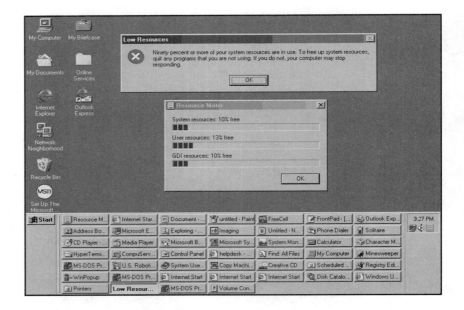

If you find that your system resources are getting low, here are some ideas that will send the Resource Meter bar up:

➤ Close any applications you won't be using for a while.

➤ If your applications support multiple open documents, close files you aren't using.

➤ Run DOS applications full-screen rather than in a window.

➤ Turn off application objects you don't use, such as toolbars, rulers, and status bars.

➤ Minimize any running applications you aren't using.

➤ Turn off desktop wallpaper and animated cursors.

Miscellaneous Ideas for Optimizing Memory

To help get the most out of your machine's workspace, here are a few pointers for maximizing memory in Windows 98:

If you have other applications running, close them one at a time until your application will start. This, I suppose, is the most obvious (but the least convenient) solution. If you have any running applications that you really don't need, shut them down. The bigger the application, the more memory you'll save.

Don't load stuff at startup. Other memory-stealers are the programs that get loaded at startup. This includes both the programs stuffed into your Startup folder, and any

DOS programs that are loaded via AUTOEXEC.BAT and CONFIG.SYS. Double-check everything that's being loaded to see if you really need all that stuff.

Delete the contents of the Clipboard. When you cut or copy a selection in a Windows 98 application, the program stores the data in an area of your computer's memory called the Clipboard. If you're working with only a few lines of text, this area remains fairly small. However, cutting or copying a graphic image can increase the size of the Clipboard to several hundred kilobytes or more. If you've run out of memory, a chubby Clipboard may be the culprit. To trim the Clipboard and release most of this memory, try one of the following methods:

➤ If you have an application running, highlight a small section of text (a single character or word will do) and select **Edit | Copy**. This replaces the current Clipboard with a much smaller one.

➤ Select **Start | Programs | Accessories | System Tools | Clipboard Viewer**. When the Clipboard Viewer window appears, select the **Edit | Delete** command.

Load larger applications first. Because of the way Windows 98 uses memory, you can often start more programs if you load your larger Windows 98 applications before your smaller ones.

Run the Help system's Memory Troubleshooter. The Memory Troubleshooter can help with certain kinds of memory mishaps. Select **Start | Help** and, in the Windows Help window, make sure the **Contents** tab is displayed. Now open the **Troubleshooting** book, and then the **Windows 98 Troubleshooters** book. Select the **Memory** topic.

Shell out the bucks to buy more memory. The ultimate way to beat memory problems, of course, is simply to add more memory to your system. (Although, as you've seen, you still need to make sure that your system resources don't get too low.) Happily, memory prices have fallen over the past couple of years, so adding a megabyte or two shouldn't break your budget. If you do decide to take the plunge, contact your computer manufacturer to find out the best kind of memory to add to your system.

The Hot Rod Hard Disk

By far the biggest bottleneck on your system is your hard disk. Windows spends much of its life hauling data from the hard disk to memory, and then sending it back again. If its transportation routes are clogged or too chaotic, even the fastest hard disk will run like a dachshund through cheese dip.

To help you avoid such a fate, the next few sections offer some helpful techniques that'll ensure your hard disk works as hard as it can.

First, A Summary

Before getting to the new stuff, let's take a second to review the Windows 98 hard disk beautification features that I covered in detail in *The Complete Idiot's Guide to Windows 98*:

ScanDisk   Run this program regularly to ensure that your hard disk maintains its fighting trim. (Select **Start** | **Programs** | **Accessories** | **System Tools** | **ScanDisk**.)

Disk Defragmenter   Use this program to make sure all your hard disk files are stored as efficiently as possible, which means your programs and documents will load faster. (Select **Start** | **Programs** | **Accessories** | **System Tools** | **Disk Defragmenter**.)

Disk Cleanup   You use this utility to rid your hard disk of unnecessary files that are just wasting space. (Select **Start** | **Programs** | **Accessories** | **System Tools** | **Disk Cleanup**.)

DriveSpace   This program safely compresses the data on your hard disk so that it takes only about half the space. This lets you fit more data on the disk, but it does slow things down a tad. (Select **Start** | **Programs** | **Accessories** | **System Tools** | **DriveSpace**.)

Checking Your System's Performance Level

The first step down the road to hard disk health is to make sure your system is "configured for optimal performance," as the geeks like to say. To check this out, first use either of the following techniques:

➤ Right-click **My Computer** and then click **Properties**.

➤ Open Control Panel and launch the **System** icon.

In the System Properties dialog box, display the **Performance** tab. If all is well, this tab will display the message **Your system is configured for optimal performance**. On the other hand, the tab may complain that a drive or two is using **MS-DOS compatibility mode**, as shown in the following figure. If this happens, there are a couple of ways to proceed:

➤ The culprit here is often a line or two in either **CONFIG.SYS** or **AUTOEXEC.BAT**. Try renaming these files so that Windows 98 doesn't load them at startup. (In Chapter 1, see the section "What's All This About **CONFIG.SYS** and **AUTOEXEC.BAT**?".)

➤ Contact your computer manufacturer's tech support department, tell them about the message in the Performance tab, and ask if they have newer device driver files that will correct the problem.

The Performance tab looks like this when your system isn't at its best.

A System Swap Meet: The Swap File

Do you know how much memory your system has? If not, the Performance tab in the System Properties dialog box tells you. (In the previous figure, see the **Memory** line near the top.) As I said before, the amount of memory in your system is absolutely crucial to overall performance.

What happens if Windows runs out of memory? That may not seem possible, but with today's multi-megabyte programs and large data files, systems with "only" 16MB of memory will run out of RAM (random access memory; the full geek name for memory) sooner rather than later. Does this mean you're stuck?

Not at all, because Windows 98 does a smart thing: It converts a chunk of your hard disk into what's known in the trade as *virtual memory*. That is, it configures this hard disk real estate so that it looks and acts just like regular RAM (a.k.a. *physical memory*). Windows 98 then proceeds to shuffle files and data between regular RAM and the virtual memory area, as needed. Because data is constantly swapped between memory and the hard disk, this virtual memory area is known as the *swap file*. (And, yes, it is just a single—albeit large—file on your hard disk.)

The less RAM you have in your system, the more important Windows 98's virtual memory features become. That's because if you're dealing with a relatively small amount of physical RAM, Windows 98 can still create a swap file and, therefore, enable you to open many more programs than you could otherwise. No matter how much RAM you have, however, Windows 98 will still create a swap file and will still use it for tossing data back and forth. To make this process as efficient as possible, you need to optimize your swap file. This section shows you how to do just that.

Before I show you how to change the swap file settings, here are some ideas to keep in mind for maximum swap file performance:

Use the hard disk with the most free space. The best way to ensure top swap file performance is to make sure that the hard disk containing the swap file has lots of free space. This extra space gives the swap file enough room to expand and contract as needed. (If you want to use a different hard disk for your swap file, I'll show you how to do this in the next section.)

Use the hard disk with the fastest access time. If you have multiple physical hard disks on your system, make sure that the swap file is using the disk that has the fastest access time.

Defragment the swap file's hard drive. File fragmentation slows down everything on your system, including the swap file. For best results, keep the disk drive containing the swap file defragmented.

Use an uncompressed hard disk. In some cases, Windows 98 can store the swap file on the compressed drive. Swap file performance suffers if you do this, however, so it's best to use an uncompressed drive for the swap file.

Mystery Disk Activity Solved!

Have you ever heard your hard drive humming when you're not using your computer? It might seem like your system is possessed, but it's really just Windows 98 performing some housekeeping chores. In particular, Windows 98 begins compacting the swap file as soon as you haven't used your computer for a minute.

The first thing you might want to do is track the swap file size. If you see that this size is approaching the amount of free space left on the disk, you should free up some disk space to ensure that the swap file has complete flexibility. Follow these steps:

1. Select **Start** | **Programs** | **Accessories** | **System Tools** | **System Monitor** to load the System Monitor.
2. Select **Edit** | **Add Item** to display the Add Item dialog box.
3. In the **Category** list, highlight **Memory Manager**.
4. In the **Item** list, highlight **Swapfile size**.

5. Click **OK**. The following figure shows System Monitor displaying the Swapfile size value in a chart. (To get the specific values in the status bar, click the chart.)

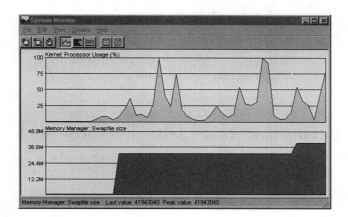

Use System Monitor to keep track of the swap file (disk cache) size.

In Windows 98, virtual memory is a "self-tuning" feature, so in most cases you won't have to change a thing. At times, however, you might need to adjust some swap file settings. For example, you might want to change the hard disk used by the swap file. Here are the steps to follow to make adjustments to the swap file:

1. Open the System Properties dialog box and select the **Performance** tab, as described earlier.

2. Click the **Virtual Memory** button. Windows 98 displays the Virtual Memory dialog box.

3. Activate the **Let me specify my own virtual memory settings** option. As you can see in the following figure, the controls below this option become available.

Use the Virtual Memory dialog box to adjust the swap file settings.

4. Use the **Hard disk** drop-down list to specify a different hard disk.

5. Use the **Minimum** spinner to set the smallest possible size, in megabytes, for the swap file, and use the **Maximum** spinner to set the largest possible size. What values should you use? For optimal performance, set both values equal to about three times the amount of memory in your system. If you have 16 megabytes of RAM, for example, set both values to **48**.

6. Click **OK**. Windows 98 displays a dire (but ignorable) warning and asks if you're sure you want to go through with this.

7. Click **Yes**

Cache and Carry: Another Hard Disk Performance Boost

As I mentioned earlier, when you launch programs and documents, Windows 98 gathers the necessary files from the hard disk and stuffs them into memory. However, some tall-forehead type realized that Windows spent much of its time retrieving the same data over and over again. Wouldn't it make sense, this brainiac wondered, if Windows set aside a little snippet of memory to store recently used or frequently used bits of data? If a program requests some data, Windows would then check this area to see whether the data was already there. If so, great: just move it into the regular memory area, which is a *lot* faster than having to load it from the hard disk.

This snippet of memory is known in GeekLand as the *cache*. The cache not only holds frequently used data, but it also does two other things:

➤ It "reads ahead" to get the data that sits next to the stuff that was just retrieved. Since most data is stored sequentially on the hard disk, there's a good chance that the next bit of data will soon be needed, as well.

➤ It "writes behind" by holding changed data in the cache until the system has nothing better to do, and then it writes the data to disk.

Although Windows 98 doesn't offer any direct way to adjust the size of this cache, there are some adjustments you can make to improve performance. To make some adjustments to the hard disk cache, follow these steps:

1. Open the System Properties dialog box and select the **Performance** tab, as described earlier.

2. Click the **File System** button to display the File System Properties dialog box.

3. Make sure that the **Hard Disk** tab is selected, as shown in the following figure.

4. In the **Typical role of this computer** drop-down list, select **Network server**. (Yes, I realize that your computer isn't a "network server," but that doesn't matter here.)

5. Make sure the **Read-ahead optimization** slider is all the way over to the right (**Full**).

6. Click **OK** to return to the System Properties dialog box.

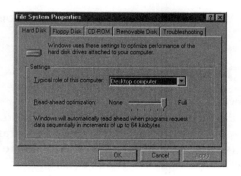

Use the Hard Disk tab to adjust how the hard disk cache works.

7. Click **Close**. Windows 98 prompts you to restart your computer.

8. Click **Yes**.

While You're At It: Adjusting the CD-ROM Cache

Windows 98 also maintains a separate cache that works with CD-ROM drives to improve performance. Again, there are a couple of things you can adjust for the CD-ROM cache. Here's what you do:

1. Open the System Properties dialog box and select the **Performance** tab, as described earlier.

2. Click the **File System** button to display the File System Properties dialog box.

3. Select the **CD-ROM** tab shown in the next figure.

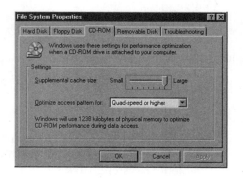

Use the CD-ROM tab to adjust parameters for the CD-ROM cache.

4. Move the **Supplemental cache size** slider all the way to the right (Large).

5. In the **Optimize access pattern for** drop-down list, select **Quad-speed or higher** (no matter what the speed of your CD-ROM drive).

6. Click **OK** to return to the System Properties dialog box.

7. Click **Close**. Windows 98 prompts you to restart your computer.

8. Click **Yes**.

Happier Hard Disks the FAT32 Way

How does Windows 98 know where to find files on your hard disk? For that chore, it uses something called the *file allocation table*, or FAT, for short. The FAT is a sort of "file filing system" that keeps track of where each chunk of a program or document is located. For technical reasons (see the "Techno Talk" sidebar if you're interested), the larger the hard disk, the more inefficient the FAT system becomes.

Why Large Hard Disks Are Inefficient

To see why large hard disks are inherently inefficient, you need to understand how Windows 98 stores files. When you format a disk, the disk's magnetic medium is divided into small storage areas called *sectors*, which usually hold up to 512 bytes of data. Hard disks typically contain hundreds of thousands of sectors, so it would be too inefficient for Windows 98 to deal with individual sectors. Instead, Windows 98 groups sectors into *clusters*, the size of which, as you'll see, depends on the size of the disk. The FAT actually keeps track of which clusters are used by each file.

One of the hard disk facts of life is that every formatted disk, from 40MB pipsqueaks to 4GB behemoths, can't have any more than 65,536 clusters. This means that the larger the hard disk, the larger the cluster size. For example, a 100MB disk uses cluster sizes of 2,048 bytes, while a 2GB disk uses 65,536-byte clusters.

The key point is that Windows 98 always allocates entire clusters when storing files. Suppose you have a file that uses 2,000 bytes. On the 100MB disk, that file would be stored in a single 2,048-byte cluster, with the extra 48 bytes as wasted space. In the 2GB disk, however, the same file takes up an entire 65,536-byte cluster, thus wasting a whopping 63,536 bytes!

To help reduce this inefficiency, Windows 98 includes a revamped FAT system called FAT32. This new system has many advantages, but the biggest is that it stores files much more efficiently than the old FAT system. How much more? Well, Microsoft estimates that, on average, users will gain an extra 28% of disk space by switching over to FAT32, which isn't bad at all.

To make this switch as painless as possible, Windows 98 comes with a utility called Drive Converter that will convert a regular FAT disk (sometimes called a FAT16 disk) into a beefed-up FAT32 disk. It's perfectly safe. Although, on the downside, the conversion isn't reversible. Here's how it works:

1. Select **Start** | **Programs** | **Accessories** | **System Tools** | **Drive Converter (FAT32)**.

2. The initial Drive Converter dialog box gives you an overview of the conversion process. Click **Next** to continue. Now Drive Converter prompts you to choose the drive you want to convert, as shown in the following figure.

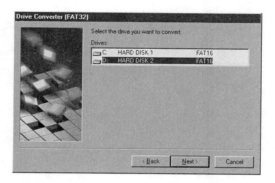

Use this Drive Converter dialog box to choose the drive you want to convert.

3. Highlight the drive you want to convert to FAT32 and click **Next**.

4. Drive Converter warns you that the new FAT32 drive will not be accessible from other operating systems. Say "duh" and click **OK**.

5. Drive Converter now checks for incompatible virus programs and disk utilities. If Drive Converter finds any incompatible programs, it displays a list and gives you further instructions. Click **Next** when you're ready to continue.

6. Drive Converter gives you an opportunity to back up your files. If you want to take advantage of this, click the **Create Backup** button. When that's done and you're back with Drive Converter, click **Next**. Drive Converter tells you it has to restart your computer.

7. Click **Next**. Drive Converter reboots your machine in MS-DOS mode and then performs the conversion. Along the way, you see a long checklist of tasks that Drive Converter is performing. The entire process shouldn't take more than a couple of minutes.

8. When it's done, Drive Converter reboots your computer again, loads Windows 98, and reports that the conversion was successful. Click **Next**. Drive Converter now tells you that it will run Disk Defragmenter to ensure that your files are stored optimally.

9. Click **Finish** to launch Disk Defragmenter.

To see for yourself that your drive was converted, right-click the drive in My Computer or Windows Explorer and then click **Properties**. In the dialog box that appears, the **File system** value will now read FAT32, as shown in the next figure.

After converting your drive, the properties sheet for the drive now tells you that the file system is FAT32.

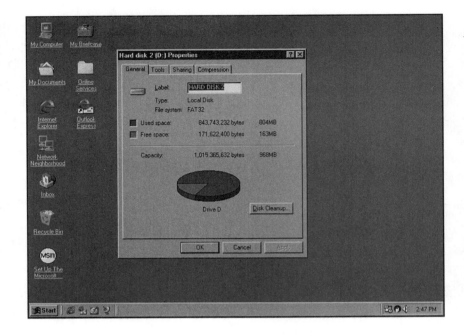

Putting the Whip to Windows Video

I'll be discussing Windows 98 video in detail in Chapter 21, "Graphics Gadgetry: Working with Video Cards and Monitors." For the purposes of this chapter, however, you should know that even a minimal video resolution of 640 pixels across by 480 pixels down means that your graphics board has to manipulate 307,200 individual bits of light. Bump up the resolution to 1,024×768, and the total number of pixels leaps to a whopping 786,432.

With several hundred thousand pixels to keep up with (and, in some cases, several thousand or even several *million* colors as well) today's video adapters can put a strain on even the most muscular CPU. If you find yourself constantly waiting for screens to update, the following tips may help:

Don't use more than 256 colors if you don't have to. Unless you need them to do graphics, using more than 256 colors will only slow you down unnecessarily. To make your display instantly several times faster, switch to a 256-color driver. If you really don't care what your screen looks like, you'll get the best performance with 16 colors.

Try different display drivers. Many video adapters come with several drivers for each mode. Try different drivers to see if any of them give you better performance.

Also, video manufacturers are constantly tweaking their drivers to get improved performance. See if you can get the latest upgrade.

If you're considering upgrading your adapter beyond Super VGA, look into boards with accelerators or coprocessors. Many of the newer high-resolution video adapters come with extra chips (or, in some cases, full-fledged micro-processors) that assume much of the graphics processing donkey work. This improves performance for two reasons:

➤ The routines on the boards that process the graphics data are highly optimized for these tasks. They can handle basic tasks, such as drawing lines, much faster than your normal system.

➤ They free up your computer's main processing unit for other tasks.

These boards are a little more expensive, but they may be worth the extra cash for video that's three to five times faster.

Get a video card with as much memory as you can afford. Video cards like to have lots of memory, as well. If you can afford it, get a card with 4MB or even 8MB of on-board memory.

From Here

This chapter showed you a few ways to get Windows 98 into the fast lane. You learned how to use the Resource Meter and other methods to maximize memory. You learned a whole bunch of ways to hop up your hard disk, and you learned how to take video performance up a notch or two.

Chapter 18, "A Windows Lifeline: The Emergency Boot Disk," shows you how to create, populate, and use an emergency boot disk.

THIS WON'T HURT A BIT...

A Windows Lifeline: The Emergency Boot Disk

In This Chapter

➤ Understanding boot disks

➤ Creating an emergency boot disk

➤ How to use the boot disk

➤ Creating a virus-checking boot disk

➤ Getting your system back on its feet with System Recovery

For many years, computer problems ranked right up there with death and taxes as constants in life. Working with a computer meant always having a nagging worry in the back of your mind that the temperamental beast was going to give up the ghost at any minute. Happily, modern computers are much more reliable and will usually give you years of faithful service before the inevitable slide into decrepitude.

That's not to say that trouble will never rear its bothersome head. Some wag once said that there are two types of computer users: those who have had a system crash and those who *will* have one crash. So it pays to be prepared for the worst, and one of the best preparations you can do is to create an emergency boot disk. This chapter explains what these boot disks are all about and shows you how to create and use them.

Boot Disk Basics

Let's begin with a bit of boot disk background. Specifically, I'll answer three common questions:

➤ What is a boot disk?

➤ Why bother with a boot disk?

➤ How does a boot disk work?

To answer the first question, a boot disk is a specially configured floppy disk. The basic idea is that if your computer won't start (*boot* in geekspeak), you insert the boot disk, turn on your machine, and then a scaled-down (i.e., DOS-prompt-only) version of Windows 98 loads from the disk. This at least gives control of your machine back to you so that you can investigate the problem.

The next couple of sections answer the other two questions.

Why Do You Need an Emergency Boot Disk?

The short answer to this question is "In case of an emergency." Yes, as I said, computers are more reliable these days, but there are still all kinds of reasons a hard disk can go south:

General wear and tear: If your computer is running right now, its hard disk is spinning away at 5,400 to 10,000 revolutions per minute. That's right, even though you're not doing anything, the hard disk is hard at work. Because of this constant activity, most hard disks simply wear out after a few years.

The old bump-and-grind: Your hard disk's hardware includes "read/write heads" that are used to read data from and write data to the disk. These heads float on a cushion of air just above the spinning hard disk platters. A bump or jolt of sufficient intensity can send them crashing onto the surface of the disk, which could easily result in trashed data. If the heads happen to hit a particularly sensitive area, the entire hard disk could crash.

Power surges: The current that's supplied to your PC is, under normal conditions, relatively constant. It's possible, however, for your computer to be assailed by massive power surges (for example, during a lightning storm). These surges can wreak havoc on a carefully arranged hard disk.

Power outages: If a power outage shuts down your system while you're working in Windows, you will almost certainly lose some unsaved data, and you might (in extremely rare cases) lose access to your hard disk as well.

Viruses: Unfortunately, computer viruses are all too common nowadays. Although some of these viruses are benign—they display cute messages or cause characters to "fall off" the screen—most are downright vicious and exist only to trash your valuable data.

Bad programming: Some not-ready-for-prime-time software programs can end up running amok and destroying large chunks of your hard disk in the process. Luckily, these rogues are fairly rare these days.

There are some "ounce of prevention" maintenance chores you can perform to avoid doing the "pound of cure" thing. For example, running ScanDisk regularly will keep your hard disk looking good and will alert you to potential trouble. Also, get a good anti-virus program and use it religiously, particularly if you download files from the Internet.

What happens if, despite your best efforts, your hard disk goes down for the count? This is bad news because Windows 98 normally uses your hard drive to start itself up when you turn on your computer. Therefore, no hard drive means no Windows 98, which means no work (or play, for that matter). If you have an emergency boot disk, however, you just insert it in drive A and reboot your computer. Since the boot disk tells Windows 98 to boot from the floppy disk instead of the hard disk, you regain at least some control over your machine. You (or some nearby computer whiz) can proceed to investigate the problem. Not only that, but the boot disk also contains some programs that you (or your troubleshooting guru) can use to diagnose the problem. For example, the boot disk includes the ScanDisk program.

> *Check This Out...*
>
> **Revue Head**
> Microsoft Plus! 98 comes with the MacAfee VirusScan anti-virus program. I showed you how to use it in Chapter 5's "VirusScan: Inoculating Windows Against Viruses" section, page 61.

How Does It Work?

The next time you start your computer, keep your eye on disk drive A. A few seconds after you throw the switch, the drive light should come on briefly. This means the drive is being set up for use, and once that's done, the light goes out again. A few seconds later, though, the light reappears. When the light comes back on, your system is looking to see if there's a floppy disk in the drive. If there is, the computer attempts to load Windows 98 from the floppy disk. If the disk contains the proper files—specifically, the Windows 98 *system files*—Windows 98 loads, but you'll see an A:\> prompt instead of the usual Windows 98 screen. This process is called *booting from a floppy*.

Forging and Using the Emergency Boot Disk

Now that you understand why an emergency boot disk is a good thing and how it works, it's time to get down to the practical matters of creating and using the disk. The next few sections will tell you everything you need to know.

Building the Boot Disk

The Windows 98 Setup program offers to create a boot disk (Windows 98 calls it a *startup disk*) during the installation process. If you skipped that step, or if you didn't install Windows 98 yourself, here are the steps to follow to create one of these disks:

1. Select **Start | Settings | Control Panel**. Control Panel reports for duty.

2. Open the **Add/Remove Programs** icon to get the Add/Remove Programs Properties dialog box onscreen.

3. Select the **Startup Disk** tab, shown in the following figure.

You use the Startup Disk tab to create the startup disk (duh).

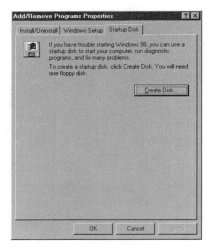

4. Click the **Create Disk** button. Windows 98 displays a dialog box asking you to insert the Windows 98 installation disc.

5. Insert the disc and click **OK**. After a few seconds, you're prompted to insert a disk in drive A, as shown in the next figure.

When you see the Insert Disk dialog box, insert a disk in drive A.

6. Pick out a disk that doesn't have any files on it that you need (Windows 98 will obliterate all the current info on the disk), insert it, and click **OK**. Windows 98

chugs away for a minute or two while it creates the startup disk. When it's done, it returns you to the Add/Remove Programs Properties dialog box.

7. Click **Cancel** to return to the Control Panel.

How to Use the Emergency Boot Disk

To be safe, you should probably give the boot disk a whirl to make sure it works properly. To do this, follow these steps:

1. Insert the boot disk in drive A.
2. Select **Start | Shut Down** to display the Shut Down Windows dialog box.
3. Activate the **Restart** option and click **OK**.
4. Windows 98 shuts down, and then restarts the system. After a while, you'll see the following menu appear:

```
Microsoft Windows 98 Startup Menu
=================================


    1. Start computer with CD-ROM support.
    2. Start computer without CD-ROM support.
    3. View the Help file.


    Enter a choice:
```

5. If you have a CD-ROM drive, press **1**. Otherwise, press **2**.
6. Press **Enter**.

From here, the boot disk does its thing, and you'll see all kinds of strange, hieroglyphic messages on the screen.

First, support for your CD-ROM is installed (assuming you chose option 1 in the menu). Then the disk creates something called a "RAM drive." This is a slice of memory (RAM) that's set aside to use as a disk drive. For example, if your hard disk is drive C and your CD-ROM is drive D, the RAM drive will be set up as drive E.

Once that's done, you see the following message:

```
Preparing to start your computer.
This may take a few minutes. Please wait...
```

After a minute or two, you see the following message and then are dropped off at the A:\> prompt:

```
The diagnostic tools were successfully loaded to drive E.
```

281

What's this all about? These "diagnostic tools" are programs you can run from the command line. The boot disk copied them to the RAM drive (drive E in the above example). If this were a real emergency, you would use these programs to investigate and, hopefully, fix the problem.

How do you get to the RAM drive? You type the following command and press **Enter**:

drive:

Here, *drive* is the letter of the RAM drive that the boot disk created. For example, to get to drive E you type **e:** and press **Enter**.

The following table lists the diagnostic tools that the boot disk parked on the RAM drive.

File name	What you use it for
ATTRIB.EXE	To set or clear file attributes (see Chapter 2's "A Fast Look at File Attributes" section).
CHKDSK.EXE	To check for disk errors (although SCANDISK is a better choice for this).
DEBUG.EXE	To test and debug executable files. This is an advanced utility and should not be used unless you know what you're doing.
EDIT.COM	To edit text files (such as the **CONFIG.SYS** and **AUTOEXEC.BAT** configuration files).
EXTRACT.EXE	To extract files from the cabinet (**.CAB**) files on the Windows 98 CD-ROM.
FORMAT.COM	To format a disk.
SCANDISK.EXE	To scan and repair a disk.
SYS.COM	To transfer Windows 98 system files to a disk.
UNINSTAL.EXE	To uninstall Windows 98 (if you installed over an existing version of Windows).

To find out how these programs work, type the name of the program (you don't need the extension) followed by a space and /?, as in this example:

scandisk /?

When you press **Enter**, you see information on how to run the program from the DOS prompt.

When you're done, remove the startup disk and press **Ctrl+Alt+Delete** to restart your machine and get back to Windows 98.

Creating a VirusScan Emergency Disk

I mentioned earlier that one of the things that can swipe the knees out from under your hard disk is a virus. If you have Microsoft Plus! 98, its VirusScan component can check for and eradicate viruses before they wreak their havoc. However, if you're lax in your virus scanning duties, or if some newfangled virus comes along that VirusScan doesn't recognize, your hard drive may go kaput.

To recover, you need to bypass your hard disk at startup and run the virus checker from the A:\> prompt.

Bypass my hard disk? That sounds like a job for the boot disk!

You're right, it is.

But VirusScan is a Windows program. How do I run it if I'm sitting at the A:\> thingy?

Luckily, VirusScan comes with a command line version that's happy to work from the DOS prompt. The easiest way to get this virus checker on a boot disk is to create a "VirusScan Emergency Disk." This is a boot disk that contains the necessary files for scanning and fumigating viruses.

Note that there isn't enough room on the Windows 98 Startup disk for these files, so you need to create a separate boot disk. The first thing you have to do is set up a blank floppy disk with the Windows 98 system files. Here's how:

1. You'll be formatting the disk, which destroys all data, so pick out a disk that has nothing valuable on it, and then insert the disk in drive A.

2. In My Computer or Windows Explorer, make sure drive A is *not* open. (Windows 98 won't let you format the disk if the drive is open.)

3. Right-click drive A, and then click **Format**. The Format dialog box appears.

4. Activate the **Full** option.

5. Activate the **Copy system files** check box (see the following figure).

Before creating the VirusScan Emergency Disk, you have to format a floppy with the Windows 98 system files.

5. Click **Start**. Windows 98 formats the disk, and then copies the system files.

6. Click **Close**.

So far so good. Now leave the disk in drive A and follow these steps to create the VirusScan Emergency Disk:

1. Select **Start | Programs | Microsoft Plus! 98 | McAfee VirusScan | Create VirusScan Emergency Disk**. The McAfee Emergency Disk Creation Utility dialog box pops up.

2. Click **Continue**. The program asks you to insert a disk in drive A.

3. You've done that already, so just click **OK**. The program wisely checks the floppy disk for viruses, and then starts tossing files onto the disk.

4. When the copying is complete, the program asks you to "write-protect" the disk, which ensures that the disk can't be altered (particularly by a virus). For a 3 1/2-inch disk, write-protection is controlled by a small, movable tab on the back of the disk. To write-protect the disk, slide the tab toward the edge of the disk.

5. Click **OK**.

To use this disk, first turn your computer off, insert the disk, and then turn the machine back on. (The on/off thing is to ensure that no viruses remain lurking in the electronic weeds.) You'll eventually see a **Did you cycle the power off and on?** prompt. Press **Y** to continue. When the program tells you it's ready to begin scanning, press any key to get things going.

If Worse Comes to Worst: Using System Recovery

What happens if your system crashes and, after you boot to the floppy, none of the diagnostic tools can put your digital Humpty Dumpty together again? The first thing you should do is take your machine back to the manufacturer or to your local computer repair shop to see if it can be fixed.

If that doesn't do it, you have no alternative but to format (or replace) your hard drive and start from scratch. However, you don't have to laboriously reinstall Windows 98 and your applications. With some advanced planning, you can use the new System Recovery utility to both reinstall Windows 98 and return your hard drive to its pre-crash state.

System Recovery consists of three pieces:

PCRESTOR.BAT: After you format your hard drive, boot from your startup disk and run this batch file. **PCRESTOR.BAT** performs several chores, but its main task is to start the Windows 98 Setup program with various switches and parameters.

MSBATCH.INF: This is an information file that specifies a number of settings and parameters used by Setup. In particular, this file tells Setup to run the System

Recovery Wizard. **System Recovery Wizard:** After Windows 98 is reinstalled, this Wizard loads automatically to take you through the rest of the recovery process, including restoring the files from your system backup.

To use System Recovery successfully, you must assume your machine will crash one day and make the necessary preparations. More specifically, you must follow these guidelines:

➤ Create a Windows 98 startup disk.

➤ Perform a full backup of the hard disk that contains the Windows system files.

➤ Your main Windows 98 folder must be **C:\WINDOWS**.

System Recovery is one of those tools that you hope you never use. However, if the day does come when your system needs to be recovered, you'll be glad to know that doing so takes just a few steps:

1. Boot your system using the startup disk. When the Startup Menu appears, make sure you select option 1 (**Start computer with CD-ROM support**).

2. If you're still using your old hard drive, format drive C by typing **format c:** and pressing **Enter**. (When FORMAT asks if you're sure, press **Y** and **Enter**. Note that the formatting will take quite a while.)

3. Create a folder named **WIN98** on your hard disk by entering the following commands (type one command at a time, and press **Enter** after each one):

    ```
    c:
    md \win98
    ```

4. Insert your Windows 98 CD-ROM.

5. Copy the Windows 98 Setup files from the CD-ROM to this new folder by entering the following command (replace *drive* with the letter of your CD-ROM drive) and pressing **Enter**:

    ```
    copy drive:\win98\*.* c:\win98
    ```

6. Enter the following commands (again, replace *drive* with the letter of your CD-ROM drive):

    ```
    copy drive:\tools\sysrec\pcrestor.bat c:\
    copy drive:\tools\sysrec\msbatch.inf c:\
    ```

7. At this point, the DOS prompt should be C:\>. If it's not, enter the following commands:

    ```
    c:
    cd\
    ```

8. Type **pcrestor** and press **Enter**.

9. Once you've read the welcome message, press any key. The Windows 98 Setup begins.

10. Once Setup is complete, the System Recovery Wizard loads, as shown in the following figure. The initial dialog box offers an overview of the process, so click **Next**. System Recovery prompts you to enter your name and company name.

The System Recovery Wizard takes you through the process of restoring your system to its pre-crash state.

11. Enter your name and (optionally) your company name, then click **Next**. System Recovery lets you know that it is about to restore your system.

12. Insert the backup media that contains your full system backup.

13. In the final Wizard dialog box, click **Finish**. System Recovery launches Microsoft Backup.

14. Use Backup to restore your files. When Backup asks if you want to restore the Registry and the hardware and software settings within the Registry, make sure you select **Yes**.

15. When the restore process is done, Backup will ask if you want to restart. Click **Yes** and, when Windows 98 restarts, your system will be completely recovered.

From Here

This chapter shows you how to prepare for a system crash by working with an emergency boot disk. I began by explaining what a boot disk is, why you need one, and how it works. From there, you learned how to create the disk and how to use it to "boot from a floppy." For good measure, I also showed you how to create a separate VirusScan Emergency Disk just in case a virus attack is the cause of your hard disk dilemma. Finally, you learned how to use Windows 98's new System Recovery feature, just in case your hard disk is a write-off.

To complete your system tools education, Chapter 19, "For the Nerd In You: Higher-End System Tools," takes a look at some of the more powerful programs found in Windows 98's toolchest.

For the Nerd in You: Higher-End System Tools

In This Chapter

➤ Getting the inside scoop on your machine with the System Information utility

➤ Ensuring system integrity with System File Checker and Registry Checker

➤ Custom startups with the System Configuration utility

➤ Pacifying warring files with the Version Conflict Manager

➤ Scheduling routine tasks with the Task Scheduler

➤ A baker's dozen (minus 7) of Windows 98's best and brightest system tools

In *The Complete Idiot's Guide to Windows 98* and so far in this book, you've seen quite a few of the system tools, including the most practical ones: Backup, ScanDisk, Disk Cleanup, Disk Defragmenter, and the Maintenance Wizard. You might think that the rest of the stuff in the System Tools menu should be labeled "For Geeks Only" and forgotten about. You'd be surprised. Although the other tool tidbits definitely have a higher-end flavor to them, they're really quite palatable and nutritious (from a system point of view). In this chapter, you'll sample a half dozen of these tools: System Information, System File Checker, Registry Checker, System Configuration utility, Version Conflict Manager, and Task Scheduler.

Knowledge is Power: The System Information Utility

One of the keys to troubleshooting a troubled system is being able to examine the computer's innards for signs of where things went awry. Windows 98 has no shortage of ways to get inside information about your machine, but the most comprehensive by far is the System Information utility. This handy little program crams into its display just about every conceivable chunk of data that relates to your system configuration. Most of this data isn't even close to comprehensible for the likes of you and me, but it can be invaluable to a technical-support engineer or computer repairperson.

To try out this utility, select **Start | Programs | Accessories | System Tools | System Information** to display the window shown in the following figure. The System Information pane on the left presents you with a list of categories. The pane on the right displays the data associated with each category.

Windows 98's System Information utility tells you everything you always wanted to know about your system.

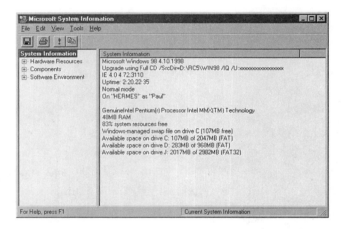

The top-level **System Information** item displays some basic data about your system. Here's a summary of what you find in the other major categories:

➤ **Resources**   These categories display information on the hardware resources used by your computer.

➤ **Components**   These categories display specific information about the devices attached to your computer. The categories include **Multimedia**, **Display**, and **Network**. There's also a **History** category that provides you with a chronological account of the changes you've made to your system.

➤ **Software Environment**   These categories are devoted to the programs, applets, and device drivers on your system. You can find out about all the device drivers installed (including version numbers and descriptions), the tasks that are currently running, the programs that run at startup, and much more.

You can also perform the following tasks within the System Information window:

➤ To save this data to a System Information file (an MSInfo file type that uses the .**NFO** extension), select **File | Save**, use the **Save Copy As** dialog box to choose a location and enter a filename (without the extension), and then click **Save**. The file you end up with is a whopper: over 1MB! Still, it's small enough to save on a floppy disk for safekeeping.

➤ To export the data to a text file, select **File | Export**, use the **Save As** dialog box to pick out a location and enter a filename (again, without the extension), and then click **Save**. The resulting file takes up about 350KB, so you could copy it to a floppy disk.

➤ To print the data, select **File | Print**. Note, however, that I don't recommend doing this since the full printout consists of approximately 100 pages!

Note, too, that the System Information window also gives you quick access to a few of Windows 98's system tools. Just pull down the **Tools** menu and select the program you want to run. Many of these tools (such as the System File Checker discussed next) can only be started from this menu, so you might want to leave System Information open for now.

A Windows Checkup: The System File Checker

If you find that Windows 98 is acting strange (stranger than usual, that is), or if frequent program crashes have got you *this* close to tossing the unruly beast out the window, a system file check may be in order. The system files are the behind-the-scenes components that Windows 98 uses to get its work done. If one of these files is corrupted or missing, or if it has been replaced with an older version by a brain-dead installation program, Windows may go wonky on you.

Windows 98's new System File Checker utility can help you prevent these kinds of problems, and recover from them if they happen. This program takes a snapshot of your system's configuration, and then uses that snapshot as a base from which to compare future configurations. If System File Checker detects corrupted, missing, or replaced system files, it can restore your system to a previously stable configuration.

To run System File Checker, open the System Information utility, and then select **Tools | System File Checker**. You see the window shown in the following figure.

This window appears when you launch System File Checker.

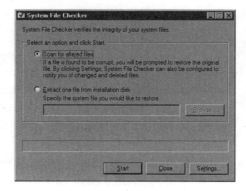

Scanning System Files for Errors

Follow these steps to scan your system files for errors:

1. Make sure the **Scan for altered files** option is activated.

2. Click **Start** to begin the check. As System File Checker goes about its duties, you may see various dialog boxes whenever the program detects a problem. For example, if System File Checker detects a corrupted file, you see the File Corrupted dialog box shown in the following figure.

You see this dialog box if System File Checker detects a corrupted system file.

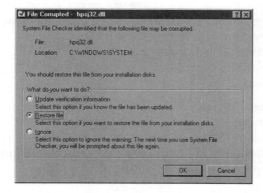

3. Here's a rundown of the options you can work with:

   ➤ **Update verification information**   Choose this option if you're sure there isn't a problem and you want System File Checker to revise its database accordingly.

   ➤ **Restore file**   If you choose this option, System File Checker displays the Restore File dialog box shown in the following figure. Click **OK** to restore the file.

   ➤ **Ignore**   Choose this option to ignore the problem.

4. When the check is complete, System File Checker displays the **Finished** dialog box to let you know. Click **OK** to return to the System File Checker window.

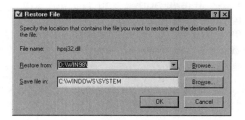

Use the Restore File dialog box to extract a system file from your Windows 98 installation files.

Extracting Files with System File Checker

One common troubleshooting technique that a tech-support engineer or other Windows guru may ask of you is to restore a missing file from the Windows 98 installation disc. Unfortunately, this isn't a simple matter of inserting the CD and copying the necessary file to your hard disk. No, that would be *way* too easy and sensible. The problem is that the Windows 98 files are stored on the CD in a number of *cabinet* files (they use the **.CAB** extension). A cabinet file is a compressed file archive that usually contains dozens of files squished together. To use one of these files, you have to *extract* it from the appropriate cabinet file.

The hard way to do this is to open the cabinet file, highlight the file you want, and then select **File | Extract**. Sound easy? It's not. The hard part is finding the right cabinet file out of the dozens that are available.

Fortunately, you can use System File Checker to easily extract a file from one of the cabinet files. Here are the steps to follow:

1. In the System File Checker window, activate the **Extract one file from installation disk** option.

2. Use the text box to enter the name of the file you want to work with. (Or click **Browse** to pick out the file using the **Select File to Extract** dialog box.)

3. Click **Start**. System File Checker displays the **Extract File** dialog box, which is identical to the Restore File dialog box shown in the previous figure.

4. Use the **Restore from** text box to enter the path to your Windows 98 installation files (or, again, click **Browse**).

5. Use the **Save file in** text box to enter the destination folder for the extracted file. This will usually be the **System** subfolder of your main Windows 98 folder.

6. Click **OK**.

7. When System File Checker reports that the file has been successfully extracted, click **OK**.

Keeping the Registry Regular: The Registry Checker

In Chapter 10, "The Registry: The Soul of the Windows Machine," you saw that the Registry was a database that Windows and Windows programs use to store configuration data. So a smoothly functioning Registry is vital for Windows to work well. For this reason, Windows 98 automatically checks the Registry files at startup for corruption, and it creates backup copies of these files. To run this check, Windows 98 uses a program called Registry Checker.

Although Windows 98 automatically runs Registry Checker at startup, you can run it any time you like. To do so, follow these steps:

1. Open the System Information utility, if it isn't already onscreen.
2. Select **Tools | Registry Checker**. The Windows Registry Checker window appears and immediately begins scanning the Registry.
3. If the Registry Checker finds an error, it replaces the current version of the Registry with the most recent backup copy. Otherwise, the program asks if you want to back up the Registry now. Click **Yes** to back up the Registry, or click **No** to skip this step.
4. If you elected to back up the Registry, click **OK** once the backup is complete.

If something's wrong with Windows 98 and it refuses to start, a Registry error may be the culprit. In this case, you should follow these steps:

1. Restart your computer and hold down the **Ctrl** key to display the Windows 98 **Startup** menu.
2. Select the **Command prompt only** option.
3. When you get to the DOS prompt, type the following command and press **Enter**:

   ```
   scanreg /autorun
   ```

4. When the scan is complete, press **Ctrl+Alt+Delete** to restart your computer.

Update Your Emergency Boot Disk

The Registry Checker is an indispensable troubleshooting tool, so I recommend adding it to your emergency boot disk (see Chapter 18, "A Windows Lifeline: The Emergency Boot Disk"). That way, if a Registry problem prevents you from accessing your hard drive, you can boot to the floppy disk and run **SCANREG /AUTORUN** to restore the Registry.

To update your emergency boot disk, use Windows Explorer or My Computer to copy the file **SCANREG.EXE** from the **Command** subfolder of your main Windows 98 folder.

Streamlining Startups with the System Configuration Utility

In Chapter 1, "Beginning at the Beginning: Windows 98 Startup Techniques," I told you about the Windows 98 startup. In particular, you learned to use the Windows 98 **Startup** menu to change the way Windows 98 loads, which can be useful for troubleshooting or bypassing startup snags. For example, selecting the **Step-by-step confirmation** command tells Windows 98 to ask you whether it should load each of its startup components. By using this method, you can often see exactly where an error crops up, and you can bypass the offending component on subsequent startups.

That's a workable technique, but it's a bit tedious. Luckily, there's another way to control the startup that's both easier *and* more powerful. It's a system tool called the System Configuration utility. To check it out, open the System Information utility and then select **Tools | System Configuration Utility**. The following figure shows the window that appears.

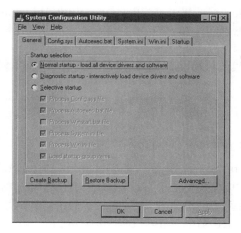

Use the System Configuration utility to define custom Windows 98 startups.

This utility modifies some of the Windows 98 startup files, so the first thing you should always do is create backup copies of these files:

1. In the **General** tab, click **Create Backup**.
2. When the program tells you that your files have been backed up, click **OK**.

If something gets messed up, click the **Restore Backup** button to put things back the way they were.

Okay, now you can play with the various settings without any worries. The whole idea behind the System Configuration utility is to give you an easy method for deciding which components are loaded at startup. To do this, the program offers six tabs:

➤ **General**   This tab offers three startup options:

> **Normal startup**   Select this option to load Windows 98 normally.

> **Diagnostic startup**   Select this option to automatically display the Windows 98 **Startup** menu at boot time.

> **Selective startup**   Select this option to enable the various check boxes below it. Deactivating any of these check boxes tells Windows 98 to bypass the component (such as **Config.sys**).

➤ **Config.sys**, **Autoexec.bat**, **System.ini**, and **Win.ini**   These tabs deal with specific startup files and offer check boxes for each component within those files. You can prevent a component from loading at startup by deactivating its check box.

➤ **Startup**   This tab lists the various tasks and modules that Windows 98 runs at startup (including any items in your Startup menu). You know the drill by now: deactivate the check boxes beside any items that you don't want loaded.

When you've made your choices, click **OK**. When Windows 98 asks if you want to restart your computer, click **Yes**.

Peace Negotiations: Using the Version Conflict Manager

In Windowsland, a *dynamic link library* (DLL) is a special file (it uses the .**DLL** extension) that contains programming code used by an application (or by Windows itself). Now consider the following DLL factoids:

➤ A program won't work if its DLL files aren't installed. Therefore, the installation programs of most applications make sure that the required DLLs are loaded onto your system.

➤ Many DLL functions are used by multiple programs, so it's not unusual for several applications to make use of the same DLL file.

➤ Many common DLL files go through several versions as features are added or improved.

So what? Well, theoretically, the installation program is supposed to check to see whether an existing version of a DLL already exists on the system. If it does, the program is then supposed to check whether that version is newer or older than the one the application comes with. If the existing file is newer, the program will usually do nothing; if the existing file is older, the program will usually replace the file. However, there are plenty of moronic installation programs that don't perform these checks and just install all their files without even so much as a how-do-you-do.

This DLL confusion was one of the major causes of program crashes in Windows 95. Realizing this, Microsoft did something about it in Windows 98. Now, when a program replaces a DLL file (or any common system file, for that matter), Windows 98 creates a backup copy. This way, if a new system file causes problems, the previous file is still available and can be restored.

Windows 98 also includes a program to make this restoration process easier: Version Conflict Manager. Here's how it works:

1. Open the System Information utility, if it isn't already lounging on the desktop.

2. Select **Tools | Version Conflict Manager**. The Version Conflict Manager window shows up, as shown in the following figure.

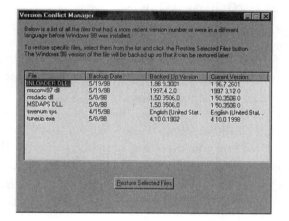

Use the Version Conflict Manager to restore system files.

3. This window lists the system files (most of which, as you can see, are DLL files) that have backup copies available. Highlight the file or files you want to restore.

4. Click **Restore Selected Files**. Version Conflict Manager restores the file and then exits.

Note that all this program does is switch the current copy of the file with the backed-up copy. Therefore, you can reverse the procedure simply by performing these same steps over again.

Hands-Free Windows: The Task Scheduler

In *The Complete Idiot's Guide to Windows 98*, I showed you how to use the Maintenance Wizard to schedule regular maintenance chores that run automatically. The engine under the Maintenance Wizard's hood is a system tool called the Task Scheduler. Its purpose in life is to act as a sort of girl Friday for Windows 98. That is, you tell the Task Scheduler to perform a particular task (such as running ScanDisk) on a particular schedule (such as daily at 3:00 a.m.), and the program handles all the dirty work for you.

The Maintenance Wizard is a nice front-end for the Task Scheduler, but the latter can handle more than just maintenance chores. Just about any Windows program is fair scheduling game, so there are lots of ways to use Task Scheduler.

Task Scheduler is really a folder on your system called **Scheduled Tasks**. To display it, you have two choices:

➤ Select **Start** I **Programs** I **Accessories** I **System Tools** I **Scheduled Tasks**.

➤ In Windows Explorer, highlight **Scheduled Tasks** in the **All Folders** list.

Adding a New Scheduled Task

To create a new scheduled task, follow these steps:

1. Open the **Add Scheduled Task** icon. This launches the Add Scheduled Task wizard.
2. The first dialog box presents an overview. Click **Next** to proceed.
3. Now the wizard takes a minute or two to scour your system and gather a list of all your programs, which it then displays in a dialog box. Click the program that you want to schedule. If the item you want to schedule isn't in this list, click **Browse**, use the **Select Program to Schedule** dialog box to choose the program, and then click **Open**. When you're ready to move on, click **Next**.
4. The wizard prompts you for a name and to choose the frequency with which this task is to be run (see the following figure). Enter a name, select a schedule option, and then click **Next**.

Enter a name and frequency for the new task.

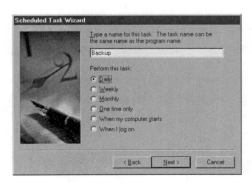

5. The next dialog box that appears depends on the schedule you chose for your task. For example, the following figure shows the wizard dialog box that shows up if you choose the Daily schedule. Specify the exact schedule you want and then click **Next**.

Set up a schedule for the task.

6. The last wizard dialog box appears. Note that this dialog box has an **Open the advanced properties of the task when I click Finish** check box. If you activate this check box and click **Finish**, the wizard opens the **Properties** dialog box for the task. See "Modifying a Scheduled Task's Properties," later in this chapter.

Working with Scheduled Tasks

The following figure shows the **Scheduled Tasks** folder with a few tasks set up. The five columns (activate **View | Details** to see them) tell you the name of the task, its schedule, the date and time of the next and last run, and the status of the last run.

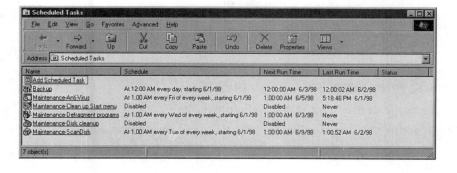

The Scheduled Tasks folder with a few scheduled tasks.

Here are some techniques you can use to work with scheduled tasks:

➤ To run a scheduled task right away, highlight the task and select **File | Run**.

➤ If a task is running, you can stop it by selecting **File | End Scheduled Task**.

➤ To remove a task, highlight it and select **File | Delete**. When Task Scheduler asks you to confirm, click **Yes**.

➤ To suspend all the scheduled tasks, select **Advanced | Pause Task Scheduler**. To resume operations, select **Advanced | Continue Task Scheduler**.

➤ If you no longer want to use Task Scheduler at all, select **Advanced | Stop Using Task Scheduler**. To enable Task Scheduler, select **Advanced | Start Using Task Scheduler**.

Modifying a Scheduled Task's Properties

Each scheduled task has various properties that control the program's executable file, how it runs, which folder it runs in, and more. To view and modify these properties, highlight a task and then select **File | Properties**. The following figure shows an example of the dialog box that appears.

The properties sheet for the scheduled Backup program.

Here are the properties you get to play with on the **Task** tab:

➤ **Run**   This is the name of the file that starts the program.

➤ **Start in**   This specifies the drive and folder that the program should use as its default.

➤ **Comments**   Use this text box to enter your own comments or notes regarding the task.

➤ **Enabled (scheduled task runs at specified time)**   This check box toggles the task on and off.

You can use the **Schedule** tab to change the task's schedule. Use the **Schedule Task** list to choose the frequency with which you want the task to run, and then use the controls that appear (which vary depending on the frequency you selected) to set the specifics of the schedule.

If you'd like to set up two or more schedules for a task, activate the **Show multiple schedules** check box. This adds a new list box to the top of the **Schedule** tab, as shown in the following figure. Click **New** to start a new schedule.

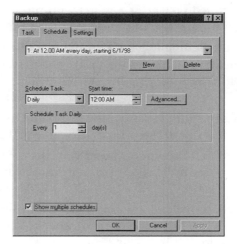

Activating the Show multiple schedules check box adds a drop-down list to the Schedule tab.

The **Schedule** tab also has an **Advanced** button that displays the **Advanced Schedule Options** dialog box. Here are the available options:

➤ **Start Date**   Use this calendar control to set the date the task starts.

➤ **End Date**   Activate this check box and then use the calendar control to set the last date this task should run.

➤ **Repeat task**   If the preset schedules aren't exactly what you need, activate this check box and then use the controls to specify a custom interval:

   Every   Set the interval in minutes or hours.

   Until   Some programs might not shut down automatically after they complete their mission. Rather than leave these programs running, you can ensure that they shut down by activating either **Time** or **Duration** and setting a cutoff point for the task.

➤ **If the task is still running, stop it at this time**   If the program is still running by the time the deadline rolls around, it might be that the program is hung or stuck. To allow for this possibility, you should leave this check box activated so that Task Scheduler shuts down the program if it's still running at the specified time.

Here's a quick look at the controls on the **Settings** tab, shown in the following figure:

➤ **Delete the scheduled task when finished**   If you want your task to run only once, activate this check box to have Task Scheduler delete it for you when the task is done.

➤ **Stop the scheduled task after *x* hours *y* minutes**   Use these controls to set an upper limit on the amount of time the task can run.

➤ **Only start the scheduled task if computer is idle for**   If you activate this check box, Task Scheduler won't run the task if you're still using your computer. Use the spinner to set the number of minutes your machine must be idle before the task begins.

➤ **If computer is not idle at scheduled start time, retry for up to**   Use this spinner to set the number of minutes Task Scheduler will wait for idle time.

➤ **Stop the scheduled task if computer is in use**   If you activate this check box, Task Scheduler shuts down the task if you start using your computer while the task is running.

➤ **Don't start scheduled task if computer is running on batteries**   When this option is turned on, Task Scheduler will check to see whether your notebook is on battery power and, if it is, it won't run the task.

➤ **Stop the scheduled task if battery mode changes**   When this check box is on, Task Scheduler will shut down a running task if your notebook switches from AC to batteries.

The Settings tab.

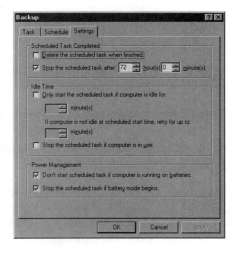

From Here

This chapter closed out your look at more Windows 98 system tools by checking out another half dozen programs: System Information utility, System File Checker, Registry Checker, System Configuration utility, Version Conflict Manager, and Task Scheduler. Although I billed these programs as "higher-end" tools, you saw that they weren't all that hard to use, and that they could be quite useful even for non-nerds.

Now it's time to switch gears a little. In Part 5, "Hardware Hootenanny: More Device Advice," I'll help you to understand the often arcane world of Windows 98's hardware support.

Part 5
Hardware Hootenanny: More Device Advice

Getting the most out of Windows 98 usually means grabbing software by the scruff of the neck and giving its options and settings a good shake. However, Windows 98 is also a creature of its hardware home, so mastering Windows 98 also means poking and prodding a peripheral or two. Fortunately, this doesn't mean you have to become a wirehead (a person with an intimate knowledge of hardware). As you'll see here in Part 5, Windows 98 has quite a few features that give you easy access to device settings and setup.

Chapter 20

Using Device Manager to Take Control of Your Hardware

Windows 98 comes with a hatful of "free" programs that you can use for word processing, graphics, and wandering the World Wide Web. However, these programs are mere accoutrements that dangle from Windows 98's *real* purpose: being an *operating system*. There are as many definitions of an operating system as there are Porsches in Silicon Valley. However, the basic idea is that an operating system acts as a kind of electronic go-between.

From your perspective, Windows 98's middleman duties include grabbing your keystrokes or mouse clicks and passing them along to the application you're using, making sure messages from your applications get displayed on the screen, and so on.

Windows 98 also has lots of internal intermediary chores to perform, such as making sure applications have enough memory and don't tread on each other's digital toes.

Hardware support also falls into this category. One of Windows 98's most crucial jobs is to translate incomprehensible "devicespeak" into something your software can make sense out of, and it must ensure that devices are ready, willing, and able to carry out software instructions.

Given the thousands of devices available, and the tens of thousands of bells and whistles on those devices, building reliable hardware support into any operating system is a monumental undertaking. Did Microsoft achieve this laudable goal with Windows 98? No, not really. But it's a huge improvement over the primitive hardware support that existed in the long-ago days of Windows 3.*x*. So, if nothing else, it will make your hardware chores easier. This chapter introduces you to Windows 98's hardware support and shows you how to wield its most useful hardware tool: Device Manager.

Understanding Device Mumbo-Jumbo

Installing software is usually a relatively painless affair. You shoehorn a setup disk into the appropriate drive, launch the installation program, and a few minutes later your program is ready to roll.

Hardware, however, is a whole other ball game. Sure, attaching a CD-ROM or a printer to the back of your machine isn't that difficult. Even coaxing internal circuit boards and disk drives into their particular slots or bays isn't a big deal, as long as you're at least minimally dexterous (and can stomach the idea of messing with your computer's innards). No, the real ulcer-causing aspect of hardware installation is the weird device settings you have to deal with. Even if you could somehow decipher the minimalist instructions that come with every device ever made, you still have to use "jumpers" and "DIP switches" to configure the hardware.

What is the purpose of all this? To coax the device into working with your hardware and to avoid conflicts with other devices. For most devices, this requires configuring three resources: the Interrupt Request Line (IRQ), the Input/Output (I/O) port address, and the Direct Memory Access (DMA) channel. The next section explains this hardware hoopla.

IRQs, I/O Ports, and Other Device Doo-Doo

Here are some brief explanations for IRQ lines, I/O ports, and DMA channels:

IRQ line   The microprocessor inside your computer gets confused easily, so it prefers to deal with one thing at a time. Therefore, devices have to electronically tap the processor on the shoulder and say, "Ahem, please deal with me now." For example, when you press a key, your keyboard has to let the processor know that a new keystroke is ready to be sent. This tapping of the processor's shoulder is called an *interrupt request* in technotalk, and the path along which the request travels from the device to the processor is called an *interrupt request line*, or IRQ.

I/O port   This is a memory address that the processor uses to communicate with a device directly. After a device has used its IRQ to catch the attention of the processor, the actual exchange of data or commands takes place through the device's I/O port address.

DMA channel   This is a connection that lets a device transfer data to and from memory without going through the processor.

The basic device dilemma here is that for your hardware to work properly, there cannot be any conflicts:

➤ Although you need a separate IRQ for each device that requires one, only 16 IRQs are available to go around. That might sound like plenty, but many of these IRQs are used by system devices. In the end, most machines have only four or five IRQs for the sound card, mouse port, video adapter, and whatever other devices are stuffed inside the machine. An IRQ conflict—either two devices trying to use the same IRQ or software that thinks a device is using one IRQ when in fact it's using another—is the cause of many hardware problems.

➤ There are 1,024 I/O ports available—more than enough to satisfy all your device needs. As with IRQs, however, no two devices can share an I/O port, so conflicts can lead to problems.

➤ Problems can arise when two devices attempt to use the same DMA channel. This is a rare problem, however, because few devices use DMA and most of the DMA channels are available.

Trying to get a handle on all these hardware acronyms is tricky. Yet, when it comes down to actually configuring these settings, things really get tough. How do you know which resources a device is currently using? If a device isn't working properly, which resource— IRQ, I/O port, or DMA channel—is causing the problem? Is the problem a conflict with an existing device, or is it that the software trying to access the device is referencing the wrong resource?

To help answer these and other questions, the world's hardware hackers realized that two things were needed:

➤ A way to easily see not only which devices are attached to your system, but also which resources they're using and whether there are any conflicts. In Windows 98, this task is handled by the Device Manager.

➤ "Smart" devices and software that can examine the resources currently being used and configure the devices accordingly. The feature that solves this is called Plug and Play.

What's this Plug and Play Stuff About?

I'll get to Device Manager a bit later (see "The Device Database: Device Manager"). For now, though, let's take a closer look at Plug and Play.

In theory, Plug and Play gives you totally automatic device setup and configuration. When you attach a new device, not only does the system recognize that it has a new member in the hardware team, but it also ensures that everyone gets along by automatically configuring things like IRQs and I/O ports to avoid conflicts.

In practice, Plug and Play works pretty well, but not perfectly. What's the difference between true Plug and Play and mere "Plug and Pray" (as some wags call it)? In order for device configuration to be completely automatic, three things must be true:

➤ Your computer must have something called a *Plug and Play BIOS*. The BIOS (Basic Input/Output System) is the code that performs the Power-On Self Test (POST) that I told you about in Chapter 1, "Beginning at the Beginning: Windows 98 Startup Techniques." If you have a system with a Plug and Play BIOS, during the POST it talks to all the Plug and Play–compatible devices on the system. It gathers the devices' resource configurations, checks for resource conflicts, and, if there are any problems, it takes steps to resolve them. Most computers sold today have a Plug and Play BIOS. If you're thinking of investing in a new system, be sure to put this type of BIOS on your "must have" list.

➤ Your computer must use only Plug and Play devices. This may be the most important aspect because a Plug and Play BIOS isn't worth a hill of beans if it doesn't have Plug and Play–compatible devices to talk to. Luckily, most new devices support Plug and Play, but you should definitely check this out when buying a new peripheral.

➤ You computer must use a Plug and Play operating system, such as Windows 98 (or Windows 95).

If you don't have all three components, Plug and Play might or might not work. If you *do* have all three, then Plug and Play works like a charm. I have the Big Three on my newest computer, and I haven't had to think about IRQs and I/O ports for months (until writing this chapter, that is).

Device Drivers: Hardware Helpers

I mentioned earlier that Windows 98 acts as a middleman between your programs and your hardware. For example, when you ask a program to print something, it's Windows 98 that negotiates the print job. However, Windows 98 doesn't actually get its hands dirty by dealing with devices directly. Instead, it calls upon a helper program called a *device driver*. This is a small chunk of programming code that is intimately familiar with the inner workings of a particular device. Windows 98 doesn't give a hoot *how* the device does its thing. Instead, it just tells the driver that it wants the device to perform a particular task ("Print this file!"). The device driver then busies itself translating the request into something the device can understand, and Windows 98 moves on to more productive matters.

Installing a New Device Driver

Windows 98 comes with all kinds of device drivers for all kinds of devices, and hardware manufacturers usually create their own versions of drivers for their devices. In fact, one of the most common hardware troubleshooting techniques is to get and install a new version of the device driver from the manufacturer. Most companies offer the latest drivers on their Web site, bulletin board system, or on a disk. Once you get the new driver, you have to install it, of course. You can use either Device Manager (see "Changing Drivers Via Device Manager," later in this chapter), or the Add New Hardware wizard. For the latter, follow these steps:

1. Select **Start | Settings | Control Panel**, and then open the **Add New Hardware** icon in the Control Panel. Windows 98 displays the first of the Add New Hardware wizard's dialog boxes.

2. Click **Next** to continue. The next wizard dialog box tells you that it will search for Plug and Play devices.

3. Click **Next**.

4. How you proceed from here depends on what the wizard finds:

   ➤ If the wizard finds one or more new Plug and Play devices, you'll eventually see a list of the installed devices. In this list, make sure you select the **No, I want to install other devices** option, and then click **Next**.

   ➤ If the wizard found new Plug and Play devices, but there are problems with those devices, you'll see a different list. In this case, activate the **No, the device isn't in the list** options, and then click **Next**.

5. The wizard now tells you that it will attempt to detect your hardware. You don't want to do this, so activate the **No, I want to select the hardware from a list** option, and then click **Next**. The wizard displays a list of hardware categories, as shown in the following figure.

6. In the **Hardware types** list, highlight the hardware category for your device and click **Next**. The wizard displays the Select Device dialog box.

7. Click the **Have Disk** button. (If you have a disk from the manufacturer, insert the disk now.) The **Install From Disk** dialog box appears.

8. In the **Copy manufacturer's files from** text box, enter the appropriate drive and folder where the device driver is stored. (Or click **Browse** to select the folder using a dialog box.) Windows 98 displays a list of possible device drivers.

The wizard displays this list of hardware categories.

9. Highlight the driver you want to install, and then click **Next**.

10. If Windows 98 asks whether you want to restart your computer, remove any floppy disks you may have inserted, and then click **Yes** to reboot and put the new driver into effect.

The Device Database: Device Manager

Back in Chapter 10, "The Registry: The Soul of the Windows Machine," I told you that Windows 98 stores all of its hardware information inside the Registry. However, although it would be possible to use the Registry Editor to adjust device settings, Windows 98 offers a much easier method: Device Manager. To display Device Manager, use either of the following techniques:

➤ Select **Start | Settings | Control Panel**, and then open the **System** icon in the Control Panel.

➤ Right-click **My Computer** and click **Properties** in the shortcut menu.

In the **System Properties** dialog box that appears, select the **Device Manager** tab. As you can see in the following figure, Device Manager gives you a nice graphical representation of your hardware.

The default display is a treelike outline that lists various hardware categories (**CDROM**, **Disk drives**, and so on). To see the specific devices, click the plus sign (+) to the left of a device category. For example, opening the **Disk drives** category displays all the disk drives attached to your computer, as shown in the following figure.

If you like, you can also view the devices according to the component to which they're connected by activating the **View devices by connection** option button.

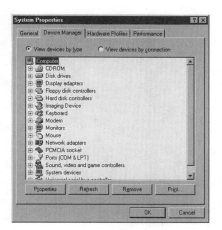

Device Manager shows you a visual representation of all the devices on your system.

Real Mode Versus Protected Mode

Device drivers come in two flavors: real mode and protected mode. A *real mode* device driver is, basically, a DOS device driver. Windows 98 uses mostly *protected mode* device drivers, which are faster, more reliable, and use less memory.

Windows 98 ships with hundreds of protected-mode drivers for specific devices. This is why, as I mentioned in Chapter 1, you can probably do away with **CONFIG.SYS** and **AUTOEXEC.BAT**, since it's their job to load real-mode drivers. In most cases, this is a simple matter of renaming your **CONFIG.SYS** and **AUTOEXEC.BAT** files (to, for example, **CONFIG.WIN** and **AUTOEXEC.WIN**) and then rebooting. Because Windows 98's Setup program made a note of all the devices in your startup files, it should automatically pick up the slack for each device by loading the appropriate protected-mode driver.

If, after trying this technique, you find that one of your devices isn't working properly, Windows 98 probably doesn't have the correct protected-mode driver. In this case, you need to make two adjustments:

➤ Restore **CONFIG.SYS** or **AUTOEXEC.BAT** (whichever one loads the necessary real-mode driver).

➤ Edit **CONFIG.SYS** or **AUTOEXEC.BAT** to comment out the lines that load real-mode drivers that *do* have a protected-mode counterpart in Windows 98. (You comment out a line by adding **REM** and a space to the beginning of the line.)

Reboot your machine when you're done. You should then contact the manufacturer of the device to obtain an updated protected-mode driver. When you get it, follow the instructions given in this section for installing new device drivers.

Opening a hardware category shows you the specific devices within that category that are attached to your computer.

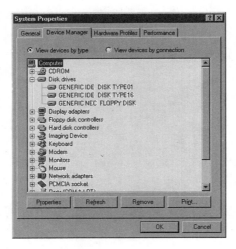

Viewing Devices by the Resources They Use

One of Device Manager's most welcome features is its capability to show you a list of your devices according to the hardware resources they use. To try this, highlight the **Computer** item at the top of the list, and then click the **Properties** button. Device Manager then displays the **Computer Properties** dialog box. Use the option buttons at the top of the dialog box to select the type of resource you want to view. For example, the following figure shows this dialog box with the **Interrupt request (IRQ)** option selected.

Use the Computer Properties dialog box to view your devices by specific resources.

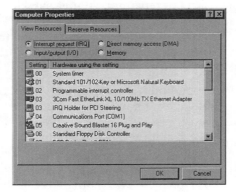

Printing a System Report

Device Manager won't do you a lick of good if you're having some kind of hardware problem that prevents you from starting Windows 98. That might never happen, but just in case it does, you should print a hard copy of the device data. Here's how you do it:

312

1. If you want a printout of only a specific hardware category or device, use the **Device Manager** list to highlight the category or device.

2. Click the **Print** button to display the **Print** dialog box shown in the following figure.

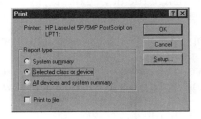

You can get a printout of your system's device information.

3. In the **Report type** group, select one of the following report options:

   ➤ **System summary**   This report gives you a summary of how the resources (IRQs, and so on) are being used on your system.

   ➤ **Selected class or device**   This report prints the driver and resource data for the highlighted hardware category or device.

   ➤ **All devices and system summary**   This report gets you both the summary of resource usage on your system and the driver and resource data for every device.

4. To make printer adjustments, click **Setup**, select the options you want from the **Print Setup** dialog box, and click **OK**.

5. Click **OK** to print the report.

Getting Rid of a Device

If your computer has a Plug and Play BIOS and you remove a device, the BIOS informs Windows 98 that the device is no longer present. Windows 98, in turn, updates its device list in the Registry, and the peripheral no longer appears in the **Device Manager** tab.

If you don't have a Plug and Play BIOS, but the device you're removing is Plug and Play–compliant, Windows 98 figures out that the device is missing and updates its records accordingly.

If you're removing a non–Plug and Play device, however, you need to tell Device Manager that the device no longer exists. To do that, highlight the device in the **Device Manager** tab and click the **Remove** button. If you've defined multiple hardware profiles (as described later in the "Setting Up Hardware Profiles" section), Windows 98 will ask whether you want to remove the device from all the profiles or just from a specific profile. Select the appropriate option. When Windows 98 warns you that you're about to remove the device, click **OK**.

Checking Out Device Properties

Like just about everything else in Windows 98, each device listed in the Device Manager has its own set of properties. You can use these properties not only to learn more about the device (such as the resources it's currently using), but also to make adjustments to the device's resources, change the device driver, alter the device's settings (if it has any), and make other changes.

To display the properties for a device, highlight the device in the **Device Manager** tab, and then click **Properties**. The following figure shows the properties for a sound card. The **General** tab tells you the name of the device and its hardware category, the manufacturer's name, and the hardware version (if known). The **Device status** group tells you whether the device is working properly. You use the **Device usage** group to add and remove devices from hardware profiles (see "Setting Up Hardware Profiles" later in this chapter).

The properties for a sound card.

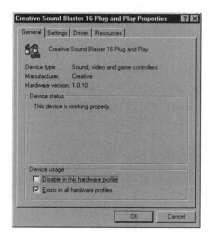

Besides this general information, a device's properties sheet includes a wealth of other useful data. Depending on the device, the properties sheet can also tell you the resources used by the device, the device driver, and miscellaneous settings specific to the device. I cover each of these items in the next few sections.

Viewing and Adjusting a Device's Resources

To view the resources being used by the device (if any), select the **Resources** tab, shown in the following figure. The two-column list shows you the **Resource type** on the left and the resource **Setting** on the right. If you suspect that the device has a resource conflict, check the **Conflicting device list** to see whether any devices are listed. If the list displays only **No conflicts**, the device's resources aren't conflicting with another device.

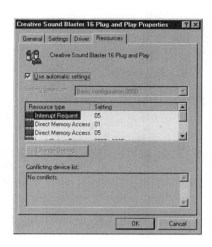

The Resources tab outlines the resources used by the device.

However, if you do have a conflict, you need to change the appropriate resource. Some devices have multiple configurations, so one easy way to change resources is to select a different configuration. To try this, deactivate the **Use automatic settings** check box, and use the **Setting based on** drop-down list to select a different configuration.

Otherwise, you need to play around with the resource settings by hand. Here are the steps to follow to change a resource setting:

1. In the **Resource type** list, highlight the resource you want to change.

2. Deactivate the **Use automatic settings** check box, if it's activated.

3. For the setting you want to change, highlight it and click the **Change Setting** button. You'll see an **Edit** dialog box similar to the one shown in the following figure. (If, instead, Device Manager tells you that **This resource setting cannot be modified**, then you're out of luck.)

Use this dialog box to change an IRQ. Other resources display similar dialog boxes.

315

4. Use the **Value** spinner to select a different resource. Watch the **Conflict information** group to make sure that your new setting doesn't step on the toes of an existing setting.

5. Click **OK** to return to the **Resources** tab.

6. Click **OK** to return to Device Manager.

7. If Windows 98 asks whether you want to restart your computer, click **Yes**.

Changing Drivers Via the Device Manager

If you need to change the device's driver (for example, if you've obtained an updated driver from the manufacturer), you can do it from Device Manager. Here's how it works:

1. In the device's **Properties** dialog box, display the **Driver** tab.

2. Click the **Upgrade Driver** button to start the Upgrade Device Driver wizard.

3. Click **Next** and the wizard displays a dialog box with two options:

   ➤ **Search for a better driver than the one your device is using now**   Choose this option to have Windows 98 search your disk drives or even the Internet for a more recent driver. If you have a disk from the manufacturer, insert it into the appropriate drive now.

   ➤ **Create a list of all the drivers in a specific location, so you can select the driver you want**   Choose this option to select a driver from a list of the devices that Windows 98 can work with.

4. Click **Next** to proceed.

5. If you asked Windows 98 to search for a better driver, the wizard displays the dialog box shown in the following figure. Activate the appropriate check boxes, and then click **Next**. If you activated the **Microsoft Windows Update** option, Windows 98 connects to the Windows Update site on the Internet. (Note that you must register your copy of Windows 98 before you can access the online driver updates.) If the wizard finds a better driver, follow the instructions onscreen to install and configure the driver.

6. If you opted to select the driver you want from the Windows 98 list, you see a dialog box similar to the one shown in the following figure. There are three ways to proceed from here:

   ➤ If the new device driver you want is shown in the **Models** list, highlight it and click **OK**.

   ➤ If you don't see the device, activate the **Show all hardware** option to display the full list of available drivers. Highlight the appropriate device manufacturer in the **Manufacturers** list, highlight the driver you want in the **Models** list, then click **OK**.

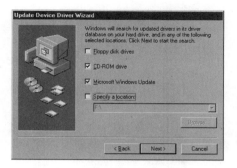

Select the locations the wizard should search for a newer driver.

➤ If you have a disk from the manufacturer, insert the disk, and then click the **Have Disk** button. In the **Install from Disk** dialog box, enter the appropriate drive and folder in the **Copy manufacturer's files from** box and click **OK**. Windows 98 displays a list of possible device drivers in the Select Device dialog box. Highlight the driver you want to install and click **OK**.

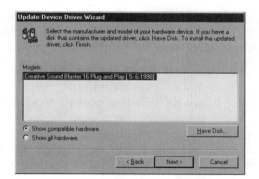

Use this dialog box to pick the new driver for the device.

7. At this point, Windows 98 will likely ask whether you want to restart your computer. Remove any floppy disks you may have inserted and click **Yes** to reboot and put the new driver into effect.

Adjusting Device Settings

Some devices have a **Settings** tab in their **Properties** dialog box that lets you set various options specific to the device. For a CD-ROM drive, for example, you can specify the drive letter to use and whether the drive runs the Windows 98 AutoPlay feature (see the figure below).

317

For some devices, you can use the Settings tab to adjust various device parameters.

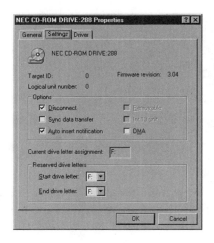

Setting Up Hardware Profiles

Software applications come and go, but hardware tends to remain the same. Even when you add or remove a computer appliance, Windows 98 merely updates its current hardware configuration to compensate.

In some situations, however, you might need to switch between hardware configurations regularly. A good example is a notebook computer with a docking station. When the computer is undocked, it uses its built-in keyboard, mouse, and screen; when the computer is docked, however, it probably uses a separate keyboard, mouse, and screen. To make it easier to switch between these different configurations, Windows 98 lets you set up each configuration as a *hardware profile*. It then becomes a simple matter of your selecting the profile you want to use at startup; Windows 98 handles the hard part of loading the appropriate drivers.

Hardware Profiles and Plug and Play

You don't need to bother with hardware profiles if your computer has a Plug and Play BIOS and you're using Plug and Play devices. Plug and Play detects any new hardware configuration automatically and adjusts accordingly. For example, Plug and Play supports hot docking of a notebook computer: While the machine is running, you can insert or remove it from the docking station, and Plug and Play handles the switch without breaking a sweat.

Here are the steps to create a new hardware profile:

1. In the **System Properties** dialog box, select the **Hardware Profiles** tab. On most systems, you see a single profile named **Original Configuration**, as shown in the following figure. This profile includes all your installed device drivers.

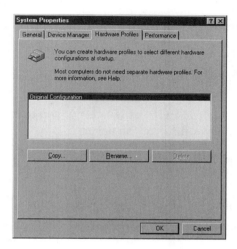

The Hardware Profiles tab lists the currently defined profiles.

2. Click the **Copy** button. Windows 98 displays the **Copy Profile** dialog box.
3. Enter a name for the new profile and click **OK**.

Now that you have multiple profiles in place, you need to tell Windows 98 which devices go with which profile. Windows 98 is now using the "Original Configuration" profile. If this is the one you want to work with, fine; just follow the steps later in this section. Otherwise, you need reboot your computer.

How does Windows 98 know which profile to use at startup? Generally, it goes by the current hardware configuration. For example, if you have a hardware profile that uses an external keyboard, Windows 98 will use this profile at startup if it detects an attached keyboard.

Note, however, that all the devices in a profile must match the physical devices present in the system before Windows 98 will use a profile automatically. If there is some ambiguity (that is, the physical devices don't match the devices specified in the profile), Windows 98 will display a menu of hardware profiles at startup. This menu will be similar to the following example:

```
Windows cannot determine what configuration your computer is in.
Select one of the following:
```

```
1. Undocked
2. Docked
3. None of the above

Enter your choice:
```

In this case, you need to select the hardware profile you want Windows 98 to use.

Once you're back in Windows 98, follow these steps:

1. Display the **System Properties** dialog box and select the **Device Manager** tab.
2. Highlight a device that you want to adjust, and then click **Properties**.
3. In the **General** tab's **Device usage** group, you may see one or more of the following three choices, depending on the device:

    ➤ **Disable in this hardware profile**   If you activate this check box, Windows leaves the device in the current hardware profile, but the device is disabled.

    ➤ **Remove from this hardware profile**   Activate this check box to take the device out of the current hardware profile.

    ➤ **Exists in all hardware profiles**   Use this check box to add or remove a device from all your profiles—even new profiles that you create later on.

The Properties dialog box for a device lets you include or exclude the device from each profile.

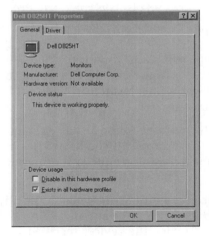

4. Click **OK** to return to the **Device Manager** tab.
5. Repeat steps 5–8 to adjust other devices.
6. Click **Close** to shut down the **System Properties** dialog box.
7. Restart your system.

From Here

This chapter introduced you to the strange world of hardware devices. I began by making you suffer through explanations of IRQs, I/O ports, and DMA channels. With your brain still screaming, I then explained Plug and Play and device drivers. Luckily, you then moved on to more practical matters, including installing device drivers and using the Device Manager. I closed by showing you how to set up hardware profiles.

Chapter 21, "Graphics Gadgetry: Working with Video Cards and Monitors," continues your hardware education by looking at two specific hardware categories: video display cards and monitors.

Graphics Gadgetry: Working with Video Cards and Monitors

In This Chapter

➤ Basic background info on video cards

➤ Letting Windows 98 know what kind of video card you have

➤ Setting the display resolution and color depth

➤ What to look for when buying a monitor

➤ Trying out Windows 98's new multiple-monitor feature

➤ How to get great graphics in Windows 98

The high-IQ types in the lab refer to Windows as a *graphical user interface*. In laymen's lingo, this means that you operate Windows by using icons and images instead of just plain text (like at the DOS prompt). The key word here is *graphical*, so one of the ways to get the most out of Windows is to make sure you're getting the most out of your system's graphics. This means playing around with two chunks of hardware: the video card and the monitor. This chapter introduces you to both components and shows you all the ways that Windows works with them.

No Guts, No Graphics: Working with Video Cards

I'll begin with the video card. The next few sections give you some video card background, show you how to install a device driver for a video card, and explain how to adjust the settings for your video card.

Understanding Video Cards

The video card—it's also known as the *graphics adapter*—is a circuit board that resides inside your computer. Its day job is to accept instructions from Windows 98 about the images that are to appear on the screen. It then passes those instructions along to your monitor for display.

It used to be that video cards relied on the microprocessor to handle most of the dirty work of graphics processing. However, most video cards sold today are *accelerated*. This means that they come with a graphics coprocessor that assumes most of the graphics duties from the main microprocessor, including time-consuming tasks such as drawing lines and circles. The coprocessor is specially designed to handle these tasks, so not only do screens update faster, but the microprocessor is relieved of a massive processing burden. For the most part, as far as graphics are concerned, all that remains for the microprocessor is to send the basic instructions to the graphics card regarding what to draw and where to draw it.

The next few sections run through some video card concepts that you need to know.

Pixel Pushing: Understanding Display Resolution

Display resolution is a measure of the sharpness of an onscreen image. Resolution is expressed as the number of pixels displayed horizontally by the number of pixels displayed vertically. (A pixel is a tiny pinpoint of light.) For example, 640×480 resolution means that there are 640 pixels across the screen and 480 pixels down the screen. Because most screen objects have a fixed size in pixels, the resolution determines how large or small an object appears, and, therefore, how much apparent room you have onscreen.

For example, suppose that you have a dialog box onscreen that is 160 pixels wide and 120 pixels tall. In a 640×480 resolution, this dialog box would take up 1/16th of the desktop area. If you switched to 800×600 resolution, however, the dialog box's dimensions would remain the same, so the dialog box would end up usurping only 1/25th of the desktop. At 1024×768, the same dialog box would fit into a mere 1/40th of the screen.

You can use the various resolutions supported by your video card to enlarge or shrink the desktop. If you move to a higher resolution, objects appear smaller, so, in a virtual sense, you end up with more room. In turn, this lets you either display more windows or make your existing windows larger. Before adjusting the resolution, however, you should keep the following points in mind:

➤ The higher the resolution, the smaller your text will appear. You need to trade extra screen real estate for text readability. (Many applications also let you "zoom" their window contents larger or smaller.)

➤ In most cases, you also need to trade color depth for resolution. Unless you have lots of video memory on your video card, the higher the resolution, the fewer colors you can display (more on this in the next section).

➤ Now match the resolution produced by the video card to that supported by your monitor. For one thing, monitors have a maximum supported resolution, so you won't be able to exceed that. For another, the size of the monitor determines the maximum comfortable resolution: The smaller the monitor, the smaller the resolution you should use. Here are my maximum resolution suggestions for various monitor sizes:

Monitor Size	Suggested Maximum Resolution
13 inches	640×480
14 inches	800×600
15 inches	800×600
17 inches	1024×768
21 inches	1600×1200

I'll tell you how to adjust the display resolution later in this chapter (see "Adapting the Adapter: Setting the Colors and Screen Area").

Counting Colors: Understanding Color Depth

Color depth determines the number of colors available to your applications and graphics. Color depth is expressed either in bits or total colors. The bits value specifies the number of bits each pixel can use to display a color. In the simplest case—a 1-bit display—each pixel could use only two colors: If the bit were 0, the pixel would show black; if the bit were 1, the pixel would show white.

The higher the number of bits, the more combinations a pixel can assume, and the more colors you have available. The minimum realistic color depth is 4-bit, which produces 16 colors in each pixel (because 2 to the power of 4 equals 16). The following table lists the fundamental color depths.

Bits	Colors
4	16
8	256

continues

continued

Bits	Colors
15	32,268
16	65,536 (High Color)
24	16,777,216 (True Color)

If you're working with mainstream business applications, 256 colors are plenty. In multimedia applications, however, you might need to jump up to 16-bit to get the best-looking output. (If you're working with photographic-quality images, you need to use 24-bit for faithful reproduction.)

I'll tell you how to adjust color depth a bit later in the "Adapting the Adapter: Setting the Colors and Screen Area" section.

The Key to It All: Understanding Video Memory

The resolution you can display and the number of colors available at that resolution are both a function of the amount of video memory that's installed on your video card. (Unlike system RAM, video RAM has nothing to do with performance.) To understand why, consider that the current state of each pixel on your screen has to be stored some-where in memory. A screen displayed at 640×480 will have 307,200 pixels and, therefore, will need 307,200 memory locations. However, each pixel also requires a particular number of bits, depending on the color depth. At a 4-bit depth, those 307,200 pixels use 1,228,800 bits, or 153,600 bytes (150KB).

The following table lists various resolutions and color depths and shows the memory required to support each combination. (The Adapter Memory column tells you the minimum amount of memory that needs to be installed in the video card.)

Resolution	Color Depth	Actual Memory in Bytes	Adapter Memory
640×480	4-bit	153,600	256KB
640×480	8-bit	307,200	512KB
640×480	16-bit	614,400	1MB
640×480	24-bit	921,600	1MB
800×600	4-bit	240,000	256KB
800×600	8-bit	480,000	512KB
800×600	16-bit	960,000	1MB
800×600	24-bit	1,440,000	2MB
1024×768	4-bit	393,216	512KB
1024×768	8-bit	786,432	1MB

Resolution	Color Depth	Actual Memory in Bytes	Adapter Memory
1024×768	16-bit	1,572,864	2MB
1024×768	24-bit	2,359,296	4MB
1280×1024	4-bit	655,360	1MB
1280×1024	8-bit	1,310,720	2MB
1280×1024	16-bit	2,621,440	4MB
1280×1024	24-bit	3,932,160	4MB
1600×1200	4-bit	960,000	1MB
1600×1200	8-bit	1,920,000	2MB
1600×1200	16-bit	3,840,000	4MB
1600×1200	24-bit	7,680,000	8MB

Telling Windows About Your Video Card

Windows 98 ships with device drivers for many of the most popular video cards, and the Setup program should install the appropriate driver for you. Even if your video card doesn't come with a Microsoft driver, it's likely that the manufacturer has released its own driver designed to work with Windows 98. (Check the vendor's Internet site or BBS to find out.) So although your old video card drivers will probably work under Windows 98, you should take advantage of the newer drivers if they're available.

Here are the steps to follow to install a video card driver:

1. Use either of the following techniques to display the **Display Properties** dialog box:
   - ➤ Select **Start | Settings | Control Panel**, and then open the **Display** icon.
   - ➤ Right-click the desktop, and then click **Properties** in the menu that appears.
2. Select the **Settings** tab.
3. Click the **Advanced** button. The video card's **Properties** dialog box appears.
4. In the **Adapter** tab, click the **Change** button. Windows 98 launches the Upgrade Device Driver wizard, which I explained in detail in Chapter 20, "Using Device Manager to Take Control of Your Hardware" in the section "Changing Drivers Via the Device Manager.")
5. Follow the wizard's dialog boxes to install your new driver, and then reboot your system.

Troubleshooting a Garbled Display

You might find that your display is a mess when you reboot after installing a new video driver. This probably means one of three things:

➤ You installed the wrong driver.

➤ The driver you're using is corrupt.

➤ The display resolution or color depth is beyond the capacity of the driver.

If this happens, you need to shut down your computer and restart in safe mode (as described in Chapter 1's "Taking Advantage of the Windows 98 Startup Menu" section).

Now hold on just a cotton-picking minute! How the heck do I shut down Windows if I can't see anything onscreen?

Excellent question! Here are the keyboard techniques to use:

➤ If the logon dialog box is displayed, press **Ctrl+Alt+Delete**, and then press **Alt+S** to select the **Shut Down** command.

➤ If you're in Windows 98, press **Ctrl+Esc**, then press **U**, then **S**, then **Enter**.

When Windows 98 restarts, you can troubleshoot the problem (for example, by selecting a different video driver).

Adapting the Adapter: Setting the Colors and Screen Area

Now that you know what display resolution and color depth are all about, you can play around with these settings in Windows 98 to see what you prefer. You use the **Display Properties** dialog box to work with these settings, so you need to get that dialog box onscreen as described earlier. Select the **Settings** tab, as shown in the following figure.

Use the Settings tab to customize your video display.

Here are the steps to follow to set the display resolution:

1. Use the **Screen area** slider to pick out a display resolution. Move the slider to the left to get a lower resolution; move the slider to the right to get a higher resolution.

2. Click **Apply**. Windows 98 lets you know that it is about to resize your desktop.

3. Say "Well, duh" and click **OK**. Windows 98 now asks if you want to keep the new setting.

4. Click **Yes** to keep the new resolution, or click **No** to go back to the old one.

Remember that, as I mentioned earlier, the maximum available resolution depends on your video hardware and the current color depth. So don't be surprised if, when you move the **Screen area** slider to the right, Windows 98 reduces the color depth (as shown in the **Colors** list).

Problem? Windows'll Fix It.

It's possible that changing to the new resolution will give your screen a nervous breakdown. If that happens, just sit tight for about 15 seconds, and Windows 98 will automatically return to the old resolution.

Here's how to set the color depth:

1. Use the **Colors** list to select a color depth.

2. Click **Apply**. Windows 98 displays the **Compatibility Warning** dialog box shown in the next figure.

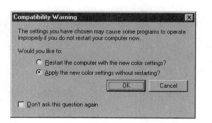

Windows 98 fires this dialog box at you when you change the color depth.

3. Select one of the following options:

   ➤ **Restart the computer with the new color settings?**   If you activate this option, Windows 98 will restart before it changes to the new color depth. Why? Well, some programs—especially games and graphics programs—expect a minimum color depth. If you go below that, you could have problems. If you're not using one of these programs (or don't plan to at this color depth), you don't need to select this option.

➤ **Apply the new color settings without restarting?**   If you activate this option, Windows 98 sets the new color depth on-the-fly. This should work fine in the majority of cases.

4. When you're ready, click **OK**. If you chose the **Restart** option, Windows 98 asks if you want to restart your computer now.

5. Click **Yes** to restart.

If you change color depth frequently, that **Compatibility Warning** dialog box quickly becomes a pain in the you-know-what. Fortunately, Windows 98 gives you two ways to set the default response for color depth changes:

➤ In the **Compatibility Warning** dialog box, choose the option you want to set as the default and activate the **Don't ask this question again** check box.

➤ In the **Settings** tab, click **Advanced**, and then make sure the **General** tab is displayed in the **Properties** dialog box that appears (see the following figure). Use the options in the **Compatibility** group to set the default behavior.

The options in the Compatibility group set the default behavior for color-depth changes.

Image Is Everything: Windows 98 and Your Monitor

Your video card is the one with the pixel-pushing prowess. However, it's your monitor that shows the end result, so it's no less an important component. This section gives you a few pointers to bear in mind when shopping for a monitor. It shows you how to change the monitor type and gives you the steps to follow to give Windows 98's multiple-monitor support a whirl.

The Eyes Have It: What to Look for in a Monitor

If you spend even a moderate amount of time sitting at your computer each day, it may seem like your hands do all the work. However, your eyes have to stare at the monitor most of that time, so they work hard, as well. Whatever the quality of your video card, if your monitor is cheap, you'll end up with a display that's uncomfortable and hard on the eyes. If you're shopping around for a monitor, here are a few things to look for:

➤ Make sure your monitor and video card can work together. For example, if you've purchased a video card that operates at 1,280×1,024 resolution, make sure that your monitor can handle that many pixels as well.

➤ Make sure that the monitor's refresh rate (also known as its vertical frequency) is 72Hz or higher. This is a measure of the number of times the screen is refreshed per second. The higher the refresh rate, the easier the display will be on your eyes.

➤ You need to make sure that the refresh rate generated by your video card matches the refresh rate supported by your monitor. One easy way to ensure refresh rate compatibility is to purchase a *multisync* monitor. These monitors can adjust themselves to the frequencies generated by the video card.

➤ Some monitors use *interlacing* to display higher resolutions. Interlacing means that the electron beam that generates the screen images doesn't paint the entire screen with each pass. (The frequency of these passes is determined by the monitor's refresh rate.) Instead, one pass will paint the odd lines, and the next pass will paint the even lines. This can cause a noticeable flicker on the screen, which will become annoying and hard on your eyes after a short period of time. You should always buy noninterlaced monitors, which paint the entire screen with each pass.

➤ The electron beam that paints the screen does so by using electrons to activate phosphors in the back of the monitor. The distance between each of these phosphors is called the *dot pitch;* it's a measure of the clarity of a monitor's image. The smaller the dot pitch, the sharper the image. Look for a monitor with a dot pitch of .28mm or less.

➤ Many of the latest monitors are Plug and Play–compatible. This means that you just need to attach the monitor's cable, and Windows 98 will recognize the new monitor automatically.

➤ To save money and energy, look for monitors that meet the Energy Star requirements. These monitors have power-saving features that can switch the monitor to a low-power standby mode after a specified number of minutes. In some cases, the monitor can even shut down automatically. (To learn how this works in Windows 98, see "Activating Your Monitor's Energy-Saving Features," later in this chapter).

Changing the Monitor Type

As I said, if you change your monitor and it is Plug and Play–compatible, Windows 98 should detect it automatically the next time you restart your machine. However, in some cases Windows 98 may not detect the monitor properly and will, instead, list it as "Unknown Monitor." If this happens, follow these steps to ensure that Windows 98 detects your monitor:

1. Open the **Display Properties** dialog box and select the **Settings** tab.

2. Click the **Advanced Properties** button. An **Advanced Properties** dialog box appears.

3. Select the **Monitor** tab, as shown in the following figure.

Use the Monitor tab to change the current monitor.

4. Activate the **Automatically detect Plug & Play monitors** check box.

5. Click **OK** to return to the **Display Properties** dialog box.

6. Click **OK** to return to the desktop.

7. Restart your computer. Windows 98 should now detect your monitor.

If your new monitor is not Plug and Play–compatible, here's how to let Windows 98 know about it:

1. Display the **Monitor** tab, as described above.

2. Click the **Change** button.

3. Use the Upgrade Device Driver wizard to select your new monitor.

Activating Your Monitor's Energy-Saving Features

Most people consider computers to be energy hogs. However, the base unit (the part with the hard drive and CPU) doesn't suck up that much juice. The only truly porcine component in the average (read: modern) computer system is the monitor. Although improvements have been made in monitor power consumption over the past few years, most displays still eat quite a bit of energy while doing their thing.

As an aid to reducing monitor power appetites, many newer monitors have built-in power-management capabilities. Using the video card, Windows 98 can send a signal to the monitor that can either blank the screen (this is called *standby mode*) or turn off the monitor altogether. Here's how to make sure your monitor's energy-saving features are activated:

1. Open the **Display Properties** dialog box and select the **Settings** tab.

2. Click the **Advanced Properties** button.

3. Select the **Monitor** tab.

4. Activate the **Monitor is Energy Star compliant** check box.

5. Click **OK** to return to the **Display Properties** dialog box.

6. Activate the **Screen Saver** tab.

7. In the **Energy saving features of monitor** group, click **Settings**. Windows 98 displays the **Power Management Properties** dialog box, as shown below.

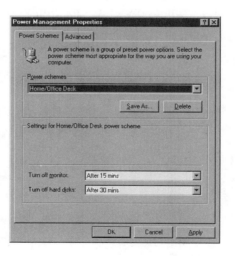

Use this dialog box to tell Windows 98 when to turn off your monitor.

8. Use the **Turn off monitor** list to select the amount of time after which Windows 98 will shut off your monitor.

9. Click **OK** to return to the **Display Properties** dialog box.

10. Click **OK** to return to the desktop.

Windows 98's Multiple-Monitor Support

Every Windows user has a list of bugbears and botherations that get under his or her skin. For many years, my personal pet peeve was a constant lack of screen space. I thought I was set for life when I moved up to a 21-inch monitor and a video card capable of displaying 16 million colors at 1,280×1,024 resolution. Now, however, I find my desktop is as crowded as ever with my word processor, email, browser, and who knows what else on the go at once.

So it will come as no surprise that one of my favorite new features in the Windows 98 package is the built-in support for multiple monitors. With two or more video cards installed in your computer and a monitor attached to each card, Windows 98 provides you with an expanded desktop. This enables you to move windows from one monitor to another, display a different set of desktop icons on each monitor, move the taskbar between monitors, have Active Desktop items visible on one monitor while you work on the other, and much more. Best of all, after you've installed your second video card, enabling multiple-monitor support takes only a couple of mouse clicks.

Multiple-monitor support is easy to set up, but only if you have the right hardware. The main video card can be any PCI card running on a Windows 98 or later device driver. For the secondary video card, however, Windows 98 is a bit more finicky. It must also be a PCI card, and it must use one of the following graphics chipsets:

ATI Mach64

ATI Mach64 GX

ATI Rage 1 & 2 (VT & greater)

Cirrus 5436, 7548, 5446

ET6000

S3 764V+ (765), Trio 64V2

S3 Aurora (S3M65)

S3 ViRGE

After you install the second video card and attach the monitor, Windows 98 should recognize the card at startup, install the necessary drivers, then reboot. When Windows 98 restarts, the secondary monitor should display the following message:

```
If you can read this message, Windows has successfully
initialized this display adapter.
```

To use this adapter as part of your Windows desktop, open
the Display option in the Control Panel and adjust the
Settings on the Monitors tab.

When Windows 98 loads, follow these steps to get the second monitor working:

1. Open the **Display Properties** dialog box and select the **Settings** tab. As you can see
   in the following figure, the **Settings** tab now has a new look. Monitor "1" is your
   main monitor/card combo, and monitor "2" is the secondary monitor/card.

*With multiple video
cards in your system,
the Settings tab takes
on a new look.*

2. Use the **Display** list to select the secondary monitor/card combination.
3. Activate the **Extend my Windows desktop onto this monitor** check box. Windows
   98 will now display a **Compatibility Warning** dialog box, which lets you know that
   some programs don't support the multiple display feature.
4. Click **OK**.

You can customize each monitor/card combo by using the following techniques:

➤ To adjust the display resolution, color depth, and so on, first use the **Display** list to
   select the monitor/card you want to work with. You can then use the other controls
   to adjust the display properties.

➤ To adjust the relative position of the two windows, drag the monitor representations
   in the **Monitors** tab.

When you click **OK** to return to the desktop, your multiple-monitor setup is ready to roll.
Go ahead and drag objects (including the taskbar) from one window to another.

From Here

This chapter closed your look at Windows 98 and hardware by examining two particular peripherals: the video card and the monitor. I began by explaining some video card concepts. Then, I showed you how to tell Windows 98 about your card, troubleshoot a garbled display, and set the display resolution and color depth. For monitors, I first gave you a few things to look for when purchasing a monitor. You then learned how to change the monitor type, work with your monitor's energy-saving features, and try out Windows 98's multiple-monitor support.

Speaking of hardware, I'll tell you a bit about networking hardware in Part 6, "More Networking Know-How." You'll also learn how to connect to and use a network, send email, and use Dial-Up Networking.

Part 6
More Networking Know-How

If you're running Windows 98 at work, chances are that your computer is connected to a whole whack of other machines in a companywide network. This connection enables several machines to share things like printers and CD-ROM drives. It also lets you set up common folders that some or all of the folks on the network can use for storage. And, of course, no networked office would be complete without an email system so employees can exchange snarky notes about the boss. The capability to do all of these network tricks and more is built right into Windows 98. The three chapters in Part 6 let you in on this network know-how.

Working with Network Connections

Back in the high-flying '80s, *networking* was the buzzword du jour. Although to the innocent observer networking appeared to be a social skill designed to augment business contacts, it was really just a high-falutin' euphemism for unabashed *schmoozing*.

Nowadays, though, the meaning of networking has changed from cocktail party conversations to computer system connections. Everywhere you turn, people are hooking computers together to see what happens. If you're a budding network administrator and you've connected a couple of machines at home or at the office, this chapter looks at some simple network stuff: setting up your computer, sharing files, sharing printers, accessing other computers, and other networking know-how.

Networking for Novices

If you'd like to take the networking plunge and connect a couple of computers for sharing files and printers (which is the simple definition of a network), Windows 98 is probably your best way to go. Why? Well, it takes most of the pain out of connecting computers, and you can share stuff with others in your network using familiar Windows Explorer tools.

When most people think of networks (if, in fact, they ever think of them at all), the image that springs to mind is one of a central, monolithic computer that contains all the data and applications and has dozens or even hundreds of "terminals" attached to it. *Workgroups*, however, are different. A workgroup is a small group of computers connected by some kind of network cable. Each computer has its own applications and data, but the other computers in the workgroup can share these resources. In this egalitarian setup, all the computers in the workgroup are treated equally; no one machine is "better" or more important than any other. In most workgroups, the computers are related to each other somehow. For example, all the computers in a company's accounting department could form one workgroup, while the marketing department might have its own workgroup.

Check This Out...

Some Net-Words

Networks in which all the machines have their own programs and data and can share these with the other computers are *peer-to-peer* networks.

A networked computer's *resources* include the disk drives, folders, programs, documents, and printers associated with that computer. The purpose of a network is to share these resources among several computers.

Each workgroup has a name (Accounting, for example), and each computer in the workgroup has its own name (this is usually the name of the person using the computer, but it can be just about anything you like). You specify the workgroup name and computer name when you set up Windows 98. In my case, I have five computers set up as a workgroup. My group name is **Olympus**, and the five computer names are **Paul**, **Karen**, **Hermes**, **Selene**, and **Zeus**.

The whole point of setting up a workgroup is so the members of the group can share their resources. For example, if you have five computers in the group but only one printer (as I do), you can set things up so that each machine can print from that one printer. Handy, huh? Similarly, you can share files, applications, and even CD-ROM drives. Does this mean that other people in the group can just play with your machine willy-nilly? Heck no, not if you don't want them to. *You* decide which resources on your computer are shared, and for extra safety, you can set up passwords to prevent undesirables and other members of your family from accessing sensitive areas.

Some Notes About Network Hardware

Your network won't work unless you have the proper hardware installed in all the computers. If you're in the market for some network knickknacks, here are a few things to bear in mind:

➤ Most network noodling is done via a *network adapter* (also known as a *network interface card*, or NIC), which is an add-on component that gets inserted into each computer. Once you plug in some network cables (more on this in a sec), the adapter takes care of the dirty work of sending data out to the network and receiving data coming in from the network. Make sure you get an *Ethernet* card.

➤ For easiest installation, make sure the card is Plug and Play–compatible (most are nowadays).

➤ For workgroup connections, use *coaxial network cable*. (Also known as *10Base-2* or *thinnet* cable.)

➤ Finally, make sure your network adapter has the proper connector for coaxial cable. This type of connector is called a *BNC connector*.

A single chapter is, of course, a pitifully small amount of space to devote to a large topic like networking. Because I can't cover everything, I'm going to assume that you have (or some cajolable networking sage has) installed the necessary network hardware in your computers.

Once the network adapter is installed, Windows 98 should recognize it automatically when you start your computer, and it will then install the necessary device drivers. If Windows 98 fails to find the adapter (if you didn't get a Plug and Play adapter, for example), you'll have to tell Windows 98 what kind of adapter you're using. Here are the steps to follow:

1. Select **Start | Settings | Control Panel**. Windows 98 displays the Control Panel window.

2. Open the **Network** icon to display the Network dialog box.

3. Click **Add**. Windows displays the Select Network Component Type dialog box.

4. Click **Adapter** and then click **Add**. The Select Network adapters dialog box appears, as shown in the following figure.

5. Use the **Manufacturers** list to highlight the manufacturer of your network adapter; use the **Network Adapters** list to highlight the adapter (you should find both things either on the box the adapter came in or in the adapter's manual); and then click **OK**.

6. You may now be asked to insert your Windows 98 CD-ROM. If so, follow the instructions on the screen until you're returned to the Network dialog box.

Use this dialog box to specify the type of network adapter you're using.

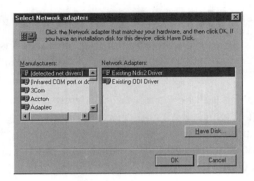

Getting Your System Network-Ready

With all that hardware hoo-ha out of the way, let's see how you set up Windows 98 for network use on the software side of things. The next two sections take you through the two main steps: identifying your computer for network purposes and setting up your computer for sharing its resources.

Establishing Your Computer's Network Identity

Your first task is to give your computer a name and address on the network. The name is what appears in Windows Explorer when you hang out in the Network Neighborhood (which I'll talk about later on). The "address" is actually the name of the workgroup that your computer is a member of.

To do this, display the Network dialog box once again (as described in the previous section), and then select the **Identification** tab, which is shown in the following figure.

Use the Identification tab to establish a network name for your machine.

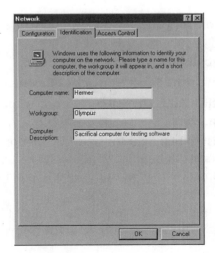

Fill in the fields as explained here:

➤ **Computer name**   Enter a network name for your computer (15 characters maximum). Ideally, you should enter a name that'll make it easy for others on the network to figure out which computer they're working with.

➤ **Workgroup**   Enter the name of your network workgroup. If you set up your own network at home or in the office, you can enter any name you like (again, use a maximum of 15 characters). Just be sure to use the same name for each computer you include in your network. If you hook into a larger network at the office, the network system administrator assigns you a workgroup name.

➤ **Computer Description**   Use this text box to enter a description for your computer (up to 48 characters). Windows 98 shows this description in some networks' lists to help others figure out which computer they're working with. This doesn't have to be anything fancy; a simple **Biff's Computer** or **Buffy's Honkin' Pentium Beast** will do.

Setting Up Sharing

If you want to be a good network citizen and share stuff on your computer with your net friends (which I'll show you how to do later in this chapter), follow these steps to activate sharing:

1. In the Configuration tab of the Network dialog box, click the **File and Print Sharing** button. The File and Print Sharing dialog box appears (see the following figure).

Activate these check boxes to share your stuff with other folks on your network.

2. Activate the two check boxes.

3. Click **OK** to return to the Network dialog box.

Okay, your machine is now pumped and primed for network use. Click **OK** to put your changes into effect. When Windows 98 asks if you want to restart your computer, click **Yes**.

Logging On to Your Network

After you set up your network and restart Windows 98, eventually you'll be pestered to enter a user name and a password, as shown in the following figure.

343

With networking installed, you'll have to negotiate this dialog box each time you start Windows 98.

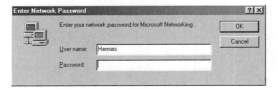

Here are the steps to follow to get through this:

1. The default name shown in the **User name** text box is the computer name you entered during setup. If you want, you can change the logon name to something different (such as, say, your first name).

2. Use the **Password** text box to enter a password if you want to prevent others from getting into your copy of Windows 98. If your network is at home, you may not want to bother with a password (you *do* trust those kids of yours, don't you?), in which case, you can leave the **Password** text box blank.

   If you do use a password, make sure you enter one that's easy for you to remember but hard for others to figure out. When you enter the password, the letters appear as asterisks (*) for security reasons (you never know who might be peeking over your shoulder!).

3. Click **OK**. The Set Windows Password dialog box appears.

4. Re-enter your password in the **Confirm new password** text box, and then click **OK**. Windows 98 finishes loading.

When you start Windows 98 in the future, all you have to do is enter your password. If, however, you change your user name, you have to repeat the whole process.

A Drive Around the Network Neighborhood

Windows 98 calls your workgroup and network the "Network Neighborhood," which certainly sounds friendly enough. Here are a couple of different ways to see what's in your Network Neighborhood:

➤ Open the desktop's **Network Neighborhood** icon.

➤ Open Windows Explorer and select **Network Neighborhood** in the All Folders list.

The following figure shows my Network Neighborhood folder. (If your screen doesn't show all the columns shown in the figure, activate the **View | Details** command.) The Name column contains the following information:

➤ **Entire Network** Open this folder to see all the workgroups that are part of the full network to which your computer is attached. (If you're just hooked up to your own workgroup, Entire Network shows only that workgroup.) Opening these workgroup folders displays the names of all the computers in each workgroup.

➤ **Some computer names** The rest of the Name column displays the names of the computers in your workgroup (including your own).

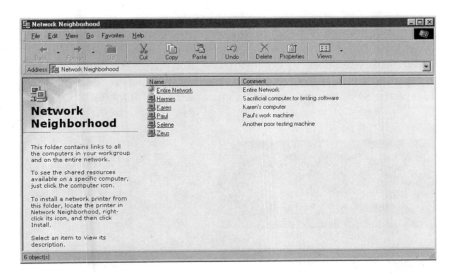

The Network Neighborhood: your computer's community.

Windows treats each of the Network Neighborhood computers as a folder. This means that you can use the usual My Computer or Windows Explorer techniques to check out what's on the various machines. For each computer, you'll see those resources that the owner of the computer has chosen to share with the network. (I'll tell you how to share your resources later in this chapter.) For example, the next figure shows the window that appears when I open the folder for the computer named **Selene**. Notice that this generous user is sharing all sorts of goodies: a CD-ROM drive, a printer, and a data folder. The other computers in the workgroup can access these resources as though the hardware and folders were part of their own systems.

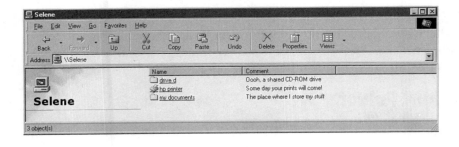

If you open the folder for a Network Neighborhood computer, Windows shows the computer's shared resources.

Actually, the level of access available for a shared resource depends on the *access rights* the sharer has granted the sharees. As you'll see later, you can prevent others from messing with your resources by giving them *read-only* access. If you run into, say, a shared folder that's read-only, you won't be able to change any of the folder's files. If you try, you'll see a curt error message telling you that **Network Access is denied**. Bummer.

It's also possible to tailor access to a shared resource by using passwords. For example, if you try to view a shared disk drive that has been password-protected, Windows 98 displays the Enter Network Password dialog box, as shown in the next figure. You won't be able to access the drive until you enter the correct password in the **Password** text box. (Note, too, that unless you want to re-enter the password every time you access this resource, you should leave the **Save this password in your password list** check box activated.)

Windows tosses this dialog box at you if a resource is protected by a password.

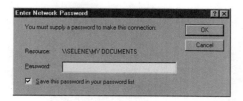

Accessing Network Resources

As I've said, one way to play with the shared resources in your workgroup is to head into the Network Neighborhood and "open" the computers you see listed. Here are two other ways to work with these resources:

➤ You can "map" a network folder so that it appears to be a disk drive on your computer. For example, let's say that your system has two floppy disk drives (drives A and B) and a hard disk drive (drive C). If you map a network folder, it will appear as drive D on your computer. If you map another network folder, it will appear as drive E, and so on. This makes it easier not only to copy and move files to and from the network folder, but also to open files on the drive. It also makes the drive accessible from the MS-DOS prompt.

➤ You can install a network printer and use it (more or less) just like a printer attached directly to your computer. (Why "more or less"? Well, there are some things you won't be able to do, such as purging other people's print jobs.)

Mapping a Network Folder

Mapping a network folder is easier done than said. Here's what you do:

1. Display the Network Neighborhood and open the computer that contains the folder you want to work with.

2. Try either of the following techniques:

   ➤ Highlight the network folder and select **File | Map Network Drive**.

   ➤ Right-click the network folder and click **Map Network Drive** in the shortcut menu.

3. The Map Network Drive dialog box appears, as shown in the following figure. The **Drive** box shows you the drive letter that Windows 98 will use to map the network folder. You can select a different letter if you like.

This dialog box tells you the drive letter that Windows will assign to the mapped network drive.

4. If you'd like this folder to be mapped every time you log on to Windows 98, make sure the **Reconnect at logon** check box is activated.

5. When you're done, click **OK**.

6. If the folder is protected by a password, you'll see the Enter Network Password dialog box. In this case, enter the correct password, and then click **OK** to map the drive.

After a few seconds, Windows opens a window for the mapped resource, and the new drive appears in Explorer's All Folders list as part of the **My Computer** folder. (For those of you who have been paying attention: yes, the mapped drive also appears in the My Computer window.) The following figure shows Windows Explorer with two mapped drives:

➤ **F on 'Paul' (G:)**   This means that drive F on the network machine named **Paul** has been mapped to drive G.

➤ **My documents on 'Selene' (H:)**   This means that the **My documents** folder on the network machine named **Selene** has been mapped to drive H.

To disconnect a mapped drive, use either of the following techniques:

➤ Highlight the mapped drive in Windows Explorer and select the **Tools | Disconnect Network Drive** command. In the Disconnect Network Drive dialog box that appears, highlight the drive you want to disconnect, and then click **OK**. If Windows 98 asks whether you're sure you want to disconnect, select **Yes**.

Windows Explorer showing a couple of mapped network drives.

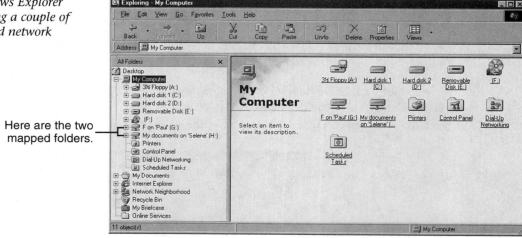

Here are the two mapped folders.

➤ Right-click the network drive and click **Disconnect** in the shortcut menu. Windows 98 disconnects the drive right away.

Using a Network Printer

One of the big advantages of setting up a workgroup in your office or home is that you can share expensive items—such as printers—among all your computers. You don't need to get a separate printer for each machine or put up with the hassle of swapping printer cables. Here are the steps to follow to install a network printer for use on your computer:

1. Display the Network Neighborhood, open the computer that has the shared printer, and then highlight the printer.

2. Select the **File | Install** command.

3. You may see a Connect to Printer dialog box mumbling something about the "server" not having "a suitable printer driver." If so, ignore the geekspeak and click **OK.**

4. If you were subjected to the Connect to Printer dialog box in step 3, you'll see a dialog box from the Add Printer Wizard. Use the **Manufacturers** and **Printers** lists to highlight the printer you want to install, and then click **OK.**

5. From here, you follow the usual steps for installing a printer. (I covered this in *The Complete Idiot's Guide to Windows 98.*)

Playing Nicely with Others: Sharing Your Resources

Networking is a two-way street. It's fine to play around with the resources on other people's machines, but only a real greedy-guts would refuse to share his own computer's resources. To avoid being shunned by your peers, you need to designate a resource or two that can be shared. Read on to learn how.

Sharing Folders and Disk Drives

If you have a CD-ROM drive or perhaps some data in a folder that the others in your workgroup are lusting after, you should put your co-workers out of their misery by sharing the drive or folder with them.

The first thing you need to decide is how you want to share your resources. For each drive or folder you share, Windows 98 gives you three choices (called *access rights*):

➤ **Read-Only** At this level, someone else who accesses one of your shared drives or folders can only copy, open, and view files. They can't move files, modify them, rename them, delete them, or add new ones.

➤ **Full** This anything-goes level gives others complete access to the files in the shared drive or folder. They can move, copy, open, view, modify, rename, delete, and even create files.

➤ **Depends on Password** This level enables you to assign separate passwords for read-only and full access.

Here are the steps to follow to share a disk drive, CD-ROM drive, or folder:

1. In Windows Explorer or My Computer, highlight the disk drive or folder that you want to share.

2. Select the **File | Properties** command, and then display the **Sharing** tab in the Properties dialog box that appears. Alternatively, you can right-click the drive or folder and click **Sharing** from the shortcut menu. The following figure shows the Sharing tab. (If your Sharing tab looks different, read the instructions that follow these steps.)

3. Activate the **Shared As** option button.

4. The **Share Name** text box shows either the letter of the disk drive or the name of the folder. Because this is what appears in the Network Neighborhood's Name column when other people access your computer, it's probably best that you leave the name as is. You should, however, enter a brief description of the resource in the **Comment** text box. (Something like "Hard disk," "CD-ROM drive," or "Crucial workgroup files" is sufficient.)

Use the Sharing tab to share a drive or folder with your workgroup pals.

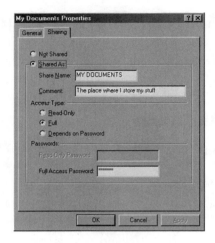

5. Select the type of access you want for this resource: **Read-Only**, **Full**, or **Depends on Password**.

6. If you want others to enter a password to access the shared drive or folder, enter the appropriate password in either the **Read-Only Password** or the **Full Access Password** text box. If you selected **Depends on Password**, you need to enter a password in both text boxes. (If you do enter a password, don't forget to let the other people in your group know what it is!)

7. Click **OK**. If you entered a password, you're asked to confirm it. In this case, re-enter the password and click **OK**. When you return to Explorer or My Computer, you see a little hand under the folder's icon. This reminds you that you've shared the folder.

Depending on the way your network is set up, you may have to use a different technique to share your resources. Specifically, if you see the version of the Sharing tab shown in the next figure, your network is set up for "user-level" access to shared resources.

As before, you activate the **Shared As** option and enter a **Comment**. Next, you need to specify which users or groups of users are allowed to access your resource. Here's how it's done:

1. Click the **Add** button to display the Add Users dialog box, shown in the next figure. The Name list displays all the users and groups that are recognized as valid by your network.

2. Highlight a user or group in the **Name** list.

3. Click **Read Only**, **Full Access**, or **Custom**.

4. Repeat steps 2 and 3 to add other users or groups to the lists.

5. When you're finished, click **OK**.

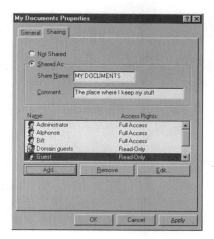

You'll see this Sharing tab if your network is set up with user-level access.

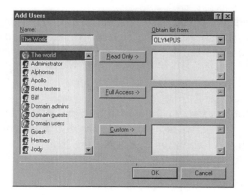

Use the Add Users dialog box to specify which users and groups should be allowed access to the resource.

6. If you added any users or groups to the Custom list, you'll see the Change Access Rights dialog box. Use this dialog box to set up specific access rights for the users. When you're finished, click **OK**.

7. When you're back at the Sharing tab, click **OK**.

Sharing Printers

Sharing a printer among several computers in a workgroup is similar to sharing folders. First, you need to open the Printers folder, either by highlighting it in Explorer's All Folders list or by selecting **Start | Settings | Printers**.

Highlight the printer you want to share, and then select the **File | Sharing** command (or right-click the printer and click **Sharing** in the shortcut menu). Windows 98 displays the printer's Properties dialog box and selects the **Sharing** tab, as shown in the following figure.

Use this version of
the Sharing tab to
share a printer with
your network cohorts.

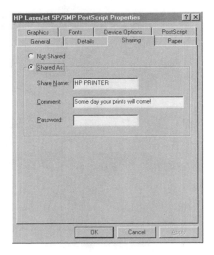

Activate the **Shared As** option, enter a **Comment**, and then enter an optional **Password**. Click **OK** to enable the share. (If you entered a password, the Password Confirmation dialog box appears. Re-enter the password and click **OK**.)

From Here

This chapter introduced you to the world of networking and showed you how to get Windows 98 set up for network use. Now that you're connected, the next chapter, "Using Windows Messaging to Exchange Email Notes," shows you how to exchange email missives with your colleagues.

Chapter 23

Using Windows Messaging to Exchange Email Notes

In Chapter 12, "Getting Your Modem's Mojo Working," I showed you how to use Windows Messaging's Microsoft Fax component to send and receive faxes from Windows 98. Windows Messaging has one other trick up its communications sleeve: it sends and receives Microsoft Mail messages over a network. This chapter shows you how to use the Microsoft Mail service to read and compose your digital network correspondence from the comfort of Windows 98.

Installing Windows Messaging and Microsoft Mail

You need to bear in mind that Windows Messaging isn't part of the regular Windows 98 package. What does this mean for would-be network emailers? There are two possibilities:

➤ If Windows 98 was installed over a version of Windows 95 that had Windows Messaging installed, then Windows Messaging will still be there and will work as advertised with Windows 98.

➤ If you upgraded over a version of Windows 95 that didn't have Windows Messaging installed, if you have a new machine, or if you upgraded over Windows 3.1, Windows Messaging won't be on your system.

The next two sections show you what to do in each scenario.

No Postoffice? No Problem!

To use Microsoft Mail, you need access to a postoffice on your network. (A *postoffice* is a central location where your incoming messages are stored.) If you're running your own network in a small office or at home, you probably won't have a postoffice set up. Happily, it's not that hard to create one. I show you how later on in the "Your Personal Postmaster-General: Setting Up a Postoffice" section. Make sure you create your postoffice before you set up Windows Messaging or Microsoft Mail.

If Windows Messaging Is Already Installed

If you see an Inbox icon on your desktop, then you know for sure that Windows Messaging is installed on your system. In this case, your first order of business is to install the Microsoft Mail service. Just plow through these steps to add the Microsoft Mail service:

1. If Windows Messaging isn't already started, either launch the desktop's **Inbox** icon or select **Start | Programs | Windows Messaging**.

2. Select **Tools | Services** to display the Services dialog box.

3. Click **Add**. Windows Messaging displays the Add Service to Profile dialog box.

4. Click **Microsoft Mail**, and then click **OK**. The Microsoft Mail dialog box appears, as shown in the following figure.

5. Type the location of your Microsoft Mail postoffice in the **Enter the path to your postoffice** text box. (If you're not sure of the path, either ask your network administrator or click the **Browse** button.)

6. In the Logon tab, enter the name of your Microsoft Mail mailbox and enter the password for that mailbox. If you want Windows 98 to log you on to that mailbox automatically, activate the **When logging on, automatically enter password** check box.

Use this dialog box to set up the Microsoft Mail service.

7. Click **OK**. Windows Messaging tells you that the service you just added won't work until you exit and restart the program.

8. Click **OK**, and then click **OK** again to return to Windows Messaging.

9. Select **File | Exit and Log Off**.

If Windows Messaging Isn't Installed

If Windows Messaging is missing in action (that is, you don't see the Inbox icon on your desktop), you must install it by hand. Easy money. First slip the Windows 98 CD into the drive, then use Windows Explorer or My Computer to open the **tools\oldwin95\ message\us** folder. When you open this folder, you see a program called **wms.exe**. Running this program will install Windows Messaging.

Once you've installed Windows Messaging, you need to follow these steps to get it ready for action:

1. Either launch the desktop's **Inbox** icon or select **Start | Programs | Windows Messaging**. Windows 98 pushes the Inbox Setup Wizard on stage, as shown in the following figure. This wizard will lead you through the entire Windows Messaging setup procedure.

2. Make sure the **Microsoft Mail** check box is activated. (You almost certainly will want to use Outlook Express for your Internet email chores, so be sure to deactivate the **Internet Mail** check box.) Click **Next >** when you're ready to ramble on.

3. You now see the Wizard dialog box shown in the following figure. This time the Wizard wants to know where it can find your network postoffice. You have a couple of options for specifying the postoffice location:

   ➤ Enter the postoffice's network address in the text box provided.

Use this Wizard dialog box to choose the services you want to use.

➤ Click the **Browse** button to display the Browse for Postoffice dialog box, open the Network Neighborhood, find the computer that contains the postoffice, and then highlight the postoffice folder (it will be called something like WGPO, or WGPO0000).

If you're not sure about any of this, your network administrator will be happy to give you the correct location. When you've got it all sorted out, click **Next >** to continue.

This Wizard dialog box begs you for the location of your network Microsoft Mail postoffice.

4. As shown in the following figure, the Wizard next presents you with a list of all the users that have accounts on the Microsoft Mail postoffice you chose in the previous step. All you need to do is highlight your name and then click **Next >**. (Don't see your name? You'll need to chastise your network administrator.)

5. The Wizard will then ask you to enter a password for your account. Type your password in the text box provided, and then click **Next >**. This ends the Microsoft Mail portion of our show.

6. From here, the Wizard will present you with dialog boxes for your Personal Address Book and your Personal Folders. In both cases, click **Next >** to move on.

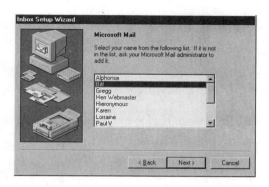

This Wizard dialog box presents a list of the users in the selected postoffice.

7. In the last Wizard dialog box, click **Finish**.

Messing Around with Messaging: A Few Email Chores

Okay, now that all that malarkey is over with and Windows Messaging is pumped up and ready to roll, you can get right down to the nitty-gritty of reading and writing email messages. If Windows Messaging isn't already up and at 'em, your first chore is to wake the program from its hard disk slumbers by either opening the desktop's **Inbox** icon, or by selecting **Start | Programs | Windows Messaging**. Enter your Microsoft Mail password, if prompted, and then click **OK** to log on.

The following figure points out a few interesting features in the Windows Messaging window that appears. (If you don't see the list of folders, activate the **View | Folders** command.)

The Inbox folder is where the messages you receive are stored.

The Message list shows you all the messages in the highlighted folder.

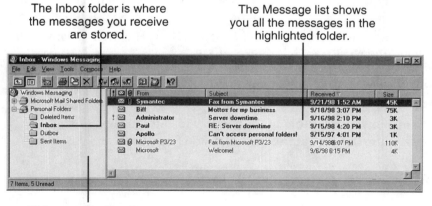

A few Windows Messaging landmarks.

This area displays the folders that you use to store messages.

Shipping Out an Email Message

Here are the steps to follow to send a Microsoft Mail message:

1. Select **Compose | New Message** (or press **Ctrl+N**). The New Message window appears, as shown in the following figure.

Either type the recipients' names here...

Use the New Message window to compose your email missive.

...or click these buttons to select names from the address book.

Use this box to enter the message text.

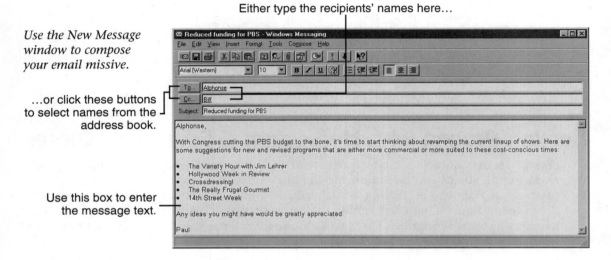

2. Use the **To** box to specify the message recipient. You have the following choices:

   ➤ Type the recipient's mailbox name.

   ➤ If you want to type multiple names, use a semicolon (;) to separate each from the others.

   ➤ Click the **To** button to open the postoffice address box. Highlight a name and click **To**. Repeat as necessary, and then click **OK**.

3. If you want to send a courtesy copy to a different recipient, use the **Cc** box.

4. Use the **Subject** box to enter a short description of your message.

5. Use the large blank box at the bottom of the window to enter the text of your message. Feel free to use the Formatting toolbar to add fancy fonts and colors to your message.

6. When your message is ready to ship, select **File | Send** (or press **Ctrl+Enter**).

Getting and Reading Your·Mail

Email is, ideally, a give-and-take, thrust-and-parry deal. So not only will you be firing out messages to all and sundry, but you'll also receive a few notes. These messages are stored in your network postoffice mailbox until you go and get them. By default, Microsoft Mail checks your mailbox for new messages every 10 minutes, but you can check for mail anytime you like. All you have to do is run one of the following commands:

➤ If Microsoft Mail is the only Windows Messaging service installed, select **Tools |
Deliver Now**.

➤ If you have multiple Windows Messaging services installed, select **Tools | Deliver
Now Using | Microsoft Mail**.

Changing the Default Checking Intervals

If need be, you can force Windows Messaging to check for new messages after a different time interval. Select the **Tools | Services** command, highlight **Microsoft Mail** in the Services dialog box, and then click **Properties**. In the Microsoft Mail dialog box, select the **Delivery** tab, enter a new value in the **Check for new mail every *x* minute(s)** text box, and then click **OK**. When you're back in the Services dialog box, click **OK** to return to Windows Messaging.

Either way, Windows Messaging connects to the postoffice and lugs back any messages that are waiting for you. The new messages then appear in the Windows Messaging Inbox folder, as shown in the following figure. For each message, the Messages list shows you the name of the person who sent the message, the Subject line, the date and time it was sent, and the size.

This symbol means that a file is attached to the message.

This symbol means it's a high-priority message.

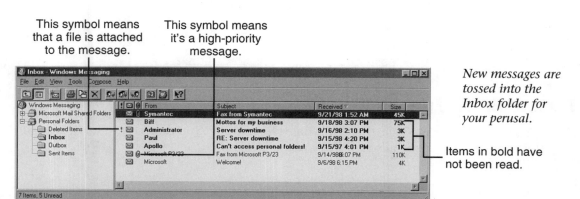

New messages are tossed into the Inbox folder for your perusal.

Items in bold have not been read.

Now that you have your stack of mail, you can read each message by highlighting it and selecting the **File | Open** command (or by just double-clicking the message or pressing **Enter**).

A new window opens to display your message, as shown in the next figure. After you've read the message, you can either close the window or use the following techniques to check out your other messages:

➤ To open the next message in the list, either select **View | Next** or click the Next Message toolbar button (**Ctrl+>** works, too).

➤ To open the previous message in the list, either select **View | Previous** or click the Previous Message toolbar button (you can also try **Ctrl+<**).

When you open a message, Windows Messaging displays it in a new window.

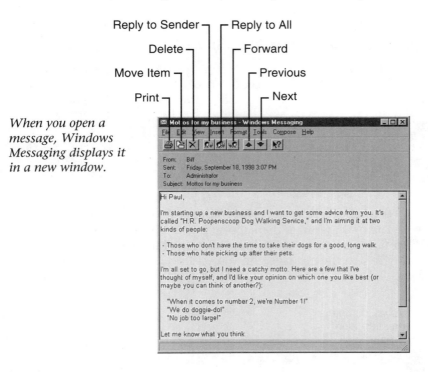

Further Email Fun

After you've read a message, there's a whole pile of things you can do with it. The rest of this chapter runs through each of these tasks.

Send a Reply

To send a rejoinder to the author of the message, either select **Compose | Reply to Sender**, or click the Reply to Sender toolbar button. (The keyboard shortcut is **Ctrl+R**.) Enter your reply in the window that appears, and then send the message as described earlier.

Send a Reply to All the Recipients

If the message was sent to several people, you can send a response to all the recipients by either selecting **Compose | Reply to All** or clicking the Reply to All toolbar button. (From the keyboard, press **Ctrl+Shift+R**.)

Forward the Message

If you'd like someone else to eyeball the message, you can forward it to him or her by either selecting **Compose | Forward** or clicking the Forward button. (Keyboard mavens can press **Ctrl+F**.)

Print the Message

To get a hard copy of the message, either select **File | Print** or click the Print button (or press **Ctrl+P**).

Delete the Message

To get rid of the message, either select **File | Delete** or click the Delete button (or press **Ctrl+D**). In this case, Windows Messaging moves the messages to the **Deleted Items** folder. (If you change your mind, there's no problem moving the message back to the Inbox. Use the technique described next.)

Move It to Another Folder

You probably won't want to leave all your messages cluttering the Inbox folder. Any messages you want to keep should be stored in a separate folder. To move a message to another folder, select **File | Move** (or click the Move Item button), use the Move dialog box to highlight the destination folder, and then click **OK**. (If you want to create a new folder along the way, click the **New Folder** button in the Move dialog box.)

Your Personal Postmaster-General: Setting Up a Postoffice

If you've got a small peer-to-peer network humming away at home or in a small office, you probably don't want to fork over a few thousand hard-earned dollars for a full-fledged mail server. Luckily, you don't have to. The Windows 98 CD comes with a utility (it's called Workgroup Postoffice) that lets you establish a simple "postoffice" that's used to store and forward Microsoft Mail messages for the network users. Note that Workgroup Postoffice is installed automatically when you install Windows Messaging.

Here are the steps to follow to create a postoffice:

1. Select **Start | Settings | Control Panel**, and then open the Microsoft Mail Postoffice icon. The Microsoft Workgroup Postoffice Admin dialog box appears.

2. Activate the **Create a new Workgroup Postoffice** option and click **Next >**.

3. The next dialog box, shown in the following figure, asks you to enter a location for the postoffice. Use the **Postoffice Location** text box to enter the drive and folder where you want the postoffice to reside. (If you're not sure, entering **C:** will do the job.) Workgroup Postoffice will create a new subfolder called **WGPO0000** that will contain the postoffice. Click **Next >** when you're ready to continue.

Use this dialog box to enter a location for the postoffice.

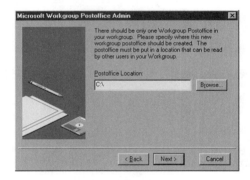

4. When Windows 98 shows you the location of the postoffice, click **Next >** again. The Enter Your Administrator Account Details dialog box, shown next, appears.

Use this dialog box to enter your name, account name, password, and other administrivia.

5. Fill in the details for your administrator account, including a password, and then click **OK**.

6. Workgroup Postoffice creates the postoffice, and then displays a dialog box to let you know. This dialog box also reminds you to share the postoffice folder so that it's accessible to others on the network. Be sure to share the folder with full access (as described in the previous chapter; see "Sharing Folders and Disk Drives"). Click **OK** when you're done.

Before other folks on the network can work with Microsoft Mail, they need to have their own postoffice accounts set up. Here are the steps to trudge through:

1. Select **Start | Settings | Control Panel**, and then open the Microsoft Mail Postoffice icon to get the Microsoft Workgroup Postoffice Admin dialog box onscreen once again.

2. Make sure that the **Administer an existing Workgroup Postoffice** option is activated and click **Next >**. The next dialog box asks you for the location of the postoffice.

3. You should see the name of your postoffice displayed (probably **C:\WGPO0000**), so click **Next >**. You're now asked to enter your administrator mailbox name and password.

4. Enter your **Mailbox** and **Password**, and then click **Next >**. The Postoffice Manager dialog box drops in, as shown in the following figure.

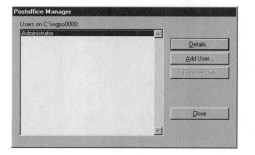

Use the Postoffice Manager to add and remove user accounts in your postoffice.

5. To create an account for a user, first click **Add User**. In the Add User dialog box, fill in the user's **Name**, **Mailbox**, **Password**, and other data. Click **OK** when you're done.

6. To make changes to a user's account, highlight the user's name in the Postoffice Manager, click **Details**, make your adjustments, and click **OK**.

7. If you want to remove a user account, highlight the user's name in the Postoffice Manager and click **Remove User**. When the Postoffice Manager asks whether you're sure, click **Yes**.

8. When your administrative duties are done, click **Close**.

From Here

This chapter gave you the scoop on using Exchange to exchange email notes with your network peers. If you travel for business, the next chapter, "Keeping In Touch: Mobile Computing with Dial-Up Networking," shows you how to connect to your network from remote locations.

Chapter 24

Keeping In Touch: Mobile Computing with Dial-Up Networking

There's an old saying that "Far folks fare well." No, I don't know what it means, either. However, folks who are far away from their company network can still fare well by using Windows 98's Dial-Up Networking program (sometimes called DUN, for short). This feature enables you to use a modem to establish a connection to your network lifeline when a physical connection just isn't physically possible (say, when you're working on the road or at home). This chapter shows you how to configure and use Dial-Up Networking. I'll also show you how to use different dialing locations and how to set up a remote Microsoft Mail session.

Setting Up a Dial-Up Networking Connection

Before the fun begins, you should know that I'm making three assumptions right off the bat:

➤ That your modem and computer are attached at the hip (electronically speaking, of course; the latest computers and peripherals come without hips).

➤ That you've clued Windows 98 in on what kind of modem you have. (I told you how to do this in Chapter 12's "Setting Up a Modem from Scratch" section.)

➤ That the Dial-Up Networking component is installed.

Setting Up the Basic Connection

Given that, let's dive right into the deep end of Dial-Up Networking. To get the show on the road, you need to follow these steps:

1. Select **Start | Programs | Communications | Dial-Up Networking**. The Dial-Up Networking window appears.

2. If this is the first time you've done the DUN thing, Windows 98 starts the Make New Connection Wizard automatically. If that doesn't happen, you see the Dial-Up Networking window, instead. Curse your luck and launch the **Make New Connection** icon by hand. You use this wizard to specify the particulars of your Dial-Up Networking session. Windows 98 calls these particulars a *connection* (or sometimes, bizarrely, a *connectoid*), and each connection contains, among other things, a name, the modem to use, and the phone number to dial.

The Dial-Up Networking Folder

The Dial-Up Networking window is actually the Dial-Up Networking folder, which is part of the My Computer folder. Therefore, it's often easier to get to the Dial-Up Networking stuff either by opening My Computer, or by selecting Dial-Up Networking in Windows Explorer's All Folders list.

3. In the first wizard dialog box, shown in the following figure, you need to fill in two things:

➤ **Type a name for the computer you are dialing** Use this text box to enter a name for the new Dial-Up Networking connection.

➤ **Select a device** If you've installed multiple modems, use this drop-down list to select the modem you want to use for this connection.

Use this dialog box to enter a connection name and choose the modem to use with Dial-Up Networking.

4. Click the **Configure** button to open up the Properties dialog box for your modem, and then activate the **Options** tab, shown in the following figure.

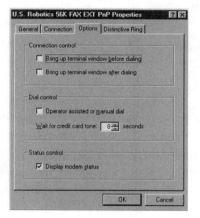

Your modem's Properties dialog box contains a few useful settings for modifying how the modem makes the connection.

5. You may not have to bother with any of the Option tab's options, but here's a quick run-down of what's available, just in case (click **OK** when you're done):

   ➤ **Bring up terminal window before dialing**   If you activate this check box, Dial-Up Networking tosses the Pre-Dial Terminal Screen your way before it makes the connection. You use this window to send commands to your modem, although it's unlikely you'll ever need to do this.

> **Note**
> I gave you the scoop on the stuff lurking in the General and Connection tabs back in Chapter 12's "Changing Your Modem's Modus Operandi" section, page 176.

➤ **Bring up terminal window after dialing** If you activate this check box, Dial-Up Networking offers the Post-Dial Terminal Screen after it makes the connection. You use this screen to send commands to the remote system. This is most often used with Internet connections. See "Do It Yourself: Creating a Dial-Up Networking Internet Connection," later in this chapter.

➤ **Operator assisted or manual dial** This check box enables you to initiate the connection by hand, which is useful in hotels and other situations where you must place a call manually or through an operator. See "Operator-Assisted or Manual Dialing," later in this chapter.

Note

To learn how to set up your modem to dial using a calling card, head back to Chapter 12's "That Long Distance Feeling: Setting Up a Calling Card" section, page 182.

➤ **Wait for credit card tone *x* seconds** If you'll be using a calling card, use this spinner to specify how long Windows should wait for the distinctive tone used by these cards.

➤ **Display modem status** When you connect to a remote system, Dial-Up Networking displays a dialog box that shows you the progress of the connection. In theory, deactivating this check box prevents this dialog box from showing up, but it doesn't seem to work in practice. Oh well.

6. When you're back in the initial Make New Connection wizard dialog box, click **Next**.

7. You use the next Make New Connection Wizard dialog box, shown in the following figure, to enter the area code, telephone number, and country code for the computer you'll be dialing. When you're finished, click **Next**.

Use this dialog box to specify the phone number for your connection.

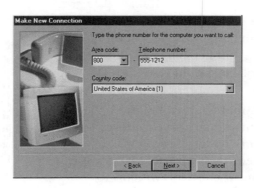

8. That'll do it: your new connection is ready to roll. In the final dialog box, click **Finish** to shut down the wizard.

Tweaking the Connection Properties

When you get back to the Dial-Up Networking window, you'll see a new icon for the connection you just created. If you ever need to make changes to the connection, highlight the connection icon, and then either select **File | Properties**, or click the Properties button in the toolbar.

In the dialog box that rears its ugly head, the General tab shows the basic data you spelled out when creating the connection. Feel free to edit this data at will.

The Server Types tab, shown in the following figure, is loaded with all kinds of high-end settings, most of which you can safely ignore. (Although you might want to ask your system administrator if anything here applies to your network.) Here's a quick look at the more useful settings:

➤ **Type of Dial-Up Server**   Use this drop-down list to specify the kind of system you'll be dialing in to.

➤ **Log on to network**   When this check box is activated, Dial-Up Networking logs you on to the remote system with the username and password you use to log on to Windows 98.

➤ **Allowed network protocols**   These check boxes specify which *network protocols* Dial-Up Networking uses with this connection. (You can think of a network protocol as a kind of language that Dial-Up Networking and the remote system use to converse with one another.) In most cases, it's best just to leave all three checked and let DUN and the remote computer figure things out for themselves. (Wondering about the TCP/IP Settings button? I'll talk about it a bit later. See "Do It Yourself: Creating a Dial-Up Networking Internet Connection.")

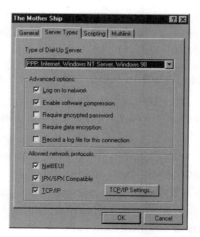

The Server Types tab contains a few useful settings.

Do It Yourself: Creating a Dial-Up Networking Internet Connection

This chapter is primarily concerned with establishing a link to your corporate network while you're on the road. However, Dial-Up Networking also moonlights as Windows 98's Internet connection machine. This section shows you how to configure Dial-Up Networking for a connection to an Internet service provider (ISP, to those in-the-know).

As you may know, the usual method for setting up an online lifeline is to use the Internet Connection Wizard. I don't know about you, but I find this wizard annoying with all its incessant questions and "baby steps" approach. When I need to get an Internet connection set up in a hurry, I bypass the wizard and just create a Dial-Up Networking connection with the sweat of my own brow.

To do this yourself, you need the following tidbits of Net data (your ISP should have provided you with all this):

➤ Your *username* (or *logon name*) and password.

➤ The phone number you use to dial in to the provider.

➤ Whether you have to type your username and password each time you log on.

➤ Whether your ISP assigns an *IP address* automatically when you log on. (Your IP address identifies your computer to the Internet community. When you request information—such as a Web page—the data is sent to your IP address.)

➤ If an IP address isn't assigned automatically, you need to know the permanent IP address (for example, 123.45.67.89) that has been assigned to your account.

➤ Whether your ISP automatically assigns the address of its *DNS server* when you log on. (A DNS server routes your requests to the appropriate Internet site.)

➤ If the DNS server address isn't assigned automatically, you need to know the permanent address of the DNS server (for example, 123.45.67.1). Most ISPs have a secondary DNS server, as well.

With all that gobbledygook in hand, follow these steps to set up a connection for your ISP:

1. Create a new Dial-Up Networking connection that specifies the phone number for your ISP.

2. When you're safely back in the Dial-Up Networking folder, highlight this new connection and select **File** | **Properties**.

3. If your ISP doesn't require you to type in your username and password each time you log on, skip to step 5. Otherwise, in the General tab, click **Configure** to display the Properties dialog box for your modem.

4. Activate the **Bring up terminal window after dialing** check box, and then click **OK**.

5. In the Server Types tab, deactivate the **NetBEUI** and **IPX/SPX Compatible** check boxes.

6. Make sure the **TCP/IP** check box is activated, and then click **TCP/IP Settings** to display the dialog box shown in the next figure.

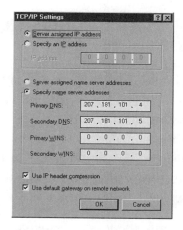

Use this dialog box to configure some TCP/IP weirdness for your ISP connection.

7. Activate one of the following options:

   ➤ **Server assigned IP address**   Select this option if your ISP assigns you an IP address automatically.

   ➤ **Specify an IP address**   Select this option if your ISP assigned you a permanent IP address. Then enter the address in the **IP address** box.

8. Activate one of the following options:

   ➤ **Server assigned name server address**   Select this option if your ISP assigns you a DNS server address automatically.

   ➤ **Specify name server addresses**   Select this option if your ISP uses a permanent DNS server address. Then enter the address in the **Primary DNS** box. If your ISP has two DNS servers, enter the address of the other server in the **Secondary DNS** box.

9. Click **OK** to return to the Server Types tab.

10. Click **OK** to return to the Dial-Up Networking folder.

Remote Network Connecting and Disconnecting

Now you're ready to make the connection. This section shows you how to connect both via your modem and via an operator-assisted call.

Placing the Call via Your Modem

In most cases, you'll want to get the modem to do your dialing dirty work for you. Here are the steps to march through:

1. Make sure that your modem is hooked up properly and, if you have an external modem, that it's turned on.

2. If you haven't done so already, get the Dial-Up Networking window on board by selecting **Start** | **Programs** | **Accessories** | **Communications** | **Dial-Up Networking**.

3. Launch your connection icon to get the connection started. Here are some of the methods you can use:

   ➤ Double-click the icon. (Single-click if you have Web integration turned on.)

   ➤ Highlight the icon, and then click the Dial toolbar button.

   ➤ If you have Web view turned on (as shown in the following figure), highlight the icon, and then click the **Connect** link.

The connection you created appears as an icon in the Dial-Up Networking folder.

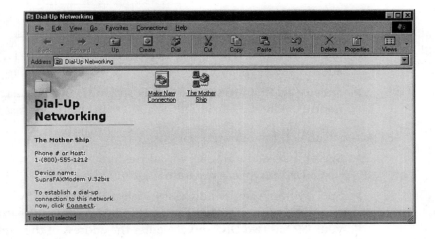

4. Windows 98 displays the Connect To dialog box in which you enter your username and password (see the next figure). If you activate the **Save password** check box, Dial-Up Networking will remember your password for future calls, which is nice.

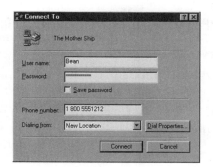

Use this dialog box to initiate the connection.

5. Click **Connect**. Dial-Up Networking dials the modem and then negotiates your logon with the remote system. When you're safely connected, the Connection Established dialog box shows up (see the next figure).

6. If you want to track the duration of your session, double-click the Dial-Up Networking icon in the taskbar (you can see the icon in this figure).

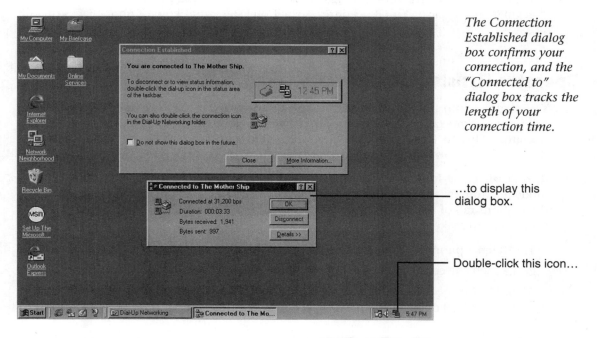

The Connection Established dialog box confirms your connection, and the "Connected to" dialog box tracks the length of your connection time.

...to display this dialog box.

Double-click this icon...

7. When you're connected, your computer becomes a full member of the network. You can access network resources, browse the Network Neighborhood, and others on the network can see your computer, as well.

8. When you've finished your online work, you need to remember to disconnect to clear the line and avoid running up long distance charges (if applicable). To disconnect, you have two choices:

➤ Display the Connected To dialog box shown in the preceding figure, and then click the **Disconnect** button.

➤ Right-click the Dial-Up Networking icon in the taskbar, and then click **Disconnect**.

Digital Phone Jack Alert!

If you find yourself on the road with your notebook computer and want to connect to your office network, watch out for the digital phone systems used by many hotels. Most modems aren't compatible with digital systems, and you'll end up frying your modem if you attempt to connect over a digital line. Unfortunately, digital phone jacks look identical to regular analog jacks. You'll need to ask the hotel staff what kind of phone jacks they use.

Operator-Assisted or Manual Dialing

You may run into situations where you don't want Dial-Up Networking to dial the phone call for you. For example, you may be in a country where calls must be placed through an operator. Happily, Dial-Up Networking can handle these kinds of "manual dial" deals. In this section, I show you how to place such a call.

Recall earlier that I told you that you can prevent Dial-Up Networking from dialing the modem automatically by activating the **Operator assisted or manual dial** check box in the Options tab of the modem Properties dialog box. Assuming you've done this, follow these steps to make the connection:

1. Attach a phone To your modem, if you haven't done so already.

2. Launch the connection icon, as described in the last section.

3. In the Connect To dialog box, click **Connect**. Dial-Up Networking displays the Manual Dial dialog box, shown in the next figure.

You see this dialog box when you attempt to connect while manual dialing is turned on.

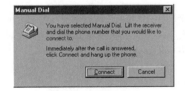

4. Pick up the telephone handset and dial the number.

5. When the remote system answers the call, click **Connect**.

6. Replace the handset.

A Better Connection: Dial-Up Networking Settings

If you think you'll be using Dial-Up Networking regularly, you should check into the various customization settings it offers. To get to these settings, select the Dial-Up Networking folder's **Connections | Settings** command. This displays the Dial-Up Networking dialog box as shown in the next figure.

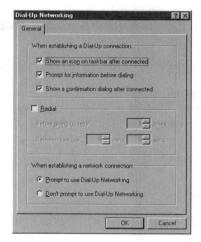

Use this dialog box to set some Dial-Up Networking options.

Most of these settings serve to make Dial-Up Networking easier to use, so frequent dial-uppers can save lots of time in the long run.

Here's what you get to play with:

➤ **Show an icon on taskbar after connected**   If you deactivate this check box, Dial-Up Networking doesn't display its taskbar icon. The taskbar icon offers the quickest way to disconnect, so I recommend leaving this setting activated.

➤ **Prompt for information before dialing**   If you turn off this setting, Dial-Up Networking doesn't display the Connect To dialog box. So long as you never have to twiddle with the connection settings, deactivating this option saves you a step.

➤ **Show a confirmation dialog after connected**   Deactivate this option to force Dial-Up Networking not to heave the Connection Established dialog box at you once you're connected.

➤ **Redial**   If the server is busy or temporarily down for the count, your connection won't connect. Instead of retrying the connection by hand, you can tell Dial-Up Networking to retry at regular intervals by activating this check box.

➤ **Before giving up retry *x* times**   Use this spinner to specify the maximum number of redial attempts.

➤ **Between tries wait *x* mins *y* secs**   Use these spinners to specify the number of minutes and seconds to pause between each retry.

➤ **Prompt to use Dial-Up Networking**   When this option is activated and you attempt to access a network resource (such as a mapped drive) while disconnected, Windows 98 will ask if you want to connect using Dial-Up Networking.

➤ **Don't prompt to use Dial-Up Networking**   Activate this option if you prefer that Windows 98 not prompt you to establish a connection.

Accessing Microsoft Mail Remotely

In Chapter 23, "Using Windows Messaging to Exchange Email Notes," I showed you how to configure Microsoft Mail to send and retrieve messages over your network. For those times when you want to perform email chores while you're on the road, you can set up Microsoft Mail to use a remote Dial-Up Networking connection. This section shows you how it's done.

Before proceeding, you should create a new Windows Messaging profile for your remote Microsoft Mail sessions:

1. Select **Start | Settings | Control Panel** to display the Windows 98 Control Panel.

2. Open the **Mail** icon.

3. In the dialog box that appears, click the **Show Profiles** button.

4. In the Mail dialog box, make sure that **Windows Messaging Settings** is highlighted, and then click **Copy**. The Copy Profile dialog box, shown in the next figure, appears.

Use this dialog box to enter a name for your new profile.

5. Type a name for the remote Microsoft Mail profile (such as **Remote Microsoft Mail Profile** or something equally uncreative), and then click **OK**.

6. Click **Close** to return to the Control Panel.

7. Start Windows Messaging and select **Tools | Options** to display the Options dialog box.

8. In the General tab, activate the **Prompt for a profile to be used** option, and then click **OK**.

With your new profile in place, restart Windows Messaging and, when the Choose Profile dialog box appears, select the remote Microsoft Mail profile you created. Click **OK**.

You now need to configure a few properties for your remote connection:

1. Select **Tools | Services** to display the Services dialog box.

2. Click **Microsoft Mail**, and then click **Properties**. Windows Messaging displays the Microsoft Mail dialog box.

3. In the Connection tab, activate the **Remote using a modem and Dial-Up Networking** option.

4. Select the Dial-Up Networking tab.

5. Select your Dial-Up Networking connection in the **Use the following Dial-Up Networking connection** drop-down list.

6. In the Remote Configuration tab, make sure that the **Use Remote Mail** check box is activated.

7. Click **OK**.

8. When Windows Messaging tells you that you have to log off to put the changes into effect, click **OK**.

9. Click **OK** to close the Services dialog box.

10. Select **File | Exit and Log Off**.

As you learned in the last chapter, Windows Messaging checks your mailbox at regular intervals, grabs any and all messages that are waiting for you, and dumps them in your Inbox folder. This isn't the case when you're working remotely (that is, when you're using the Remote Mail feature). Instead, you have to connect to your network and then download your messages. Here's how it works:

1. Start Remote Mail by selecting **Tools | Remote Mail**.

2. The first item on the Remote Mail agenda is to download the headers of the waiting messages. (Message headers include information such as the author's name and email address, the Subject line of the message, the date and time the server received the message, and the size of the message.) To do this, select **Tools | Connect** to display the Connect to Server dialog box, shown in the following figure. You have five options:

➤ **Send mail** Activate this check box to have Remote Mail send any messages that are waiting in your Outbox folder.

➤ **Receive marked items** Later you'll see that after you get the message headers, you can mark the ones for which you want to retrieve the entire message. Activate this check box to tell Remote Mail to retrieve those marked messages.

➤ **Update view of mail headers** Activate this check box to get the latest message headers.

➤ **Download address lists** Activate this check box to download the latest address list from your Microsoft Mail postoffice.

➤ **Disconnect after actions are completed** If you activate this check box, Remote Mail disconnects from the server after the download is completed.

Use this dialog box to tell Remote Mail what you want it to do when the connection is established.

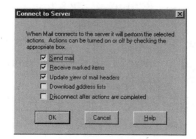

3. When you've made your selections, click **OK**. After a few seconds (or minutes, depending on how many messages you have), the Remote Mail window displays the headers of the waiting messages, as shown in the next figure.

When you connect, Remote Mail grabs the message headers and displays them in the window.

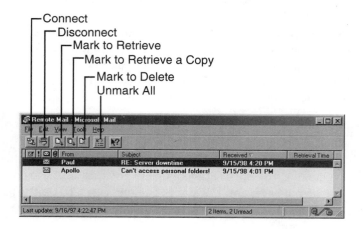

4. Now you need to decide which messages you want to retrieve. Here are the techniques to use:

   ➤ To mark a message for retrieval, highlight it and select **Edit** | **Mark to Retrieve**, or click the Mark to Retrieve toolbar button.

   ➤ To retrieve only a copy of a message (the original stays on the server), highlight it and select **Edit** | **Mark to Retrieve a Copy**, or click the message and click the Mark to Retrieve button.

   ➤ To delete a message, highlight it and select **Edit** | **Mark to Delete**, or click the message and click the Mark to Delete button.

   ➤ To start over, select **Edit** | **Unmark All** or click the Unmark All button.

5. When that's taken care of, you can transfer the marked messages by selecting **Tools** | **Connect**.

6. In the Connect to Server dialog box, make sure that the **Receive marked items** check box is activated.

7. Click **OK**.

8. When you're back in the Remote Mail window, select **Tools** | **Disconnect** (or click the Disconnect button) to sever the connection to the server.

9. Select **File** | **Close** to return to Windows Messaging.

From Here

This chapter showed you how to use Dial-Up Networking to become a road warrior instead of a road worrier. This ends your advanced Windows education. I hoped you learned a lot along the way, and that you had some fun doing it. If you're looking to do post-graduate work, check out the various Web sites and newsgroups listed in Appendix B, "More Windows 98 Online Resources."

Speak Like a Geek: More Windows Words

8.3 filename rule   The old DOS filename rule in which a name must follow these guidelines: A primary name consisting of no more than 8 characters, followed by a period (.), followed by an extension of no more than 3 characters.

Active Desktop   The newfangled Windows 98 *desktop*, which lets you replace the static desktop of Windows 95 with one that can hold Web pages and miniprograms (such as a clock, a stock ticker, or a weather map).

ASCII text file   A file that uses only the American Standard Code for Information Interchange character set (techno-lingo for the characters you see on your keyboard).

AUTOEXEC.BAT   A special *batch file* that runs a series of commands at system startup. These commands usually load programs into memory and set a few parameters that are used by devices and other programs. See also *CONFIG.SYS*.

AutoPlay   A CD-ROM feature that automatically starts a CD program as soon as you insert the disc in the drive.

backup job   A Microsoft backup file that includes a list of files to back up, the type of backup to use (*full*, *differential*, or *incremental*), and the backup destination.

batch file   A file that runs a series of DOS commands.

bit   This is the fundamental unit of computer information. Inside the computer, data is stored using tiny electronic devices called gates, which each hold one bit. Gates can be either on (electricity flows through the gate) or off (no electricity flows through). For human consumption, a gate that's on is represented by the number 1, and a gate that's off is represented by 0. These 1s and 0s are the bits. Put 8 of these bits together, and you get a byte, which holds a single character of data. For example, the letter "Z" is represented by the following 8-bit byte: 1011010.

boot   Computer geeks won't tell you to start your computer, they'll tell you to "boot it." The term boot comes from the phrase "pulling oneself up by one's own bootstraps," which refers to the fact that your computer can load everything it needs to operate properly without any help from the likes of you and me.

boot disk   A floppy disk that includes the Windows 98 system files. When you start your computer with a boot disk in drive A, the system bypasses your hard disk and loads a DOS prompt–only version of Windows 98.

bps   Bits per second. The rate at which a *modem* or other communications device spits data through a phone line or cable.

browser   A program that you use to *surf* sites on the World Wide Web. The browser that comes with Windows 98 is called Internet Explorer.

byte   Computerese for a single character of information. So, for example, the phrase *This phrase is 28 bytes long* is, yes, 28 bytes long (you count the spaces, too). See also *kilobyte*, *megabyte*, and *gigabyte*.

channel   A special World Wide Web site that features changing content that is sent automatically to your computer at predefined intervals. See *subscription*.

classic view   The folder view used with Windows 95. That is, you click an icon to select it, and you double-click an icon to launch it. See also *Web view*.

clickstream   The "path" a person takes as they navigate through the World Wide Web.

Clipboard   An area of memory that holds data temporarily during cut and paste operations.

cluster   A section of a hard disk that's used to store some or all of a file. Clusters usually consist of multiple *sectors*. See also *file allocation table*.

color depth   A video card setting that determines the number of colors available to your applications and graphics. Color depth is expressed either in *bits* or total colors. See also *display resolution*.

COMMAND.COM   The DOS command interpreter, which displays the DOS prompt to let you enter DOS commands and translates those commands into a language DOS can understand.

CONFIG.SYS   Contains instructions that are run at startup and are used mostly to configure some of the devices attached to your computer. See also *AUTOEXEC.BAT*.

connection settings   A collection of settings that your *modem* uses in order to communicate successfully with a remote system. There are three types of connection settings: *data bits*, *stop bits*, and *parity*. When setting up a connection to a remote system, you need to make sure that these three settings match the parameters expected by the remote computer.

cool switch   Pressing Alt+Tab to switch from one open window to another.

COM port   See *serial port*.

data bits   In *modem* communications, the number of bits the remote system uses to define a character of information. Although your computer uses 8 bits to define a character, many remote systems are non-PC computers that use a different number of bits (7 is quite common).

data files   The files used by you or your programs. See also *program files*.

data transfer rate   The fastest rate at which a *modem* can send data. The data transfer rate is measured in *bps*. The current standards for the data transfer rate are 28,000 bps on the low end and 56,000 bps on the high end.

delay   The amount of time it takes for a second character to appear when you press and hold down a key.

demodulation   The process used by a *modem* to convert tones received over a phone line into digital data (*bits*) that the computer can understand. See also *modulation*.

device driver   A small program that controls the way a device (such as a mouse) works with your system.

differential backup   Backs up only files in the current *backup job* that have changed since the last *full backup*. See also *incremental backup*.

directory   See *folder*.

directory server   An Internet database of email names and addresses. You can use Outlook Express to search a directory server for a name or address.

display resolution   This is a measure of the sharpness of an onscreen image. Resolution is expressed as the number of *pixels* displayed horizontally by the number of pixels displayed vertically. For example, 640×480 resolution means that there are 640 pixels across the image and 480 pixels down the image. See also *color depth*.

DMA channel   A connection that lets a device transfer data to and from memory without going through the microprocessor.

download   To receive a file from a remote computer.

drag   To press and hold down the left mouse button and then move the mouse. See also *special drag*.

drag-and-drop   A technique that you use to run commands or move things around; you use your mouse to *drag* files or icons to strategic screen areas and drop them there. See also *special drag*.

dynamic link library   A special file (it uses the .DLL extension) that contains functions and routines used by a program or by Windows.

Easter egg   An animation built into an application that displays the names of the programmers and other people who worked on the applications. Also known as a *gang screen*.

embed   An *object linking and embedding* technique that inserts data within a destination document without requiring a separate file. The data contains information about the application used to create the data, so the data can be easily edited. See also *link*.

extension   The part of the filename to the right of the period. Windows 98 uses the extension to determine the *file type* of a file.

external DOS command   A DOS command that exists as a separate, standalone program. See also *internal DOS command*.

external modem   This type of modem is a standalone box that you connect to a *serial port* on your computer with a special cable. External modems have several advantages over their *internal modem* cousins. For one, an external modem is easily shuffled between computers. For another, most external modems have a series of LED indicators on their front panel that tell you the current state of the modem. These lights are useful trouble-shooting tools. On the downside, external modems require a separate power source (which is usually a huge wall wart), and they tend to be more expensive than an equivalent internal modem.

FAT   See *file allocation table*.

FAWOMPT   Frequently Argued Waste Of My Precious Time. See also *holy war*.

file allocation table   A table that Windows 98 uses to keep track of where a file's *clusters* are stored on a hard disk.

file transfer protocol   A method that two computers connected via a *modem* use to coordinate file *downloads* and *uploads*.

file type   A categorization that specifies the general content and format of a file (for example, "Text Document"). See also *extension*.

floppy disk   A portable storage medium that consists of a flexible disk protected by a plastic case. Floppy disks are available in a variety of sizes and capacities.

flow control A routine that defines how the computer and a *modem* communicate with each other so that incoming data is received properly (or put off if the computer isn't quite ready to handle the data). There are two types of flow control: software and hardware (the latter is the one most commonly used these days).

focus The window that has the attention of the operating system (that is, Windows 98).

folder A storage location on your hard disk in which you keep related files together. If your hard disk is like a house, a folder is like a room in the house.

font A character set of a specific typeface, type style, and type size.

format To set up a disk so that a drive can read its information and write information to it.

fragmented When a single file is chopped up and stored in separate chunks scattered around a hard disk. You can fix this by running Windows 98's Disk Defragmenter program.

full backup Backs up all the files in the current *backup job*. See also *differential backup* and *incremental backup*.

gang screen See *Easter egg*.

GB See *gigabyte*.

gigabyte 1,024 *megabytes*. Those in-the-know usually abbreviate this as "GB" when writing, and as "gig" when speaking. See also *byte*, *kilobyte*, and *megabyte*.

hardware profile A specific device configuration. You use hardware profiles to switch Windows 98 easily from one hardware configuration to another.

holy war An endless debate on the merits of one thing versus another, where people use the same arguments over and over, and nobody's opinion ever budges even the slightest one way or the other. See also *FAWOMPT*.

hover To place the mouse pointer over an object for a few seconds. In most Windows applications, if you hover the mouse over a toolbar button, a small banner shows up that tells you the name of the button.

HTML Hypertext Markup Language. It's used to create Web pages. HTML consists of a few codes that tell a Web browser how to display the page (format text and paragraphs, define links, and so on).

I/O port A memory address that the processor uses to communicate with a device directly. After a device has used its *IRQ* to catch the attention of the processor, the actual exchange of data or commands takes place through the device's I/O port address.

in-place editing An *OLE* 2 technique used when editing an inserted object (see *in-place inserting*). Instead of displaying the source application in a separate window, certain features of the destination application's window (such as the menu bar and toolbar) are temporarily hidden in favor of the source application's features.

in-place inserting An *OLE* 2 technique used when inserting an object. As with *in-place editing*, certain features of the destination application's window are temporarily hidden in favor of the source application's features.

incremental backup Backs up only files in the current *backup job* that have changed since the last *full backup* or the last *differential backup*.

infrared port A communications port, usually found on notebook computers and some printers. Infrared ports enable two devices to communicate by using infrared light waves instead of cables.

internal DOS command A DOS command that is part of COMMAND.COM. See also *external DOS command*.

internal modem This type of *modem* is a circuit board that sits inside your computer. Many people prefer this type over *external modems* because no external power source is required, it's one less device taking up valuable desk space, no external serial port is used up, and they tend to be less expensive.

Internet A *network* of networks that extends around the world. By setting up an account with an Internet service provider, you can access this network.

interrupt request A signal sent to the computer's microprocessor by a device that is ready to send or receive data. See also *interrupt request line*.

interrupt request line The path along which an *interrupt request* travels from the device to the processor.

intranet The implementation of *Internet* technologies for use within an organization rather than for connection to the Internet as a whole.

IR Short for infrared. See *infrared port*.

IRQ See *interrupt request line*.

Jaz drive A special disk drive that uses portable disks (about the size of *floppy disks*) that hold 1 *gigabyte* of data.

Kbps One thousand bits per second (*bps*). Today's modern *modems* transmit data at either 28.8 Kbps or 56 Kbps.

KB See *kilobyte*.

kilobyte 1,024 *bytes*. To be hip, always abbreviate this to "K" or "KB." See also *megabyte* and *gigabyte*.

LAN See *local area network*.

link An *object linking and embedding* technique that inserts data within a destination document and maintains a link back to the original data. If the original data changes, the inserted copy gets updated, as well. See also *embed*.

local area network   A *network* in which all the computers occupy a relatively small geographical area, such as a department, office, home, or building. All the connections between computers are made via network cables.

maximize   To increase the size of a window to its largest extent. A maximized application window fills the entire screen (except for the taskbar). A maximized document window fills the entire application window.

Mbps   One million bits per second (*bps*).

MB   See *megabyte*.

megabyte   1,024 *kilobytes* or 1,048,576 *bytes*. The cognoscenti write this as "M" or "MB" and pronounce it "meg." See also *gigabyte* and *kilobyte*.

minimize   To remove a program from the desktop without closing it. A button for the program remains on the taskbar.

modem   An electronic device that enables the transmission and reception of computer data over telephone lines. The word *modem* was coined by crashing the words *modulation* and *demodulation* together.

modulation   The process used by a *modem* to convert the computer's digital data into a wave that's capable of being transmitted across a telephone line. In essence, *bits*—the 1s and 0s that compose digital data—are converted into special signals that can be represented as tones that the phone system can transmit. See also *demodulation*.

MS-DOS mode   A special operating mode in which Windows 98 hands over complete control of the computer to a DOS application. This is useful for games and other resource hogs that refuse to play nicely in a Windows DOS session.

multitasking   The capability to run several programs at the same time. Figuratively speaking, this simply means that Windows 98, unlike some people you may know, can walk and chew gum at the same time.

network   A collection of computers connected via special cables or other network media (such as *infrared ports*) to share files, folders, disks, peripherals, and applications. See also *local area network*.

nooksurfer   A person who keeps going to the same Web sites over and over and rarely checks out new sites.

object linking and embedding   A Windows technology that lets you share data between applications. See also *link* and *embed*.

OLE   See *object linking and embedding*.

parity   A form of error checking that the *modem* uses to see whether the data it just received was corrupted along the way.

pixel   A tiny pinpoint of light. The images on your monitor are composed of hundreds of thousands of pixels. The actual number depends on the *display resolution*.

Plug and Play   A hardware technology that enables devices to be set up and configured automatically.

port   The connection into which you plug the cable from a device such as a mouse or printer.

POST   See *Power-On Self Test*.

Power-On Self Test   A procedure that runs when you start your computer. This procedure checks the system's hardware and sets up the hardware for use.

RAM   Random access memory. The memory in your computer that Windows 98 uses to run your programs. See also *virtual memory*.

RAM drive   A splice of *RAM* that is used as a disk drive.

repeat rate   After the initial delay, the rate at which characters appear when you press and hold down a key.

right-click   To click the right mouse button instead of the usual left button. In Windows 98, right-clicking something usually pops up a *shortcut menu*.

RS-232 port   See *serial port*.

safe mode   An operating mode that loads a stripped-down version of Windows 98. This is useful for working around a problem that causes Windows not to start properly.

sector   A magnetic storage unit on a formatted disk. See also *cluster*.

serial port   The link between your computer and your *modem*. For an external modem, this link usually comes in the form of a serial cable that runs from the port to a plug in the back of the modem. For internal modems, the serial port is built right into the modem's circuitry. They're called "serial" ports because they transmit and receive data one bit at a time, in a series. (This is opposed to working with data in "parallel," in which multiple bits are transmitted simultaneously.)

shortcut   A special file that points to a program or a document (the *target*). Double-clicking the shortcut starts the program or loads the document.

shortcut menu   A menu that contains a few commands related to an item (such as the *desktop* or the *taskbar*). You display the shortcut menu by *right-clicking* the object.

special drag   To *drag-and-drop* an object using the right mouse button. Once you drop the object, Windows 98 displays a menu of choices (such as Move or Copy).

Startup menu   A menu of Windows 98 startup options. You invoke this menu by holding down Ctrl while your computer *boots*.

stop bit   In *modem* communications, an extra bit that's tacked on to the end of the *data bits*. It's job is to tell the remote system that it has reached the end of this particular chunk of data. Different systems look for stop bits with different lengths.

subscription   A method of checking for new or changed data on a World Wide Web site or *channel*. The subscription sets up a schedule for checking a particular site to see whether it has changed in any way since the last time it was checked.

surf   To travel from site to site on the World Wide Web.

swap file   A file on your hard disk that Windows 98 uses as *virtual memory*.

system menu   A menu, common to every Windows 98 window, that you use to manipulate various features of the window. You activate the Control menu by clicking on the Control menu box in the upper-left corner of the window or by pressing Alt+Spacebar (for an application window).

system resources   A memory area that Windows 98 uses to keep track of things like the position and size of open windows, dialog boxes, and your desktop configuration (wallpaper and so on).

target   The original item that a *shortcut* points to.

terminal emulation   A method of translating computer input and output so that your computer acts as though it is a terminal connected to the remote system. When you use your *modem* to connect to a remote computer, you are, essentially, operating that computer from your keyboard and seeing the results onscreen. In other words, your computer has become a "terminal" attached to the remote machine. It's likely, however, that the remote computer is completely different from the one you're using. It could be a mainframe or a minicomputer, for example. In that case, it isn't likely that the codes produced by your keystrokes will correspond exactly with the codes used by the remote computer. Similarly, some of the return codes won't make sense to your machine. So for your computer to act like a true terminal, some kind of translation is needed between the two systems.

text editor   A program that lets you edit files that contain only text. The Windows 98 text editor is called Notepad.

three-fingered salute   The Ctrl+Alt+Delete key combination, which displays the Close Program dialog box. This is useful for shutting down programs that are locked up tight. Also known as the *Vulcan nerve pinch*.

upload   To send a file to a remote computer.

virtual memory   A chunk of hard disk real estate—known as a *swap file*—that has been tarted up to look and act like *RAM*. This enables you to load more programs and documents beyond the amount of physical RAM on your system.

Vulcan nerve pinch   See *three-fingered salute*.

waves How sounds are transmitted across telephone lines, so they're crucial for understanding how *modems* work. When you speak into a telephone, a diaphragm inside the mouthpiece vibrates. This vibration is converted into an electromagnetic wave that mirrors the original sound wave created by your voice. This wave travels along the telephone lines, and at the destination, electromagnets in the receiver vibrate another diaphragm that reproduces your voice.

Web integration The integration of World Wide Web techniques into the Windows 98 interface. See *Web view*.

Web view The folder view used when *Web integration* is activated. With this view, you *hover* the mouse over an icon to select it, and you click an icon to launch it. See also *classic view*.

word wrap A word processor feature that automatically starts a new line when your typing reaches the end of the current line.

Zip drive A special disk drive that uses portable disks (a little smaller than a *Jaz drive* disk), which hold 100 *megabytes* of data.

ZIP file A compressed archive file that contains one or more files that have been compressed together to save space.

More Windows 98 Online Resources

Although I've crammed as much useful Windows 98 information as I could into this book and *The Complete Idiot's Guide to Windows 98*, there's just no way to cover absolutely everything. Besides, the Windows world is in a constant state of flux, so keeping up with what's new is a full-time job. To help you keep your head above the Windows waters, this appendix presents a list of some online sites that offer practical information, the latest news, and first-rate shareware and other files.

The World Wide Web

There's no shortage of Windows 98 pages on the Web, but many of these pages are pure dreck. The following is a list of the Windows 98 Web pages I think you'll find useful. First, some links to pages on Microsoft's Web site:

Windows 98 Home Page

URL: **http://www.microsoft.com/windows98/**

Content: Files, how-to, news, shareware, troubleshooting

Comments: This is the place to begin all your Windows 98 Web wandering (see the following figure). All the latest Windows 98 news from Microsoft, updates, new Windows 98 programs—it's all here.

The Windows 98 Home Page.

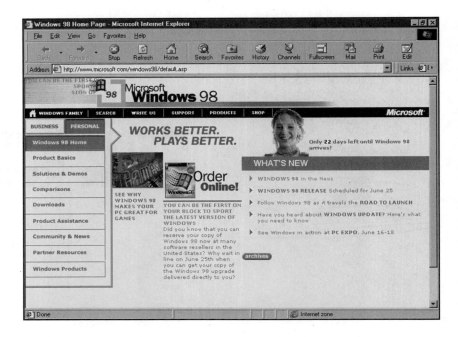

Microsoft Technical Support Search

URL: **http://support.microsoft.com/support/**

Content: How-to, troubleshooting

Comments: If you're scratching your head over some weird Windows 98 behavior, chances are someone else has found the same thing and has asked Microsoft Tech Support about it, and the engineer has posted a solution in the Microsoft Knowledge Base. This Web site lets you search the Knowledge Base and other support contents (see the next figure) to track down a problem you might be having. Note that you have to register with Microsoft to use this site.

Windows 98 Software Library

URL: **http://www.microsoft.com/windows/software.htm**

Content: Files

Comments: This site contains miscellaneous Windows 98 files from Microsoft, including updated components, device drivers, and more.

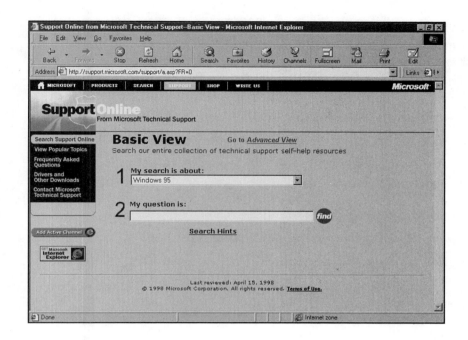

This Web page lets you search the Microsoft Knowledge Base and other files for Windows 98 information.

Here are a few more links to other Windows 98 pages:

32BIT.com

URL: **http://www.32bit.com/**

Content: Files, how-to, news, shareware

Comments: This site is dedicated to 32-bit operating systems and has extensive Windows resources, particularly shareware.

Allen's Windows 95 Applications List

URL: **http://www.winappslist.com/**

Content: Files, shareware

Comments: An extensive collection of Windows software arranged in over 40 different categories.

Consummate Winsock Apps List

URL: **http://cws.internet.com/**

Content: Files, shareware

Comments: Not just your average list of Windows 98 shareware and files. This site sticks out from the crowd thanks to the in-depth reviews given to each program by the site's proprietor: Forrest Stroud.

DOWNLOAD.COM

URL: **http://www.download.com/PC/Win95/**

Content: Files, how-to, news, shareware, troubleshooting

Comments: At the time of writing, this site was still geared toward Windows 95, but I expect you'll find Windows 98 resources by the time you read this.

PC World Magazine's Windows 98 Page

URL: **http://www.pcworld.com/workstyles/win95/index.html**

Content: How-to, news, troubleshooting

Comments: A huge list of Windows articles from the pages of PC World magazine. Includes a search engine.

PCWin Resource Center

URL: **http://pcwin.com/**

Content: Files, how-to, news, shareware, troubleshooting

Comments: A nice collection of Windows 98 software.

Tech Support Guy

URL: **http://www.cermak.com/techguy/**

Content: How-to, troubleshooting

Comments: Thousands of troubleshooting articles, many of which are related to Windows problems. Can't find your answer? Ask the Tech Support Guy!

TUCOWS

URL: **http://tucows.mcp.com/window95.html**

Content: Files, shareware

Comments: One of the premier download sites for Windows 95/98 shareware (see the following figure). Approximately 70 separate software categories.

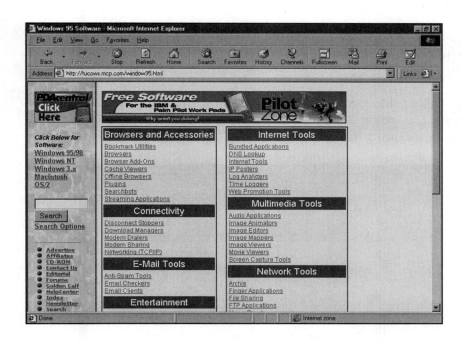

Available in many places around the Web, TUCOWS offers a huge collection of Windows 95 and 98 applications.

Windowwatch

URL: **http://www.windowwatch.com/**

Content: News

Comments: Subtitled "Electronic Windows Magazine of the Internet," this site keeps you up-to-date on the latest developments in the Windows world.

Windows 98 Megasite

URL: **http://www.winmag.com/win98/**

Content: Files, how-to, shareware

Comments: This site is run by Windows Magazine and includes discussion groups, reviews, and access to the rest of the Windows Magazine Web site.

WindowsCentral

URL: **http://www.windowscentral.com/**

Content: How-to, news, troubleshooting

Comments: This is one of the busiest Windows sites on the Net thanks to its large collection of tips and features related to the Windows world.

WinFiles.com

URL: **http://www.winfiles.com/**

Content: Files, how-to, shareware

Comments: This site has loads of useful links, and the shareware collection is second to none. The site's clever layout is designed to resemble the Windows 98 interface (see the following figure).

Winfiles.com contains lots of useful how-to links and a superb Windows 98 shareware collection.

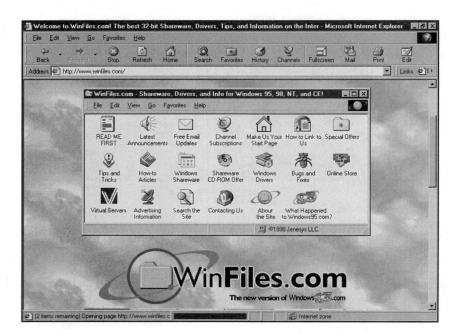

Usenet Newsgroups

If you need help with a specific Windows 98 question, fumbling around various Web sites looking for the answer might not be the best way to go. In some cases, posting a question to the appropriate Usenet newsgroup is often a better approach. The following table summarizes newsgroups that focus on Windows 95 and that are available through regular channels. (Note that no Windows 98 newsgroups were available when I wrote this.)

Newsgroup	Description
alt.os.windows95.crash. crash.crash	The name sounds like a joke, but this group has plenty of serious posts related to troubleshooting issues.

Newsgroup	Description
comp.os.ms-windows.apps. compatibility.win95	This is the place to look for help related to applications that won't run under Windows 98.
comp.os.ms-windows.apps. utilities.win95	This group deals with issues related to the Windows 95 accessories.
comp.os.ms-windows.networking. win95	Check out this group if you need help with networking, Internet access, or other connectivity issues.
comp.os.ms-windows.setup.win95	This group covers setup, configuration, and installation issues.
comp.os.ms-windows.win95.misc	This is a catchall group for other Windows 95 issues. A word of warning: This is a very busy group with hundreds of posts each day.
comp.os.ms-windows.win95. moderated	A high-signal, low-noise group that posts about one-tenth the number of messages that go through the misc. group.
comp.os.ms-windows.win95.setup	Another group related to installation. No, I don't know why there are two of them.

Microsoft also runs its own newsgroups. To view them, set up your newsreader to use the server msnews.microsoft.com. The table below lists the newsgroups that deal with Windows 98 topics.

Newsgroup	Description
microsoft.public.win98.apps	Deals with issues related to running applications in Windows 98.
microsoft.public.win98.comm.dun	Covers installation, configuration, and use of Dial-Up Networking.
microsoft.public.win98.comm.modem	Deals with issues related to modems, serial ports, HyperTerminal, Phone Dialer, and general telephony.
microsoft.public.win98. disks.general	Primarily a forum for disk drive issues, especially questions related to ScanDisk, DriveSpace, and DoubleSpace.
microsoft.public.win98. display.general	Discussions related to video cards and monitors.
microsoft.public.win98. display.multi_monitor	Covers Windows 98's support for multiple monitors.

continues

continued

Newsgroup	Description
microsoft.public.win98.fat32	Deals with the FAT32 file system.
microsoft.public.win98. gen_discussion	Miscellaneous Windows 98 topics.
microsoft.public.win98.internet	General Windows 98 Internet topics.
microsoft.public.win98.internet. active_desktop	Questions and answers related to the Active Desktop.
microsoft.public.win98.internet. browser	Discussions related to Internet Explorer and other browsers.
microsoft.public.win98.internet. netmeeting	Covers all aspects of NetMeeting conferencing.
microsoft.public.win98.internet. outlookexpress	Deals with email and newsgroup issues in Outlook Express.
microsoft.public.win98.internet. windows_update	Questions and answers related to the Windows Update Web site.
microsoft.public.win98. multimedia	Discussions on audio, video, and other multimedia.
microsoft.public.win98. multimedia.directx5	Covers multimedia topics related to DirectX version 5.
microsoft.public.win98. networking	Installation, configuration, and troubleshooting of Microsoft and NetWare networks.
microsoft.public.win98. performance	Deals with overcoming poor Windows 98 performance.
microsoft.public.win98.pnp	Windows 98's Plug and Play support.
microsoft.public.win98.power_mgmt	Questions and answers related to power management.
microsoft.public.win98.printing	Discussions about printing in Windows 98.
microsoft.public.win98.pws_4	Covers Personal Web Server.
microsoft.public.win98.scanreg	Deals with Windows 98's Registry Checker system tool.
microsoft.public.win98.setup	Covers issues related to Windows 98 installation.
microsoft.public.win98.setup.win31	Questions and answers related to upgrading to Windows 98 from Windows 3.1.
microsoft.public.win98.shell	Discussions on the Windows 98 shell and user interface.
microsoft.public.win98. sys_file_check	Covers the System File Checker utility.

Newsgroup	Description
`microsoft.public.win98.taskscheduler`	Deals with the Task Scheduler utility.
`microsoft.public.win98.webtv`	Questions and answers related to WebTV for Windows.

More Symbols: The Windows ANSI Character Set

Back in Chapter 9's "Linguistic Leaps with the United States-International Keyboard Layout" section, I talked about how to get characters and symbols other than those you can pound out directly on your keyboard. This appendix presents a complete list of those symbols. Windows eggheads call this the *Windows ANSI Character Set*.

To enter these characters into your applications, you can use either of the following methods:

➤ For the ANSI numbers 33 through 127, you can either type the character directly using the keyboard or hold down the Alt key and type the ANSI number using the keyboard's numeric keypad.

➤ For the ANSI numbers 128 through 255, hold down the Alt key and use the keyboard's numeric keypad to enter 0 followed by the ANSI number. For example, to enter the registered trademark symbol (ANSI 174), you would press Alt+0174.

Code	Text
33	!
34	"
35	#
36	$
37	%

continues

continued

Code	Text
38	&
39	'
40	(
41	)
42	*
43	+
44	,
45	-
46	.
47	/
48	0
49	1
50	2
51	3
52	4
53	5
54	6
55	7
56	8
57	9
58	:
59	;
60	<
61	=
62	>
63	?
64	@
65	A
66	B
67	C
68	D
69	E
70	F
71	G
72	H

Code	Text
73	I
74	J
75	K
76	L
77	M
78	N
79	O
80	P
81	Q
82	R
83	S
84	T
85	U
86	V
87	W
88	X
89	Y
90	Z
91	[
92	\
93	]
94	^
95	_
96	`
97	a
98	b
99	c
100	d
101	e
102	f
103	g
104	h
105	i
106	j

continues

continued

Code	Text
107	k
108	l
109	m
110	n
111	o
112	p
113	q
114	r
115	s
116	t
117	u
118	v
119	w
120	x
121	y
122	z
123	{
124	|
125	}
126	~
127	N/A
0128	–
0129	N/A
0130	,
0131	*f*
0132	„
0133	…
0134	†
0135	‡
0136	ˆ
0137	‰
0138	–
0139	‹
0140	Œ
0141	N/A

Code	Text
0142	N/A
0143	N/A
0144	N/A
0145	'
0146	'
0147	"
0148	"
0149	•
0150	–
0151	—
0152	~
0153	™
0154	_
0155	›
0156	œ
0157	N/A
0158	N/A
0159	Ÿ
0160	N/A
0161	¡
0162	¢
0163	£
0164	¤
0165	¥
0166	¦
0167	§
0168	¨
0169	©
0170	ª
0171	«
0172	¬
0173	–
0174	®
0175	¯

continues

continued

Code	Text
0176	°
0177	±
0178	2
0179	3
0180	´
0181	μ
0182	¶
0183	·
0184	¸
0185	¹
0186	º
0187	»
0188	–
0189	–
0190	–
0191	¿
0192	À
0193	Á
0194	Â
0195	Ã
0196	Ä
0197	Å
0198	Æ
0199	Ç
0200	È
0201	É
0202	Ê
0203	Ë
0204	Ì
0205	Í
0206	Î
0207	Ï
0208	–
0209	Ñ
0210	Ò

Code	Text
0211	Ó
0212	Ô
0213	Õ
0214	Ö
0215	x
0216	Ø
0217	Ù
0218	Ú
0219	Û
0220	Ü
0221	Y
0222	_
0223	ß
0224	à
0225	á
0226	â
0227	ã
0228	ä
0229	å
0230	æ
0231	ç
0232	è
0233	é
0234	ê
0235	ë
0236	ì
0237	í
0238	î
0239	ï
0240	ð
0241	ñ
0242	ò
0243	ó
0244	ô

continues

continued

Code	Text
0245	õ
0246	ö
0247	÷
0248	ø
0249	ù
0250	ú
0251	û
0252	ü
0253	y
0254	_
0255	ÿ

Index

421

optimizing, *see* perfor-
mance tuning
Organize Favorites com-
mand (Favorites menu),
196
organizing favorites,
195-196
Outbox (Outlook Express),
214
Outlook Express, 213
  customizing
    dial-up options, 229
    general options, 228
    layout, 226
    message columns,
      225-226
    Preview pane, 227
    toolbar, 227
  directory service, 224
  folders
    compacting, 215
    creating, 214
    Deleted Items, 214
    deleting, 215
    Drafts, 214
    Inbox, 214
    moving, 215
    Outbox, 214
    renaming, 214
    Sent Items, 214
  Inbox Assistant,
    222-223
  messages
    filtering, 222-223
    fonts, 218
    reading, 221
    sending, 215-217
    signatures, 220
    stationery, 219
    vCards, 220-221

P

page transitions, 209
parity, 174
passwords
  chat rooms, 238
  networks, 344
Paste command (Edit
  menu), 34
Paste Link command (Edit
  menu), 39
Paste Special command
  (Edit menu), 39
Paste Special dialog
  box, 39
pasting data
  Clipboard, 34
  MS-DOS sessions, 51
  OLE, 38-39
  shortcuts, 22
paths, displaying, 30
Pause Service command
  (Properties menu), 251
pausing scheduled tasks,
  297
PC World Magazine Web
  site, 394
PCRESTOR.BAT file, 284
PCWin Resource Center
  Web site, 394
peer-to-peer networks, 340
performance tuning,
  266-267
  FAT32 system, 272-273
  memory
    CD-ROM cache,
      271-272
    hard drive cache,
      270-271
    swap files, 267-270
  tips, 264-265
  video cards, 274-275

Personal Web Manager,
  249
Personal Web Server
  configuring, 249-250
  folders, 253-254
  home pages
    creating, 251-253
    publishing, 256-258
  installing, 247-248
  limitations, 247
  log files, 256
  Personal Web Manager,
    249
  requirements, 246
  return codes, 257
  services, starting/
    stopping, 251
  virtual directories
    creating, 254-255
    default documents,
      255-256
Personal Web Server
  command (Send To
  menu), 257
photos
  brightness/contrast, 70
  cropping, 69
  downloading from
    digital cameras, 69
  flipping, 70
  red eye, eliminating, 70
  rotating, 70
  saving, 71
  scanning, 69
  softening edges, 70
  tint, 70
  zooming in/out, 69
  see also graphics
Picture It! Express,
  69-71
pictures, *see* photos;
  graphics

429

X-Z